DAVID BOULTON

THE
TROUBLE
WITH
GOD

Building the Republic of Heaven

for

my grandsons Joe and Tom
born in the first and third years of the new millennium,
who may one day be interested
to find out
what their grandfather thought
about God, life and
the republic of heaven

Copyright © 2005 O Books
O Books is an imprint of The Bothy, John Hunt Publishing Ltd.,
Deershot Lodge, Park Lane, Ropley, Hants, SO24 0BE, UK
office@johnhunt-publishing.com
www.O-books.net

Distribution in:
UK
Orca Book Services
orders@orcabookservices.co.uk
Tel: 01202 665432 Fax: 01202 666219 Int. code (44)

USA and Canada
NBN
custserv@nbnbooks.com
Tel: 1 800 462 6420 Fax: 1 800 338 4550

Australia
Brumby Books
sales@brumbybooks.com
Tel: 61 3 9761 5535 Fax: 61 3 9761 7095

New Zealand
Peaceful Living
books@peaceful-living.co.nz
Tel: 64 7 57 18105 Fax: 64 7 57 18513

Singapore
STP
davidbuckland@tlp.com.sg
Tel: 65 6276 Fax: 65 6276 7119

South Africa
Alternative Books
altbook@global.co.za
Tel: 27 011 792 7730 Fax: 27 011 972 7787

Originally published in the UK in paperback under the same title in 2002

Text: © David Boulton 2005 (Reissue)

Design: BookDesign™, London

ISBN 1 905047 06 1

A CIP catalogue record for this book is available from the British Library.

Printed in the USA by Maple-Vail Manufacturing Group

DAVID BOULTON

THE TROUBLE WITH GOD

Building the Republic of Heaven

BOOKS

WINCHESTER UK
NEW YORK USA

CONTENTS

PREFACE TO SECOND EDITION

I BEGAN WRITING the first edition of *The Trouble with God* in September 2001, immediately after the terrorist attack on New York on the 11th of that month. It was published a year later in the UK only and the print run was sold out before the US Presidential election in 2004. Rather than simply reprint, my publisher, John Hunt, proposed a revision for a wider public, including the United States. This second edition is the result.

I have made some amendments, especially in Part 3 where I have considerably expanded what was the final chapter, turning it into two. I hope this has strengthened and clarified my argument for "seeking first the republic of heaven". Elsewhere I have tried to reflect and respond to changes in public awareness since 2001. For instance, to most non-American readers of the first edition the notion of "the Rapture" would have been new and strange. After President Bush's re-election, and as a result of the worldwide reporting of the critical part played by fundamentalist Christianity in his campaign, the Rapture is more familiar - if no less strange.

For this edition I owe a special debt of gratitude to Tom Hall of Foster, Rhode Island, an Associate Fellow of the Westar Institute, California, who as an anonymous text editor for Westar's Polebridge Press has polished the prose of many more distinguished writers than myself. I asked Tom to cast his eye over my text and draw my attention to any idioms that might puzzle American readers, divided as they are from the English by a common language. One result is that Americans will be spared baffling encounters with fridge mountains, off-the-peg solutions, and po-faced attitudes. But Tom went far beyond his brief and tidied up my grammar and syntax. The result is that the second edition is certainly a stylistical improvement on the first. Where infelicities remain, they are likely to be the result of any final revisions made after Tom's eagle eye had turned to other projects.

I am grateful too to the newly published poet Brian Boulton (see page 29) for correcting some imperfectly remembered Biblical references, thereby demonstrating that he has managed to out-perform me in retaining the detail of what we were taught in Gospel Hall and Crusader Class.

Since I am writing for the general reader rather than the scholar I have chosen not to clutter the page with footnotes. Where appropriate, I have cited sources within the main text. I have also added an index for easy reference.

As in the first edition, my Biblical quotes are generally from the Authorised or King James Version. I am aware that Americans in particular are more familiar with modern translations and may be bemused, if not scandalised, when they read of the Lord speaking through Balaam's ass rather than his donkey. But the old AV is wired into my being, and I would no more choose to read the gospels in the language of my daily newspaper than I would settle for reading a modernised version of Shakespeare. This simply indulges my literary taste. The main exceptions are where the citations come within quotations from other writers.

American readers will notice that I have not americanised my spellings: on our side of the Atlantic we favour a saviour rather than harboring a savior. At least we don't have *that* trouble with God.

David Boulton

INTRODUCTION

FOR WELL OVER a century now, God has been causing trouble. In those parts of the world where people have been encouraged to think for themselves and reflect on the meaning of life, the universe and everything, he's both troublesome and in trouble.

In the most powerful country in the world, the United States of America, conservatives and liberals fight for possession of his name – and, with his name, his power. Few in the land that still holds to a myth of settlement by Pilgrim Fathers actively disbelieve in God. But the God who is daily urged to bless America above all other nations? The God whose robe is the stars and stripes, whose canopy is the space filled by TV-evangelists? The God of Swaggart, Robertson, Graham and Bush? A neo-con God, a fag-hating God, a God of battles who leads his people into war, with the cross of Jesus going on before?

For many, yes – but not for all. Not for the millions who sense that there must be a different God, a better idea of God, a God who has escaped the clutches of fundamentalist pastors and power-in-the-blood politicians. The God, maybe, of Jefferson and Paine, of the enlightenment tradition. A God who is big trouble precisely because he challenges us to rethink what God and God-language mean in a world "swept with confused alarms of struggle and flight / Where ignorant armies clash by night".

But if God spells one kind of trouble in the USA, he troubles the rest of the English-speaking world more by his absence than his presence. Once upon a time he was taken for granted as the ultimate source of meaning, purpose, the good. He was the alpha and the omega in a world that had to have had a beginning and must surely have an end. He was the guarantor of justice, seeing to it that sinners who escaped their just deserts in this world would get their come-uppance in the next. He was the promise that, despite all appearances, all would be well and all manner of things would be well – at least for those who stayed on-message. Only the fool said in his heart that there was no God. Only the worldly–wise doubted his omnipotence, omniscience, omnipresence, and all the other "omnis" that were claimed for him by his retinue of priests and acolytes. But in secular Europe, Canada, Australia, New Zealand, all that is past. God's realm is a foreign country, to be visited on occasional breaks, where we admire the scenery, tour the sights and revel in the quaint local customs until it's time to come back to the real world.

We all know how the statistics tell a radically different story, according to which side of the Atlantic Ocean you happen to be counting in. In the United States, where church and state are good friends but not wedded, local community churches still do the business on Sundays.* Cross the ocean and you find institutional religion on an apparently unstoppable slide, this church broken into shards by paedophile priests, that chapel obsessed by the roof fund, this one emptying because it believes in nothing in particular, that one keeping up numbers only by selling false certainties and comfortable lies. Yes, the church, synagogue, temple, gurdwara or meeting-house may still function as a Sunday drop-in centre for the elderly, a social club, a heritage centre, an enclave of the past, but as the living embodiment of the city of God it hardly matches up to its prospectus. And since nine out of ten Europeans don't go near the place except for weddings, funerals and perhaps the Christmas carol service, who cares anyway?

In the English-speaking world, only three out of ten of us tell the pollsters we don't believe that God exists – or maybe four, or two, according to how and where the question is framed. Of the seven who say they do believe, four are not at all sure what they mean by saying so. They don't believe in the old man in the clouds, the friend for little

---

* According to a 2005 study by Fairfield University, 159 million Americans call themselves Christians, of whom 73 million (46%) are "born again" believers.

children above the bright blue sky, the monster god who flung frogs and boils and fire and water at those who disobeyed his commandments, or a god-man Jesus who died, descended into hell, rose again, ascended into heaven, and lives and reigns today. The God they say they believe in is Some Thing: their creed, "Well, there must be Some Thing ..." They know not who or what their Some Thing may be, but they feel it is more likely, and certainly more comfortable, than No Thing. So they search for this Some Thing in the expanding Mind, Body and Spirit section of their local bookshop, in crystals, fragrances and bottled spiritualities sold by hireling priests of the Age of Aquarius, in horoscopes, the occult, a drugs scene promising out-of-this-world mind-blowing experiences – anywhere, it seems, except amid the encircling gloom of their local church. So the God of Abraham, Isaac and Jacob, the Almighty, maker of heaven and earth, the Ancient of Days, pavilioned in splendour and girded with praise, is slowly dissolved into a wispy, gaseous Some Thing, to be appealed to in emergencies and, above all, to stave off the terror of No Thing, no purpose, no meaning...

That's half the story. But the trouble with God is that, like other old soldiers, he never dies, he only fades away. And he doesn't fade to nothing. When the composer Gustav Mahler – Jew, Catholic and atheist in turn – writes a mighty, impassioned symphony to celebrate life, he calls it The Resurrection. When cosmologist Stephen Hawkins reaches for a theory of everything he describes himself as probing the mind of God. Atonement, redemption, sacrifice, forgiveness – the fundamentals of God-language, of theology, of life itself – remain, yesterday, today and for ever the stuff of novels and newspaper stories, movies and soaps. Our secular age may declare that God is dead, but it won't let him lie down and rest in peace.

The language of faith – its symbols, metaphors and mythologies – is written on our bodies, wired into our souls, embedded in our poetry, painting and music. That's the trouble with God. We are not at all sure that we believe in him any more, or that we know what believing in him means, but he haunts us – or maybe just laughs at us

– from his exile or his grave. And that's the enigma, the paradox, I want to explore in this book. If the God of your fathers is alive and well for you, if you feel your faith is securely anchored, if you know your name is written in the Lamb's Book of Life, I am probably not writing for you. And if you can't for the life of you imagine why any rational person in this day and age would want to offer more than a yawn or sneer in response to God-talk, you'll find more congenial stuff in the sports pages of today's newspaper.

I'm writing for those who, in Stevie Smith's words, cannot "bear much longer the dishonesty / Of clinging for comfort to beliefs we do not believe in", who will not "allow good to be hitched to a lie", for those who sense that there are other worlds, but know they are all this one. For those who understand that we each live one life, and that it is many lives. For those who believe in God as they believe in Hamlet and Mr Pickwick and Mozart's Countess Almaviva, but are as skeptical of divine providence or intervention as they are of the influence of fairy godmothers and things that go bump in the night. If we have abandoned, or been abandoned by, a God "out there", we can be true to the imagined God of our true fictions, of whom we can still sing "This is my story, this is my song", the God who is woven into our everyday language and culture. This God may be trouble, but he is harder to escape – if, indeed, it is escape we are seeking.

That is what I'm going to try to explore. I am no sage, and I have no new theological theory or philosophical nostrum to offer, no secret formulae snatched from the vaults of the Knights Templar or the crystal balls of Mystic Meg. Read me for mystical enlightenment and you'll be lucky if I light your candle, let alone your fire. I'm going to improvise some variations on the theme of the trouble with God, and I'm going to draw on my own experience as journeyman journalist and broadcaster to give the improvisations shape and life, as best I can. If I take the reader through a series of tableaux featuring Bible classes in Gospel Hall, ban-the-bomb marches against Armageddon, talking hell and damnation with Ian Paisley, the gospel of Christian atheism, my shameful role in bringing Margaret Thatcher to power, and how God appeared to me on Dover beach to reassure me that he doesn't exist but nevertheless demands my soul, my life, my all, it is not because I imagine my reader has any interest in my autobiography, but because these are the concrete situations in which I've had to face up to the trouble with God – or the fact that God is in big trouble.

In the first part of this book I write about my own journey from religious fundamentalism to what I'm calling "religious humanism" (a term which may generate more heat than light, but which hopefully serves to signal a reasonable faith without outmoded supernaturalism). In the second, I turn from my own to God's journey, as pictured in the Bible, from badly behaved tribal monster-deity to a God for the modern world, incarnated within the wholly human spirit. And in the final part I write about the republic of heaven, which is our goal when kingdoms are no more, and all the responsibility is ours.

I'll start at Gospel Hall...

PART ONE

MY STORY

When I was a child, I spake as a child, I understood as a child, I thought as a child: but when I became a man, I put away childish things.

— 1 Corinthians 13:11

CHAPTER 1

Gospel Hall

I am H–A–P–P–Y,
I am H–A–P–P–Y,
I know I am,
I'm sure I am,
I'm H–A–P–P–Y.
– Sunday School chorus

I AM AT my computer keyboard in my first–floor study in our Yorkshire Dales farmhouse, deep in England's green and pleasant countryside. Surrounding me, on the table, shelves, chairs, floor, are the piles of books, newspapers and journals, clippings, letters, bills and detritus which I try to convince my wife is a perfectly rational, if untidy, filing system, awaiting only the final consummation of actually being allocated to a file.

To my left, through two lights in a steeply sloping roof, I can look up the rough fell, dotted with safely grazing sheep, over the broken wall which was the upper limit of the farm till a seventeenth–century occupant of our croft cleared a new "intack" to reclaim a few more acres on the slopes of Yorkshire's highest mountain, Whernside; and to my right a wider window gives me views past our stable, cow–house and barn, down to the river 'Big Beck' and the old stone bridge that crosses it, past the one–time Quaker meeting–house with a 1702 date stone over its porch, and then up the crazily winding "coal road" or "driving road" which was scored on the landscape two or three centuries ago by miners and drovers, and now carries cars, straining in bottom gear, up to Dent station, the highest in England, before pitching and tossing through some of England's wildest moor and mountain country. There are white blobs of sheep everywhere. The trees are still green, the meadows still golden after a late hay–cut. Michael Irving, who has the little field over Big Beck, is driving his tractor up and down, down and up, hauling a muck spreader which flings clods of well–seasoned cow muck in corn–circle patterns over the "fog" – the after–growth once the hay is taken. The sun is shining. Summer is short in these parts, but it seems to be gracing us with its presence for just a little longer.

It is September 11, 2001. Suddenly I am called downstairs to look at the television. I watch the first of the twin towers disappear, floor by floor by floor, in a puff of black powder, like an extra–special effect in a digital action movie.

And then the images of horror, repeated over and over again, a nightmare loop: the first plane smashing into the first tower, caught by a camera crew filming some road works in the street below; its disappearance into a plane–shaped hole; the fireball; the second plane and second fireball; the falling masonry and falling men and women; the collapsing towers and resultant death cloud making its terrifying, merciless progress through streets of shops and shoppers, offices and office workers, fires and firefighters... and the same again, and then again, and then in slow motion, and then cut to music.

A day or two later I read in the paper the prayer found in the highjacker Mohamed Atta's luggage:

> Oh God, open all doors for me. Oh God, who
> answers prayers and answers those who ask you, I
> am asking you for your help. I am asking you for
> forgiveness. I am asking you to lighten my way...

God, I trust in you. God, I lay myself in your hands.
I ask with the light of your faith that has lit the
whole world and lightened all darkness on this earth,
to guide me... We are of God, and to God we return.

It is the prayer of a man about to commit mass murder. It is
also a prayer I might have heard years ago at one of our Gospel
Hall meetings...

Gospel Hall was where God lived when I was a little boy. It was
a decidedly unpretentious home for a heavenly father. Sandwiched
between two suburban houses in a quiet residential street in Ashford,
Middlesex, fifteen miles south–west of London, it was built of wood
and corrugated iron, resembling an army billet–hut left over from
World War One rather than a place of worship. Inside, the boards were
half–covered in coconut matting. At one end, near the door, stood a
stove in the middle of the floor, its black and stained cast–iron flue
rising to a bare wooden roof. At the opposite end was the preacher's
platform, never referred to as a pulpit, since the word smacked of
"churchianity" – an evil scarcely to be whispered. Between stove and
platform were rows of plain wooden benches, never referred to as pews.
Two doors, one on each side of the platform, led to a perfunctory
kitchen, a toilet and a meeting–room at the back of the hall. There was
no adornment: a cross, a stained–glass window, any hint of vestments,
priestcraft or the beauty of holiness would have been anathematized as
the distractions of the Devil. The only wall decorations were faded
posters with Bible texts: "For God so loved the world..."; "Believe on the
Lord Jesus Christ, and thou shalt be saved"; "How sweet it is for
brethren to dwell together in unity...", and pictures of men in the desert
in long colourful robes and long colourless faces, often surrounded by
sheep. A large round clock ticked its smug, relentless way to Judgment
Day. I remember best the smell: of damp wood, damp coconut matting,
stacks of damp "Golden Bells" hymn books, damp ashes in the stove.
This was where we spent our Sundays: at the breaking–of–bread

meeting (never referred to as communion) in the morning, at Sunday school with Mr Stone and Mrs Burr in the afternoon, and at the gospel meeting in the evening, the last of which was open to all comers, though none but the saints (as the regulars called themselves) ever came. The gospel was preached in obedience to Christ's command to go into all the world, but the saints expected the world to come to Gospel Hall, and it showed some reluctance to make the trip.

This, then, was the meetinghouse of the Brethren, better known as Plymouth Brethren from the Devonshire town where the movement was said to have begun. It had originated in the evangelical revival of the early nineteenth century when groups of conservative Christians from the mainstream protestant churches began meeting on Sunday mornings as non–denominational fellowships, breaking bread together, reading the Bible, organizing prayer meetings and generally seeking to remodel themselves on the early church as depicted in the Acts of the Apostles. By the 1830s their dominant personality was a former Church of Ireland clergyman, John Nelson Darby, usually referred to in hushed tones as plain "JND", the Brethren's very own John Wesley, who travelled the British Isles and Europe on horseback, preaching a strictly Calvinist gospel and founding new meetings in conformity with his own uncompromising principles. By the 1840s Darby was decreeing that "separation from evil is God's principle of unity", and in "evil" (or Error as he preferred to call it) Darby included virtually all Christians outside his own fold.

His constant refrain was "Come ye out from among them and be ye separate". This was a step too far for some of the early Brethren, and the movement soon split into "Open" and "Exclusive" factions, each denouncing the Error of the other. The "Exclusives" subsequently splintered into at least eight different sects, arguing over such abstruse points as whether Jesus was the Son of God before or after his incarnation. It was rumoured, when we were children, that one group had split away after an argument as to whether or not Jesus had a beard (but this story may have been spread by my brother Brian and me, under the slogan "Jesus shaves..."). By the 1940s there were Kelly Brethren, Lowe Brethren, Raven Brethren, Craggs Brethren (known to us children as "the Scraggles") and smaller groups each named after the zealous splitter who had led them out of Error. Sometimes conferences were organized to explore reunion, and it transpired that neither side could remember what the argument had been about in the first place. At one such conference, our group had formed a reunited fellowship of the Kellys and the Lowes, henceforth known among the saints as the Kelly–Lowes – though they had nearly split again when the ex–Loweites wanted to call the new coalition Lowe–Kellys. In the United States, the different splinters shunned the cult of personality and labelled themselves Brethren I, Brethren II, and so on up to Brethren VIII. For some reason, probably because they were seen as ancient and therefore obscurely sacred, it was considered crucially important to use Roman numerals.

None of the Brethren factions had paid ministers or officials, and in their fierce rejection of priesthood, clergy and church hierarchy they bore a superficial resemblance to the Quakers. Indeed, some conservative evangelical Quakers had seceded to the Brethren in the 1830s. What this lack of structured accountability meant in practice was that the most dominant personalities ruled the roost, and when dominant personalities clashed, each tended to take his own following with him (no dominant females among the Brethren!) into yet another schism. But if their rejection of priesthood and hierarchy called to mind the anticlericalism of the Society of Friends, there were critical points on which the two nonconformist groups were (and are) worlds apart. The Brethren's Calvinist theology and Biblical literalism kept them closer to the evangelical mainstream; their emphasis on the literal and imminent Second Coming of Christ was quite different from the Quakers' conviction that Christ had already returned in the lives of his followers; and Brethren rejection of "the world" prevented them from taking part in any of the reform projects – abolition of slavery, prison reform, and the humanitarian causes that the Quakers and liberal churches were coming to see as part of a "social gospel". ("Social", and especially "socialism", were high in the Brethren's lexicography of demonic terms. My parents were severely chastised for shopping at the Co–op).

But the most obvious point of difference was over the position of women. Where Quakers had given women a role of near–equality from the movement's beginnings in the seventeenth century, the Brethren were definitely *brethren!* Women were expected to attend meetings, but were prohibited from officiating at the breaking of bread, speaking, praying aloud or contributing a Bible reading (except in occasional women–only meetings, where there could be no implied challenge to divinely instituted male supremacy). Nor could they preach at gospel meetings. A Plymouth sister was required to keep silent in church and subordinate herself to her brethren as the brethren subordinated themselves to their God.

My father and mother were Brothers by accident. My mother was one of a large Wolverhampton family, and in her teens, in the 1920s and early thirties, she made friends with a group of girls who attended "the meeting" in Cleveland Street. She did not know it was called a Brethren meeting and she knew nothing of the Open/Exclusive schism. What she knew was that it provided lively young company and safe sociability in a context where Bible study and prayer meetings, flavoured with tuneful Moody and Sankey hymns and choruses, were a seamless part of the fabric of life as it was lived in respectable lower middle–class families in middle England. She was "converted", "saved", "born again"; she "asked the Lord Jesus into her heart". And when a young man kept coming into the sweet shop where she worked, and eventually plucked up courage to ask if she would like to join him on his motorbike, she took up position on the pillion, put her arms around his waist, and steered him in the direction of Cleveland Street where he too, under the influence of his new love, pledged himself in due course to live "a new life in Christ". Initially, I suspect, the pledge was made in hopes of closer intimacy with his newly beloved; but I have no doubt that his subsequent commitment to the Brethren and their ways was genuine.

Alas, salvation did not deliver perfection. My mother suffered from a recurring health problem that put her in hospital from time to time. When her young man also fell ill with flu, he wrote a letter that would have shocked the Brethren into more prolonged and anguished prayer meetings had they ever come to hear of it. "I'm in bed and you're in bed", he wrote, "so we're both in bed together!" As is the way in this wicked world, even among the ransomed and redeemed, it wasn't long before the wish became the deed, with certain predictable consequences. Fleeing the disapproval of family, friends and Brethren, the compromised couple left Wolverhampton for the relative anonymity of Ashford, deep in London's suburbia, married hurriedly in a registry office, and lay low till I duly appeared, no doubt explained away to the folks at home as a wholly unexpected premature arrival, if not quite the product of an immaculate conception.

Settled in Ashford, and soon with two young boys (a third, and then a girl, were to follow), Lily and Charlie looked around for a Christian fellowship where they could recapture what they had enjoyed at Cleveland Street, and so discovered Gospel Hall. It was many months before they found that the Ashford meeting was Exclusive rather than Open like Cleveland Street, but by that time a mesh of new friendships had them securely "in fellowship". In any case, they couldn't for the life of them see any significant difference between the factions. My parents were neither of them nit–picking theologians who would worry whether Jesus was Son of God before, after or during his incarnation, or care a bean whether or not he had sported a beard like Brother Woolley or cheeks as smooth and virginal as those of Sister Gladys Williams. It was enough that members cared for and supported each other as an extended family, and this became even more important to my mother as my father joined the army in 1939 and was absent from the family home for much of World War II, "killing Germans" as we boys proudly told our friends (though his duties were clerical – he was a trainee accountant – and he never saw service at the front. He would have preferred to save Germans rather than kill them, or at least save them first). By 1942, when I was seven and my brother Brian five, we were spending our Sunday afternoons in the back room of Gospel Hall, where Mrs Burr and her sister Nelly Slark ran the junior Sunday school and taught us to sing:

> *Gentle Jesus, meek and mild,*
> *Look upon a little child.*
> *Pity my simplicity,*
> *Suffer me to come to thee...*

In those wartime years when we were very young, God and Jesus were family friends, spoken to familiarly, and participants in our games no less than in our worship. Every morning our mother plucked a text–for–the–day from our "Gospel Tidings" or "Gleanings of Gladness" calendar on the wall, smiling if the omens were good, looking faintly apprehensive if not. God, we were promised, *always* answered prayers. When I once asked God to chase away a dog that scared me on my way to school with its aggressive barking, and the dog had stayed put and barked even more ferociously, I complained that God hadn't answered *that* prayer. Oh yes he had, I was told, and the answer was No. He was, after all, the God of dogs as well as children, and in his loving kindness he had to let them have their fun too.

This aberration apart, God and Jesus were our playmates, our protectors, and our allies against the Germans. We were aware, sometimes uncomfortably, that the heavenly duo could always see us, even though we couldn't see them. I don't remember that it worried me too much that they saw me when I was naughty, but I did hope they were not looking when I was on the lavatory. Brian and I sometimes played God and Jesus, I, by virtue of seniority, being God, and Brian taking the supporting role as my Son. We squatted on the high back of our sitting room sofa, imagined as our heavenly home, and looked down with fixed seraphic smiles on our humble creation below. Once, when God proposed sending Jesus down to earth to save poor sinners,

Jesus refused to go and had to be pushed, falling with an undignified bump. Jesus wept, and God was given a smacked bottom. On another occasion, refusing to abandon roles, Jesus complained bitterly to his mother that God had locked him in the pantry. Mother was not shocked by these games. It was enough for her that her children were growing up in such intimacy with the Lord.

A primary article of our family creed, and one not widely shared among the Brethren, was that our God had a sense of humour. He enjoyed a good laugh. Charlie Boulton drew much of his own playfulness directly from the Bible. The smallest man in the world? Bildad the Shuhite, of course! Why Isaiah? Because one eye's 'igher than the other! A favourite game of ours was challenging the grown–ups to find animals in hymns. They soon got through lambs and lions, mother's "pity mice in Plicity" and father's "Oh what needless pain we bear", but we trumped him with "God is walking his porpoise out". Moving on from animals to items of clothing, obvious references to coats, shoes, armour were trumped with "As pants the hart for cooling streams" (which scored an animal too). We even risked body parts: feet, arms, hands, mouth, lips, heart came quickly, but we were puzzled by the embarrassed giggles that followed our contribution of "Here I raise my Ebenezer" (it was knees we had in mind) and we knew we had gone too far with "He is my ark and arsenal". If this sounds a far cry from the popular understanding of a Plymouth Brethren upbringing as all puritan piety and pain, that is because our experience was nothing like that of poor Edmund Gosse as recorded in *Father and Son*, his classic account of Brethren family life in Darby's day. Ours was a happy childhood in the bosom of a happy and loving family.

Our mother, Lily, was a strong–minded woman. She was never happy with the subordinate position that the Brethren – if not God himself – had assigned to women, knowing, I am sure (though she certainly never said so) that some of the women in the meeting had a more mature understanding of the Bible than many of the men, and would have given better "addresses" (never referred to as sermons). Hymns were her speciality, and all her housework – cooking or washing,

ironing or making the beds – was done to the accompaniment of a
verse, or often just a line, from her favourites. There were standards such
as "All things bright and beautiful" and, "In heavenly love abiding", and
gems from the evangelical repertoire like "Low in the grave He lay"
(which I heard, rather mystifyingly, as "low in the gravy...") and "Take
my life and let it be Consecrated Lord to Thee...

> *Take my Love: my Lord, I pour*
> *At thy feet its treasure–store.*
> *Take myself and I will be*
> *Ever, only, all for Thee.*

"Blessed assurance" was another regular:

> *Perfect submission, perfect delight,*
> *Visions of rapture burst on my sight.*
> *Angels descending bring from above*
> *Echoes of mercy, whispers of love.*

She was by no means sexually unaware, but I'm sure it never occurred
to her to link the ardent devotions of these hymns (all, as it happens,
written by women) to suppressed female desire. E P Thompson famously
attacked Methodist hymns for wallowing sado–masochistically in the
"fountain filled with Blood drawn from Emmanuel's veins", and other
commentators have noted what Valentine Cunningham calls, in these
same hymns, "the enormous female desire to see and meet and know
and be embraced by Christ", where "rapture is the recurring word".
Oblivious of such notions, Lily Boulton would sing

> *I am thine, O Lord, I have heard Thy voice*
> *And it told Thy love to me:*
> *But I long to rise in the arms of faith*
> *And be closer drawn to thee.*

and

I need Thee, O I need Thee:
Every hour I need Thee.
O bless me now, my Saviour:
I come to Thee.

Often, one hymn would slip seamlessly into another, and on into yet another. Sometimes a single line would be endlessly repeated. To this day I know nothing of what precedes or follows the line "Here I raise my Ebenezer...", but she raised it over and over again. My sister Celia, whenever she brought school friends home for tea, had to beg mother to suppress her tendency to burst into ecstatic songs of praise. She found it excruciatingly embarrassing when, serving the jelly and ice cream, mother would break into "Jesus wants me for a sunbeam" till hissed to silence and apologies. A minute later, another snatch would be heard from the kitchen: "Here I raise my Ebenezer...".

Many years later, as she lay dying in hospital, her three sons and her daughter sat at her bedside singing these hymns with her from memory. It did not matter to us, nor did it any longer matter to her, that the words no longer implied belief in any religious doctrine. What they did do was express love and thankfulness. Poet and unbeliever D H Lawrence wrote a moving essay, "Hymns in a Man's Life", dwelling on the power of hymns to penetrate the depths of consciousness with more raw emotion than any other form of poetry. My mother would not have wanted us to read Lawrence: but she would have agreed with him on that.

On the rare, happy occasions when our father was home on leave, he would say grace at mealtimes, always in the same words: "We thank thee Lord for all thy goodness to us, and for this food. Amen". The Brethren did not believe in set prayers, read or memorized from books, but it clearly never occurred to him that his grace was as formulaic as anything from the despised Book of Common Prayer, if less elegant than Cranmer's text. For us, giving thanks in this way was as ordinary and everyday an occurrence as listening to the war news on the radio or peeling off the "Gleanings of Gladness" text–for–today. When Brian and I wrote a play dramatizing one of Richmal Crompton's *Just William* stories, we had the Brown family lowering their heads and closing their eyes at the dinner table while Mr Brown intoned, "We thank thee Lord for all thy goodness to us and for this food amen". We could not imagine how else it would be possible to begin a family meal.

In the last year of the war our lives suddenly changed. German V1 bombers and V2 rockets were bombarding London, and Ashford was in their flight path. When our house in Village Way was badly shaken by a nearby explosion which deposited deadly chunks of twisted metal in our garden, mother decided it was time to get us to safety until the Lord of the Allied Hosts had given Hitler a good seeing–to. So we were evacuated – to Liverpool! Merseyside had been ravaged earlier in the war, and derelict bomb sites were everywhere. Liverpool was a city *from* which thousands of children had been evacuated, but its war was over, and Hitler's last throw was concentrated on London. We went to live with our Auntie Ena in a large house in Faulkner Street, not far from the huge, unfinished Anglican cathedral, which Ena, although a devout Methodist, told us was God's house. So He too had been evacuated, and a quick comparison with Gospel Hall suggested that He hadn't done too badly out of the war.

Returning to Ashford when it was all over, we discovered that Gospel Hall was no more. It had been burnt to the ground. Some said it was an incendiary bomb, others that the Lord's enemies in the local neighbourhood were to blame, driven to distraction, perhaps, by endless repetition of "I'm H–A–P–P–Y" wafting through their windows. But Brother Roberts confided to my mother and newly demobilized father his dark suspicion that Brother Woolley was behind it. Brother Woolley was considered by Brother Roberts to be in league with Error. What's more, he had once been discovered smoking in the lavatory, desperately trying to waft away the telltale fumes. When it later transpired that the insurance policy was in Brother Woolley's name, Brother Roberts' suspicion hardened to conviction. "As a Brother," he confided in my mother, "of course I love him. But as a man I *loathe* him."

God, it seemed, was now numbered among the homeless. Where, then, were we to find Him? The parish church up the road was certainly not His home: it was far too worldly. As for the Roman Catholic church we passed every day on the way to both day school and Sunday school, that was the Devil's own territory, a place of dreadful incantations and holy smoke, presided over by the Whore of Babylon, whoever she might be. From my tenth birthday in 1945, God and Jesus would never be quite as uncomplicated or intimate, never quite as trouble free, as they had seemed when they ran the universe from our Gospel Hall.

CHAPTER 2

The Rapture:
from Gospel Hall to White House

When the roll...
Is called up yon... der,
When the roll...
Is called up yon... der,
When the roll...
Is called up yon... der,
When the roll is called up yonder I'll be there.
– Sunday school chorus

IN MOST EVERYDAY respects, despite the peculiarities of my Brethren upbringing, my childhood was not so very different from that of other children growing up in lower middle–class British suburbia in the mid–twentieth century. Most of my friends went to Sunday school, if not to church or chapel. We all supposed we believed in God, and were quite sure that he spoke English rather than alien tongues like German or Japanese. We all took it for granted, in a quite untroubled way, that we would go to heaven if we were good (and gave our hearts to Jesus) and to hell if we were bad (and didn't). These were the givens of life in an England which, while it had long been retreating from old–time religious certainties, still had some way to go before arriving at the post–Christian secularism of the end of the century.

But one thing marked out children like me from the rest. It wasn't the more visible oddities of Brethrenism, nor even the eccentricities of a broader evangelicalism, with its total immersion in the Bible. It was our belief, indeed our certain knowledge, that Jesus was coming back, and coming back very soon. The Second Coming was the dominant feature of our lives. And it wasn't some distant prospect, hidden in the mists of time–future. It was imminent. We were living in the Last Days. Every tick of the clock might be the last we ever heard. If he didn't come tomorrow, it would probably be the day after; if not this week, the next. Every activity was organized on a "DV" basis: *Deo volente*, God willing. Next Sunday's gospel meeting would take place only "if he should tarry". We did not doubt that while in his mercy he might tarry a few weeks, even a few months, he would not be in a mood to tarry much longer. His return was promised in God's Word. It was to be preceded by "wars and rumours of wars", and the papers were full of nothing else. Brothers who generally warned against newspaper reading as a dangerous flirtation with the affairs of "the world" would surreptitiously scan the headlines for confirmation of their conviction that The Rapture was nigh, and in much excitement they would put their evidence before the saints.

What would actually happen at the Second Coming? At the sound of the Last Trump, Jesus would appear in the clouds. The graves would open, and the dead in Christ would rise to meet him. We, the living in Christ, would follow them to glory. So far, so Biblical: The first epistle to the Thessalonians (4:16–17) tells how:

> the Lord himself shall descend from heaven with a shout, with the voice of the archangel, and with the trump of God: and the dead in Christ shall rise first: Then we which are alive and remain shall be caught up together with them in the clouds, to meet the Lord in the air.

But the Brethren's principal founder, John Nelson Darby (1800–32), had elaborated Paul's poetic promise into a detailed doctrine of "dispensationalism", prescribing precisely how, if not quite when, all this would happen. As he and his followers told it, we few would be taken, the many would be left. The train driver who believed would fly heavenwards from his cab, leaving his train and its unbelieving passengers to run on till it hit the last buffers. Driverless cars belonging to taken saints would career into lorries driven by the unregenerate. The unbelieving batsman at the cricket crease would face an empty space where a moment earlier there had been a believing bowler. The unbelieving lover in his bed, the unbelieving brother, sister, friend, would suddenly find themselves alone in a God–forsaken world. And it would serve them right for not believing. However, in his mercy, God would offer one last chance of repentance during "the Tribulation" (derived from Revelation), which would last seven years. That would end with the Third Coming and the start of the Rapture proper, when Jesus would return one last time to reign on earth as he did in heaven, and we would return with him to help run the place, co–partakers in his power and glory.

That I might not be one of the elect, the lucky few, the happy band of Brothers who would rise to meet Christ in the clouds, did not occur to me. I had Blessed Assurance, the foretaste of glory divine. I sang:

> *When the trumpet of the Lord shall sound, and time shall be no more,*
> *When the morning breaks, eternal, bright and fair;*
> *When the saints of God are gathered over on the other shore,*
> *When the roll is called up yonder – I'll be there!*

And we prayed, in the words of another hymn:

> *Each happy morning Thou dost give,*
> *I have one morning less to live.*
> *Then help me so this day to spend*
> *To make me fitter for my end.*

My end, of course, being a new beginning.

While my parents and the grown–up Brothers believed all this most sincerely, they didn't necessarily allow it to get in the way of normal prudent planning. So they put their savings in the bank, built their careers, insured their homes, planned next year's holidays, and ignored the command to "take no thought for the morrow", just like their nice but godless neighbours. But it was different with children – at least, with this child. I took the Rapture very seriously indeed. Since Jesus was coming for me any moment, probably before the weekend, there was clearly no point in school work, no point in homework, no point in education, qualifications, career. Like Peter Pan, I would never grow up. The Rapture would get me first. In vain, my mother and father tried to convince me that, although there was no doubt whatever that he *would* come, he *really would*, I would be prudent to take on board the thin possibility that he might choose to delay longer than we all expected, if only to give the unbelievers one more chance. But I thought he'd given them all the chances they needed, especially Alan Windebank, the school bully, and I was confident that Jesus wouldn't see much point in delaying matters a moment longer than necessary.

There were times, admittedly, when I felt somewhat let down by the postponement of paradise: for instance, when I was punished for not getting my homework done, or caught out in some misdemeanor which I had supposed would not be discovered till after the Rapture. There were also times when I fervently hoped the tarrying would last a little longer: before birthdays, or Christmas and summer holidays. And when I first found the courage to invite a Brethren girl I rather liked to come out with me (to a school production of Shaw's *Androcles and the Lion*, which irreverent work the Brethren would have considered scandalously unsuitable, since it featured early Christians being eaten), I prayed hard that God would hold back till I had had the pleasure of sitting next to her and perhaps brushing my hand against hers... "Even so, come quickly, Lord" – but not *too* quickly.

Do I exaggerate? Probably. The coming Rapture was a good excuse for not getting on with what I was supposed to be getting on with, for not pursuing my studies, and for mischievously frustrating the wishes and ambitions of parents and teachers. But the vivid expectation of that Second Coming pursued me all through my early teenage years and, allied with a natural laziness and stubborn reluctance to engage in hard work, helped ensure an undistinguished school record and no chance of further education.

Meanwhile, with Gospel Hall a pile of cinders, we had to find somewhere else to spend our Sundays. For a time, we were dispatched to a Baptist Sunday School in a "tin tabernacle" little different from Gospel Hall, where the emphasis was on learning chunks of the Bible by rote. It seemed a drag at the time, but it furnished my mind with some of the finest poetry in the English language, thanks to the efforts of Brother–turned–Baptist Mr Stone, a door–to–door insurance salesman who boasted that he never read any book but the Bible and that God had given his personal assurance that he would go to heaven when he died – if the Lord didn't come first.

On Sunday evenings, we went by bus the five miles to the nearest Kelly–Lowe Gospel Hall, in Hounslow, where we kept the faith and sang the good old hymns.

There was the solemn warning:

> *Life at best is very brief,*
> *Like the falling of a leaf,*
> *Like the binding of a sheaf –*
> *Be in time!*

And our lament for the nearly–but–not–quite–saved:

> *Almost persuaded, now to believe!*
> *Almost persuaded, Christ to receive!...*
> *Sad, sad that bitter wail:*
> *Almost... but lost!*

I remember a tramp coming into the meeting one evening and trying to ingratiate himself with the Brethren by joining in the hallelujahs, amens and praise–the–Lords which punctuated the preacher's invitation to shun evil companions, disdain bad language and subdue dark passions. After the meeting, one or two Brethren tried to hustle him out, but my father stopped them. Seizing the moment, the tramp told him a sob story about being far from home and not having the money to pay for the train ticket that would restore him to the bosom of his pious, God–fearing family. Father produced a pound note, and the tramp made a hasty exit with one last triumphant hallelujah. The Brethren remonstrated with my father: "He'll take us all for fools. He'll be back". Father replied quietly, "I'd rather he take us for fools than hypocrites". I remember his words, and their silence.

On summer evenings we would carry the gospel message to a wider world, setting up a collapsible soap–box platform and a tiny treadle organ outside The Bell public house in Hounslow high street, where the regulars' strains of "The Old Bull and Bush" or "Four and twenty virgins came down from Inverness" would be drowned out by our fervent counterpoint:

> *Are you washed, are you washed*
> *In the blood, in the blood,*
> *In the soul–cleansing blood of the Lamb?*
> *Are your garments spotless, are they white as snow?*
> *Are you washed in the blood of the Lamb?*

There was more blood in our hymnal than in the local abattoir:

> *There is a fountain filled with blood*
> *Drawn from Immanuel's veins,*
> *And sinners plunged in that blest flood*
> *Lose all their guilty stains...*

As our captive revellers emerged from the pub and swayed towards the nearest bus stop, we asked them:

> *Would you be free from your burden of sin?*
> *There's power in the blood, power in the blood!*
> *Would you o'er evil a victory win?*
> *There's wonderful power in the blood!*
> *Yes, there's power, power, wonder–working power*
> *In the precious blood of the Lamb!*

We continued to break bread on Sunday mornings, meeting now in the front room of Mrs Burr's house in Parkland Grove, Ashford. We were a dwindling band, and after Brother Roberts passed on to his reward my father was often the only man present, and therefore the only one permitted to announce a hymn or reading, to pray aloud, and of course to break the bread and pour the wine. Musical instruments being anathema at the Lord's table, the hymns were sung unaccompanied, with Nelly Slark pitching the first note. I doubt that we made a joyful noise – half a dozen earnest but tuneless elderly ladies, a couple of men who strangled the high notes, and two boys who couldn't wait till it was over and we were on our way back to Sunday dinner. The meeting became, I suspect, as much an ordeal to our parents as it was to us.

When we outgrew Mr Stone's Baptist Sunday school we joined the local Crusaders. This was a union of Bible classes, originally admitting only boys attending public school (which, in Britain, means *private* school: don't ask *why*), as there were thought to be plenty of missions to the lower classes but few catering for the special needs of future captains of industry. (There was a Crusaders Union for girls, too, but this split over the theological question of whether or not the girls should be allowed to wear lipstick. Mother became a Girls Crusaders' leader and was against lipstick – but even more against making its prohibition a necessary condition of salvation). Brian and I made it into Crusaders by virtue of passing the 11–plus scholarship, which got us into the elitist Hampton Grammar School, while scholarship failures had to be content with the Crusaders' more proletarian equivalent, the Covenanters. Occasionally the rules were relaxed, as happened when my father remonstrated with George Lane, our Crusader leader, for refusing membership to the academically challenged son of the local pet shop owner. There was no class system in heaven, he argued, so why have one here below?

The Crusaders movement was strongly Bible based and evangelical, but non–denominational. The Brethren disapproved of our attending, as we risked contamination by Error, but my father and mother stood firm. Classes were held on Sunday afternoons in a dilapidated house in Church Road, Ashford, which was literally falling down around us. One Sunday we noticed that the piano, energetically pounded by chorus master Eddie Fifield, was swaying up and down like a seesaw. The floor beneath it had broken away from its pinnings and was springing like a trampoline. No–one thought to organize repairs, and Eddie continued to rise and fall for many a Sunday afternoon, till one day the adjoining lavatory disappeared into the basement, after which it was thought prudent to contact the landlord before the piano and Eddie followed it into the bottomless pit. The landlord was a local speculator who was only waiting for the roof to fall in before demolition and redevelopment. It was a race between the Rapture and the rupture.

What we enjoyed most about Crusaders, apart from the bouncing piano and the disappearing loo, was summer camps. Every year we joined fellow Crusaders from all over the country, pitching our tents in wonderful farmland sites at Polzeath in Cornwall or Studland Bay, Dorset. Camp games, camp fires and camp grub were interspersed with camp Bible readings and emotional invitations to "give your hearts and lives to Christ". I did so – every year. Mine was the most given–away heart in Ashford: I couldn't resist. So every summer's end I returned home re–renewed and re–redeemed, and sometimes it lasted a whole week. But by the time school term began again I was scrimping on my homework and hoping the unaccountably delayed Rapture would get me off the hook.

When I left school at sixteen, having failed to qualify for the sixth form and hope of a university place, I also broke with the Brethren. One Sunday morning, as we walked along Village Way towards Mrs Burr's house for our breaking–of–bread meeting, my father carrying his Bible in one hand and the Hovis loaf and bottle of plain, unsanctified plonk in the other, I told him this would be my last attendance. He was upset, but not angry. He suggested I tell the meeting myself rather than disappear without a word. So when the bread and wine had done their rounds, I told them I wouldn't be coming again, that I would never forget them, and that I hoped still to

> *Dare to be a Daniel,*
> *Dare to stand alone,*
> *Dare to have a purpose firm*
> *And dare to make it known.*

Mrs Burr said she would pray for me. Nelly Slark said she always knew I'd have to go one day. Gladys Williams cried. They had all been Brethren since the turn of the century. Their fathers knew JND. They still fully expected that their eyes would see the glory of the coming of the Lord. But I had begun to wonder if the great appointment in the sky would ever be kept, and I found I was more interested in life before death than after it. I wondered too whether the "worldly pleasures" I had been urged to shun were as wicked as I'd been told. My father sometimes played Mozart and Beethoven on his wind–up gramophone, and I was entranced: was all music really worldly and wicked? I had not only touched a girl's hand but actually held it for a second or two, and one glorious night I had accidentally brushed against a blouse stretched over a soft warm breast. (I met its owner again forty years later. She remembered too). I knew there was a world out there that I must explore. So I left Mrs Burr's on Sunday mornings and the Hounslow Gospel Hall meetings on Sunday evenings, and dared to be a Daniel elsewhere.

The Rapture joined the tooth fairy and Santa Claus as relics of the childish things I put away as manhood loomed. It remained in my consciousness as one of the more eccentric marks of an eccentric little sect, bizarre but relatively harmless. Years later I discovered that the Rapture was alive and well and living in middle America.

It turned out that, following a missionary trip to America by John Nelson Darby, a conference was organized at Swampscott, Mass., in 1876 to combat what was seen as the erosion of "fundamental beliefs" in the face of Biblical criticism, evolutionary theory and the rise of the "social gospel". Biblical "inerrancy" (the doctrine that the Bible was literally true and without error) was declared the foundation stone of the Christian religion, and the coming Rapture was emphasized as a fundamental dogma of what its followers themselves called the Fundamentalist movement. A book called *Jesus is Coming* sold more than three million copies at the turn of the century and was followed by a series of twelve books under the general title *The Fundamentals*. (A century later the Reverend Tim LaHaye and Jerry B Jenkins would produce a dozen novels in the *Left Behind* series as part of a $45 million deal including films, videos, DVDs and children's versions – unless, of course, they run out of luck and the Rapture comes first).

Initially non–denominational, fundamentalism soon spread into the Baptist and Presbyterian churches. After the First World War, independent fundamentalist churches and new fundamentalist denominations sprang up all over America. Darby's "dispensationalist" version of the Rapture was given a new lease of life when the state of Israel was created after the Second World War, since the return of the "children of Israel" to their homeland was interpreted as a sign that Biblical prophecy was being fulfilled in preparation for the Second Coming. Millions of American Christian fundamentalists, although committed by Biblical inerrancy to the New Testament view of Jews as killers of the true Messiah, now became more Zionist than the Zionists.

It only remained for these millions to be organized politically and American power would ensure that Israel's borders would be secured, the Palestinians (for which read Philistines) routed, the illegal settlement and occupation of the West Bank stabilized, and preparations for the Rapture would be complete. Billy Graham and Pat Robertson, anointed high priests of fundamentalism, set about getting a born again fundamentalist into the Oval Office. Richard Nixon was their first candidate, but he proved something of a disappointment by way of a little burglary. Ronald Reagan was better, zealous in his gleeful preparations for Armageddon. But George W Bush was better still, staking his own second coming on the support of the new Christian right. On the night of the 2004 presidential election it became apparent to a wondrous, watching world that the Rapture had made it all the way from Gospel Hall to the White House.

CHAPTER 3

"Choose you this day whom ye will serve"

Time is short, we must be speedy,
We can see the hungry filled,
House the homeless, help the needy –
Shall we blast, or shall we build?
– Peace song

I WAS A pretty poor Daniel. I didn't yet have a purpose firm, and I wasn't ready to stand alone. Having put the Brethren behind me, I tried the local Congregational church which was gaining a reputation as a lively place for teenagers to hang out. (Lonnie Donegan was singing "Sweet sixteen, goes to church, just to see the boys...". Or girls, as appropriate). The minister, Gilbert Kirby, was a warm, friendly man with a lively sense of humour, qualities that made his sermons startlingly unlike the sour or dour words I was used to from Brethren preachers. He would later head up both the London Bible College and the Evangelical Alliance, before the latter was captured for fundamentalism.

Congregational services were more formal than those at Gospel Hall. The church choir sang an anthem and the organist played a voluntary, contributions to worship which the Brethren would have considered the trappings of popery and the fornications of the Whore of Babylon. The hymns had less blood, but better tunes. After the evening service, the elderly church secretary solemnly announced that young people were welcome to congregate in the church hall "for tea and social intercourse". Here was a safe place for boys to talk to girls, and girls to boys, and when the tea and social intercourse was over, selfish genes and the first rituals of ancient mating games sorted out who would walk whom home that night. Marriages may be made in heaven, but not a few were rehearsed in "the Cong" – and there was much whispered gossip about which couples were engaged in the practice that was said to make perfect.

At eighteen I was wrenched away to do my National Service in the Royal Air Force. It was, Gilbert Kirby told me, an "opportunity to witness". The key test was whether I would have the courage to kneel at my bedside on the first night and brave the mockery of the "lewd fellows of the baser sort" who would undoubtedly be the majority of my billet mates. It was an ordeal I dreaded: never was the now fading prospect of the Rapture more devoutly wished for. But down I got, closed my eyes, and waited for the expected hail of boots and derision. Nothing happened. No one had noticed. But if my Daniel–act of daring was not remarked upon, it couldn't have been much of a "witness". What on earth was the Lord expecting of me?

Next day, however, two lads came up to me and told me they too were Christians: a Methodist and a Baptist. So we formed a small Christian fellowship to sustain each other through our square–bashing and daily exercises of running our bayonets into enemy sandbags. But none of us proved up to the responsibilities heaven had laid upon us. The Methodist was found one morning with a local girl of very different persuasion in his bed, protesting rather lamely that he couldn't imagine how she had got there. The Baptist (who was gay, though the word had yet to be applied in this context) was court–martialled for exposing himself "in a lewd and unmilitary posture" in the bathhouse. And I succumbed to the temptation of using free Sunday nights to visit the local cinema. Of the three of us, I'm sure I felt the most guilty, not least when I made my first acquaintance with Jane Russell on the big screen – and on a Lord's Day too!

Returning to Ashford after serving Queen and Country with

little distinction (I spent most of my two years as a "white cap" – an RAF police corporal – guarding a half–derelict radar installation in Lincolnshire, with no idea of what I was supposed to do if it was invaded one dark night by Russians), I was relieved to find the Cong still drawing crowds with its strategic mix of God and the joys of social intercourse. Here I met my first wife, Sylvia, while organizing a table–tennis competition, fiddling the draw to make sure she was my doubles partner. While this won me desired proximity, it also lost us whatever chance we had of winning the Cong Ping–Pong Doubles Cup, 1955, as we tended to keep our eyes on each other instead of on the ball. We married one week after brother Brian wed his Cong girlfriend, Barbara. I vaguely resented the fact that he, a full eighteen months my junior, had beaten me to the altar, especially when, at the reception, he used his best man's speech to draw on his wealth of experience of the joys and pitfalls of married life.

Gospel Hall was history, but God was as pervasively present in my life as he had ever been. After a dead–end spell as a clerk in a London export office, I had decided I wanted to be a writer. My mother had taught me my letters before I ever went to school and one of my earliest memories is of seeing the letters M–I–L–K on the milk float outside our Village Way house, and putting the four sounds together to make the mind–blowing discovery that they spelt out the very stuff the milkman delivered. I had made the connection between subject and symbol, the prerequisite of all knowledge and understanding. Thereafter I was a voracious consumer of books, even though the Brethren warned against reading anything but the Bible and the impenetrable tracts and expositions of JND. Books were magic, and I soon wanted to make magic myself, or with Brian. We started by writing our own comics, with first episodes of mystery thrillers and blood–curdling fantasies (we rarely got beyond the first episode, as we couldn't find ways of extricating our heroes from the impossible situations we had conjured up for our cliff–hanging chapter–endings). I began an epic poem on the war, but ran out of steam after a couple of bloody battles, and brought the thing to a sudden conclusion with the couplet, "And now there's nothing more to tell, / 'Xcept we won the war, and all went well". Sadly, my poetic sensibilities were mortally wounded when I was caned by my headmaster for offering as English homework an elegy on the death of King George VI which was considered both irreverent and inadequate:

> *George the Sixth, the good, the great,*
> *Once the king, he's now the late.*

(Brian unaccountably and most unfairly escaped a thrashing for a much more economical effort: "King died. Queen cried").

Hymns figured high in our repertoire, and occasionally (since we were still sure God had a sense of humour remarkably similar to our own) parodies of hymns and choruses. "Break me, melt me, mould me, fill me..." became:

> *Oh break me, squeeze me, squash me, God,*
> *Oh kick me in the belly;*
> *Tread on me, make me nothingness –*
> *A spiritual jelly...*

Then we discovered Gilbert and Sullivan, which opened the window to a whole new world of wonder rivalling that of the Bible. So we wrote an epic opera of our own, with sixty musical numbers and a hundred pages of spoken dialogue. I did the words and Brian the music, picked out with one finger on the piano and eventually played by a third–year violin student at the grand premiere (and final performance) before an audience of stupefied parents and friends. Wagner it was not – except in length. *Flymanda* (for that was its name) featured love, death, ghosts and a student witch:

> *For those who love all money*
> *And dream of growing rich,*
> *A wonderful profession*
> *Is that of student witch.*
> *The salary is generous,*

The working hours are few,
With books and spells provided,
And board and lodging too.
The work is not too difficult
And full of evil fun.
Oh the frightening trade of witchcraft
Is a very happy one.

I boil a pot of bodies
Removed from nearby tombs,
And stand a–shrieking o'er the pot
While breathing human fumes...

After the juvenilia, I had seen my first article published during my National Service days: some thoughts on the Englishness of English music (about which I knew virtually nothing) in a journal called *Musical Opinion*. Now, post–RAF, I was working on an even more un–Brethrenish subject: a history of British jazz (about which I knew only a little more), for which the publisher W H Allen had generously advanced me £200 against royalties. I edited a monthly journal, *Perspective*, for the local Christian Youth Council, and did the publicity for our Youth for Christ rallies. That was part of the trouble with God: he did make a lot of demands on one's time and energies, even if there was a lot of fun to be had in doing one's bit to advance the kingdom of heaven – and of course in those days there was no question but that it *was* a *kingdom*.

But I was aware by now of that wider world beyond courting, Jelly Roll Morton, Nanki–Poo and witnessing for the Lord. In 1956, first the Suez crisis and then the Soviet suppression of the Hungarian revolution broke through the apathy which had settled on Britain after the war and looked to be turning the fifties into the greyest and most conformist decade of the twentieth century. Both events brought crowds of young demonstrators onto the streets – a new phenomenon in post–war Britain. Suez in particular polarized opinion, forcing us to take sides. And the questions it raised were first and foremost *moral* questions. What was the *right* response to Nasser's nationalization of "our" Suez Canal? What *ethical* issues were raised by the Hungarian resistance to Soviet communism, and what *moral* consequences did it have for freedom and world peace? Such questions were not on Gilbert Kirby's agenda, nor did they create so much as a ripple on the placid surface of evangelicalism. God was working his purpose out, and his purpose had everything to do with the state of individual souls and nothing whatever to do with the state of the world.

Suez and Hungary soon opened up a much bigger issue: the Bomb. In the early fifties the Soviet Union had ended the American monopoly of nuclear power by successfully testing its own H–bomb, accelerating a nuclear arms race that threatened not only the peace of the world but the survival of the human race. By the mid–fifties both cold war camps were testing weapons of mass destruction on the ground, in the air and under the sea. Scientists warned that the mere testing, let alone actual use, of these weapons could prove catastrophic by releasing huge quantities of radioactive strontium–90 into the air we breathed and the milk we drank. There was talk of the end times: with a bang if the weapons were ever used, with a whimper if the tests continued indefinitely. We read of talks about talks to secure an international ban on tests as a prelude to international nuclear disarmament, but the endless stalemates made it clear that both sides were intent on winning the arms race rather than calling it off.

When it was clear that strontium–90 was turning up in milk supplies, it was mothers with young families who took the initiative in forming the first National Campaign Against Nuclear Weapon Tests. At the same time, a small group of peace activists began a campaign of direct action, some sailing into the Pacific testing grounds and others concentrating on a secret installation some forty miles from London near a village called Aldermaston, where a large tract of farmland had been commandeered as the site of Britain's Weapons Research Establishment (with the ominous word "Nuclear" deftly omitted from its title). By 1958 these groups had come together under the umbrella of CND, the Campaign for Nuclear Disarmament, led by Canon John Collins of St Paul's Cathedral and the veteran philosopher Bertrand Russell. The Campaign's slogan was "Ban the Bomb", and its annual Easter marches to or from Aldermaston drew tens of thousands of mainly young protesters. Similar anti–nuclear protests began in the United States under the auspices of SANE (the Campaign for a Sane Nuclear Policy) and Turn Towards Peace. The long grey night of the fifties was over and the new dawn of the sixties was at hand.

For me, as for many of my generation, the Bomb was more than a weapon of war. It was the symbol of everything that was wrong with the old world, the world of our parents and grandparents. It displaced the Devil as evil personified. To ban the Bomb was to banish evil, and build afresh:

> *Men and women, stand together!*
> *Do not heed the men of war!*
> *Make your minds up, now or never –*
> *Ban the Bomb for evermore!*

Newly married now (to my ping–pong partner), I found in the campaign a new focus for my evangelical zeal. I helped start a local branch of CND, and one of our first activities was to picket the parish church after a Remembrance Day service. Banning the Bomb did not immediately displace my activities for Youth for Christ and the Christian Youth Council (of which I had become chair). I saw them as interlinked. But that view wasn't shared by my evangelical colleagues. I had "gone political", and by doing so had compromised not only my own work but theirs. One evening I was visited by a deputation consisting of my oldest and closest friends. They asked me to choose between Christ and CND.

The Bomb, they said, was in God's hands. If nuclear war was part of his plan, there would be nuclear war, and it would be to his greater glory. Our business was saving souls, not meddling in the affairs of the world. Canon Collins may be a canon, but did that make him a Christian? As for Russell, he was a notorious atheist. And wasn't it clear that the Campaign was run by godless socialists and communists – men like Michael Foot and that scourge of fundamentalists, Methodist leader Donald Soper? What was I doing in the company of the unredeemed? Just look at the news photos of the Aldermaston marchers! Long hair, duffel coats... What were they doing in those church halls where they bedded down after each day's march? Not singing Songs of Praise, you bet!

I must drop CND, I was told, or resign from the Christian Youth Council and Youth for Christ. They had no doubt that, if I prayed about it, I would be led to the right decision. I said I would pray about it. I did. Next day I resigned from the CYC and YFC, and at the next Wednesday evening church Bible study I made sure to wear my CND badge on the lapel of my brand new but carefully crumpled duffel coat.

I was now working in London as an assistant on the Liberal Party paper, the *Liberal News*, edited by a warm–hearted but eccentric Quaker, Reg Smith. Every spare evening I spent at CND's temporary headquarters off Fleet Street, stuffing envelopes, drafting leaflets. Peggy Duff, the scruffy, chain–smoking, much–loved mother superior of the Campaign, asked me if I would help produce a new journal, *Sanity*. I became its editor, honorary at first, but full–time when the Campaign grew into a mass movement and *Sanity* started selling over 100,000 copies a month.

Crossing from the Liberals to the Labour Party, where support for nuclear disarmament was stronger, I became a founder member of the re–born Christian Socialist Movement, started on the initiative of Donald Soper, and worked with Tom Driberg on its newsletter. I had been forced to choose between Christ and the Devil. "Once to every man and nation Comes the moment to decide..." – and I had chosen Christ. But a Christ bent on healing this world, not bringing it to its knees, a Christ on the march rather than a Christ in retreat. For the first time in my life, I felt I understood what I was asking for when I prayed "Thy kingdom come, Thy will be done *on earth*". But still, you notice, a *kingdom*.

CHAPTER 4

The Cheshire Cat

*I wish you wouldn't keep appearing and vanishing so
suddenly: you make one feel quite giddy' [said Alice].
"All right", said the Cat; and this time it vanished quite
slowly, beginning with the end of the tail, and ending
with the grin, which remained some time after the rest
of it had gone.*
– Lewis Carroll (Reverend Charles Dodgson),
Alice in Wonderland

FOR SOME, the sixties started with the Beatles' first LP, for some with the trial of Penguin Books, which had dared to bring out an unexpurgated version of D H Lawrence's *Lady Chatterley's Lover*, and for others with the mini–skirt and the pill. For me, it began with the not entirely original realization that the world needed saving, and the conviction that we, the young, must be the agency by which salvation was to be accomplished. Social activism was the gospel in action, and the particular forms of social activism to which I was drawn were the Campaign for Nuclear Disarmament and the Christian Socialist Movement. For a time I continued attending the "Cong", but the occasions on which I was asked to speak or write or run something there became increasingly rare. Understandably so, as I was becoming something of an outsider, seen by my friends as in mortal peril of the sin that dared only whisper its name: "backsliding".

No longer comfortable with evangelicalism, I began looking around for a new spiritual home. The local Methodist church was run by a "modernist" Christian Socialist minister whose denial of Biblical infallibility had long scandalized the Cong, so I tried that – only to discover a sullenly conservative congregation who seemed to resent their minister's liberal theology as much as his politics. From there I tried the nearest Quaker meeting, in Staines, hoping to find something of the vibrant radicalism I had discovered among Quakers I was meeting in the peace movement. But Staines Friends were elderly, and very, very quiet. Quaker "meeting for worship" reminded me too much of the Brethren's breaking–of–bread meetings except that the Quakers didn't break bread, didn't sing hymns, and didn't read the Bible. It seemed to me that they didn't really do anything apart from observing a Trappist ritual; and when I suggested to the clerk that we hold a peace vigil in Staines one Sunday morning instead of sitting in solemn silence in a dull, dark meeting house, and was told that this would not be in "proper ordering", I left Friends (for the time being) to their own impenetrable devices.

Through CND I had met and fallen under the spell of the radical firebrand, Michael Foot. His impassioned oratory and coruscating journalism made him a role model for many in the rising generation who had lost patience with the complacency and indifference that seemed to characterize the grey old world of their parents. The son of a Liberal, nonconformist father, Michael was neither a Christian nor a pacifist. He had first come to prominence as principal author of an influential pamphlet, *Guilty Men*, which had exposed the appeasement of Hitler by right–wing politicians and press in Britain. He had edited the *London Evening Standard* during the war years, and much of his post–war journalism appeared in the small but influential independent socialist weekly *Tribune*, which he edited in the fifties. A founding member of CND, he had thrown *Tribune's* weight behind the campaign, resulting in a traumatic break with the post–war leader of the British Left, Aneurin Bevan, who opposed unilateral nuclear disarmament. Shortly after the 1959 general election, Michael invited me to join the staff of *Tribune* for three days a week, at £3 a day. Recognizing that this was hardly a living wage, he also arranged for me to do a Saturday double shift as a sub–editor, first on the Labour and Co–op Sunday paper *Reynolds News* and, when that folded, on the *Sunday Graphic* (which also folded not long after: was it something I said?). At £1 an hour for a 14–hour double shift, I entered the sixties making my bow as a radical journalist earning in total the princely sum of £23 a week before tax.

Tribune proved an ideal training ground. With a part–time editorial staff of five or six, under the hands–on editorship of Dick Clements (Michael remained a behind–the–scenes editor–in–chief), I had to learn the trades of reporter, feature–writer, political columnist, leader–writer, book reviewer, sub–editor and lay–out designer: a tough but exhilarating apprenticeship. At first I was regarded as something of a curiosity, the only professing Christian in an office where atheistic humanism was regarded as the only conceivable stance for any sane, modern, rational person. (Donald Soper had a regular column, but there was an understanding that he wouldn't mention God more than once per contribution). The office staff, led by a wonderful South London mother–earth matron named Rosie, were even warned to moderate their language when I was about, lest my innocent piety should be corrupted. This ended suddenly when I was mischievously given the newly–published unexpurgated *Lady Chatterley's Lover* to review. I took the opportunity to discuss the uses and abuses of the four–letter words that were causing all the fuss, printing them in full without resorting to coy asterisks, and Rosie discovered that my capacity to shock her was far greater than hers to shock me.

One result was that my Christianity began to be mercilessly interrogated by my colleagues. Sheila Noble, who had the relatively modest title of editorial secretary but was far more influential in the running of the paper than the job description implied, demanded, over endless cups of coffee, to know how I could *possibly* believe in God,

Jesus and all that stuff. And I began to wonder myself. I talked to Donald Soper about it, but found myself wondering if *he* really "believed": he was certainly a pretty unorthodox Methodist, and his idea of the kingdom of heaven seemed to be simply a land in which *Tribune* policies were faithfully and unquestioningly pursued. Tom Driberg, with whom I briefly edited the Christian Socialist Movement *Newsletter*, was even less helpful. *His* heaven, I gathered, would have the constitution of the Soviet Union, set to music by Stanford or Parry and sung by choirboys more knowing than their innocent faces let on. I found I couldn't give Sheila a satisfactory answer, and she – then and now one of my dearest friends – pushed her advantage mercilessly.

Then came *Honest to God*. In March 1963 the Suffragen Bishop of Woolwich, John Robinson, published his ground–breaking book which sought to give a contemporary meaning to "God", following radical continental theologians like Paul Tillich and Dietrich Bonhoeffer in de–emphasizing the nature of God as *personal* and suggesting He (still a He, though logic should have reclassified Him as an It) might be better understood as the "ground of being" or our "ultimate concern". In an article in the *Sunday Observer*, Robinson summarized his argument under what was considered in those days the scandalously provocative heading "Our Image of God Must Go". Both article and book caused a furore. The publishers, SCM Press, claimed that with 350,000 copies sold within a month of publication, and with German, French, Swedish, Dutch, Danish, Italian and Japanese translations, it "appears to have sold more quickly than any new book of serious theology in the history of the world". It certainly seemed to penetrate the parts that other theological tomes never reached. An *Observer* journalist reported that during a visit to Moscow he had been questioned by a senior apparatchik in the Kremlin about the theological concept of "ultimate concern"!

Tribune didn't often review theological books. But Robinson was a Christian Socialist and a nuclear disarmer, serving as "suffragen" or junior bishop under the Bishop of Southwark, Mervyn Stockwood. Southwark – London south of the Thames – was known as the Red Belt of the Church of England, with a high proportion of turbulent priests of a socialist persuasion. So editor Dick Clements decided to run something on *Honest to God*, and asked his token Christian staffer to tackle it.

My review appeared just over three weeks after the book came out, on April 12. After questioning the bishop's attempt to make a clear distinction between Christianity and humanism, and then trying to get to grips with his understanding of God as, in Tillich's words, "the infinite and inexhaustible depth and ground of all being", I wrote:

> Having rationalized and redefined God himself, the Bishop has to follow that process where it takes him. The prayers he reads each Sunday, traditionally thought of as communication with a personal God, have to be redefined as 'openness to the ground of our being' and 'unconditional love of the neighbour'. We are here perilously close to the sentimental meaninglessness into which Victorian modernism led, 'Each smile a hymn, each kindly deed a prayer', where words which once had well–defined meanings are stretched and redefined to such a point that they cease to mean anything because they have been made to mean almost everything. And that brings me to a final personal note.
>
> Reading *Honest to God* was for me a moving experience because it describes a path I have walked myself – which is my only qualification for writing this review. I was brought up to accept orthodox Christianity. Prayer and worship were for a long time not only real but the most real things in my life. From my belief in a personal God stemmed the conviction which shaped my political attitudes: that love, fellowship, brotherhood – call it what you will – was

written into the substance of the universe, that love *ought to be* and therefore *is* 'the last word'. And when I found I no longer believed in a God 'up there' or 'out there' these convictions remained unchanged. With Tillich I could say that the depth and ground of all being is what God means.

But at that point I began to wonder whether it was useful or honest so to stretch the meaning of words as to change their nature altogether and finally render them unserviceable. 'God' once meant something clear and definite. So did 'heaven' and 'prayer' and 'worship'. Was there any point in my continuing to use the same words but giving each of them a special, private meaning? To say 'God' instead of talking about 'the depth and ground of history' was certainly to save breath, but did not the word 'God' have so many unwelcome associations that the longer term was actually preferable?

To put the questions is to imply my answers. That is why I am no longer concerned to inject new meaning into the word 'God'. That is why I found my own attempt to be honest-to-God made me cease to apply to myself the label 'Christian'.

I can't claim these comments caused quite the stir the book itself had done, but when SCM Press rushed out a follow-up book, *The Honest to God Debate*, the editors included my review in their anthology of comments and critiques, bracketing it with two rather more substantial articles which, like mine, questioned the usefulness of the bishop's distinction between humanism and Christianity. But where I had concluded that, if Robinson's arguments were the best he could come up with to save Christianity from humanism, then I would rather be honest-to-humanism, the two contributors to whom I was linked both saw Robinson's argument as more humanist than Christian. The distinguished philosopher–theologian Alasdair MacIntyre wrote that "What is striking about Dr Robinson's book is first and foremost that he is an atheist" – and, indeed, "a very conservative atheist", even if he wouldn't renounce religious language. If this was what a bishop in the Church of England had come to, then "The creed of the English is that there is no God and that it is wise to pray to him from time to time". The right–wing *Sunday Telegraph* journalist T E Utley asked "What should happen to an Anglican bishop who does not believe in God?". Noting that Robinson had recently given evidence for the defence in the *Lady Chatterley* trial, Utley asked:

> Where… will the ravages of liberal theology end? The Devil and Hell went long ago: the position of the Blessed Virgin has been seriously undermined; God, who until last week was invulnerable, is now distinctly on the defensive. What will ultimately be left except a belief in the need for bishops, if only to give evidence in trials about obscenity and to talk to pop singers on television?

I was less concerned with the bishop's theological or ideological status than with my own. I had begun my *Tribune* review as a sort of liberal Christian, and had concluded in the course of writing the last two paragraphs that I was more of a humanist. I had persuaded myself that this conversion had been brought on not by any substantial shift in my position but in reaction against what seemed to me the bishop's cavalier use of language. In this, of course, I probably deceived myself. I had been moving for some years towards the farther edges of belief, and had finally fallen (or jumped, or been pushed) over the precipice. I had stopped believing in the God of the Brethren, the God of the evangelicals, the God of the Bible, well before I read *Honest to God.* I just hadn't realized it, or been prepared to admit it. No doubt one factor that encouraged me to "come out" as a post–Christian, and more post than Christian, was that it left me better at ease with the company I was keeping. I didn't any longer have to face Sheila's awkward questions or Rosie's head–shaking bafflement. I could be a good atheist among atheists, not so much daring to be a Daniel in the lion's den as enjoying the powerful sensation of being one of the lions.*

But if God was dismissed from my life after nearly thirty years of close companionship, my passion for seeking his kingdom remained. Nor is passion too strong a word for my dedication to building a New Jerusalem in England's green and pleasant land, and making that New Jerusalem a beacon lighting the way to a better world, another country I'd heard of long ago,

> *... Most dear to them that love her,*
> *Most great to them that know...*
> *And soul by soul, and silently,*
> *Her shining bounds increase;*
> *And her ways are ways of gentleness,*
> *And all her paths are peace.*

Socialism and the politics of non–violence, rather than prayer and supplication, looked to me to be the twin tracks of the grand highway to the kingdom. And in those golden, innocent days, that seemed a simple matter of reforming and renewing the Labour Party, then getting it voted into power. The kingdom would be won not by the Bible but by the ballot box – and committed journalism.

As the fiftieth anniversary of the outbreak of the First World War approached, I was encouraged by Dick Clements and Michael Foot to research and write a book on some forgotten heroes of that awesomely

---

* At Christmas in 2004, forty–one years after writing my review, I had dinner with John Robinson's widow, Ruth, whose friendship I had come to value when our paths crossed in the Sea of Faith movement. I mentioned that, in checking Biblical references for the second edition of this book, I missed my long–abandoned copy of *Cruden's Complete Concordance*, first published in 1737 and still the most thorough of all such reference works to the King James Version. Ruth went to her bookshelf and pulled out Bishop John's very own well–thumbed copy, signed by him, and presented it to me. It is a most treasured possession.

tragic conflict: the men whose conscientious objection to military service brought them disgrace, imprisonment, and even sentence of death by their own side. Bertrand Russell and Fenner Brockway, both veterans of the first no–conscription campaign, and both with prison records as a consequence, enthusiastically sponsored the project and jointly signed a letter to the *Observer* and other papers asking surviving conscientious objectors to send me any diaries, letters, documents or reminiscences which might help me tell their story. I received hundreds of responses, many from Quakers, whose long pacifist tradition had been put to the severest of tests, but also many more from men who had objected not on religious but humanitarian and socialist grounds.

Objection Overruled was published in 1965 by McGibbon & Kee, and soon after was made the basis of a BBC drama series, *Days of Hope*, written by Jim Allen, directed by Ken Loach and produced by Tony Garnett – then, and for many years to come, one of the most powerful creative combinations in British broadcasting, and unswervingly Marxist to boot. But the book also proved to be the vehicle by which I too stumbled into television. McGibbon & Kee was owned by Granada Television, chaired by the socialist grandee Sidney Bernstein who had inherited a cinema chain from his father and expanded it into a media empire. Granada was one of the pioneers of Britain's Independent (i.e. commercial) Television Network, and destined to become the largest and most powerful contributor to the network's output. Having read an early draft of *Objection Overruled*, Sidney invited me to join his staff, and I left print journalism for the most popular and most influential news and cultural medium in the world.

Before I had time to get to grips with television, Sidney gave me time off to fight the 1966 general election as Labour candidate for Richmond, Surrey. Leafy Richmond was a safe Tory seat and there was not the faintest risk of my ending up a Member of Parliament. But for three heady weeks I mounted soapboxes, village hall platforms and even pulpits to preach the common ownership of the means of production, distribution and exchange. I was the only Labour candidate in the country to put Clause Four of the Party Constitution on the front page of his election address. Clause Four committed the party to common ownership, and had become an embarrassment to successive leaderships long before the revisionist sixties, but for the rank and file it kept alive a dream, and they wouldn't allow it to be dropped. Hugh Gaitskell tried and failed, Harold Wilson buried it in small print, and Jim Callaghan and Neil Kinnock ignored it completely. It took Tony Blair to kill and bury it. But when I fought Richmond, my old Christian fundamentalism had given way to similar socialist certainties. When the local churches invited the candidates to address them I took some pleasure in reminding the decorous, middle–class and overwhelmingly Tory congregations that, according to the Acts of the Apostles, members of the early church "had all things common... and distribution was made unto every man according as he had need". I stopped short of reminding them that when Ananias and Sapphira secretly held on to some of their private property they were killed by act of God (Acts 4:5:11). My manifesto did not go that far. I did not win, but my vote was the highest ever recorded for Labour in the constituency – a fact that I was at the time reluctant to concede had nothing whatever to do with my romantically archaic spin on socialism, nor indeed with my own qualities as party standard–bearer, but everything to do with the national swing to Harold Wilson's softly–softly Labourism and its whispered promise (in the words of Leon Rosselson's song) to:

> ... reform the country bit by bit,
> So nobody will notice it.
> And just to show we're still sincere,
> We'll sing The Red Flag once a year.

So back to Granada, neither bloodied nor bowed. I learnt the mechanics of telling stories on screen from a rising star with whom I fell in love at first sight (my marriage to Sylvia had ended as our lives had wandered off in different directions). Anthea took longer to fall for me:

two, maybe even three days. She went on to write storylines for the top–rated soap, *Coronation Street*, and to script a masterly adaptation of Chekhov for the screen before sacrificing her own brilliant career for marriage and motherhood; but first she converted me from a print to a broadcast journalist, drumming into me the difference between telecine and videotape, and generally showing me the tricks of the trade. These included the use of a keyboard instrument called, I think, a Melotron, which produced pre–recorded sound effects to heighten filmed reports. We stopped using it when it got stuck one day on "dog being run over", which didn't always fit the story. I understand the technology has now moved on.

One of the first film stories I persuaded my bosses to let me write and produce (and one where, try as I might, I couldn't find a place for the sound of a dog being run over) was an item following the publication of a new book by Bible and Dead Sea Scrolls scholar John Allegro. Allegro argued that Christianity had originated in an halucinogenic drug cult. It was December, and my bright idea was to film small children in the local department store, just down the road from our Manchester studios, telling us what they remembered of the Christmas story. I intercut their halting and often parent–prompted references to shepherds, wise men, oxen, asses, cribs and bad King Herod with Allegro dryly summarizing his argument that Jesus was, in effect, a magic mushroom. The switchboard was jammed with angry calls. Two months later, on honeymoon in the Spanish island of Tenerife, Anthea and I found ourselves sharing our hotel with a lady who introduced herself as Mrs Mary Whitehouse, founder of a new clean–up–TV campaign. She was busy, she told us, collating complaints about a certain programme that had presented the baby Jesus as a toxic vegetable. Subsequently famous for her assaults on television sex and violence, she took her first steps to national fame by assaulting my film. You might say that Mary Whitehouse and I made our television debuts in tandem, and even shared a honeymoon.

In 1968 I joined the production team of the weekly investigative series *World in Action*, already Britain's highest–rated current affairs programme and soon to air on networks around the world, including most American PBS stations. My editors were two brilliant young high–fliers: John Birt, whose flight would take him to the Director–Generalship of the BBC, and Gus Macdonald, destined to become Scotland's leading media mogul and, with a seat in the House of Lords, one of Tony Blair's closest political aides. *World in Action* had revolutionized the staid world of television current affairs earlier in the sixties, dropping on–screen star reporters in favour of anonymous, off–vision commentary, and making use of new lightweight film cameras to get away from the artificiality of the studios and out into the real world. In the real world it found real people, and the impact of a film about, say, homelessness, was vastly increased when the protagonists were the homeless themselves rather than politicians and experts pontificating on their behalf. For campaigning, crusading journalists bent on afflicting the comfortable and comforting the afflicted, *World in Action* was the right place to be.

My first assignment was to Northern Ireland, which was in turmoil. Three years earlier, Irish Republican celebrations of the fiftieth anniversary of the 1916 Rising had produced a Protestant (or Loyalist) backlash in the form of a rash of paramilitary organizations such as Ian Paisley's Ulster Protestant Volunteer Corps and the re–formed Ulster Volunteer Force. The old IRA, dormant for some years (it had sold most of its arms to an eccentric group of adventurers calling themselves the Welsh Liberation Army), had begun to regroup and re–arm. Out of the ugly sectarian quagmire arose a Civil Rights Movement that drew its leadership from both Catholic and Protestant communities but campaigned on the streets for the rights of minorities. In Ulster, that meant campaigning for rights that the "Protestant Ascendancy" had long denied Catholics: a one–person–one–vote system in local elections and equal opportunities in housing allocation and employment. 1968 and 1969 saw march and counter march, state repression and street reaction. At the centre of it all stood the bizarre embodiment of Protestant bigotry, the Reverend Ian Paisley.

To my colleagues, and to most observers on the UK mainland, Paisley was more comic than malevolent. Bawling his incomprehensible anathemas while waving his big black Bible like a blackthorn bludgeon, he seemed a throwback to the wars of religion in a distant past, a caricature of clerical power gone mad. Who could possibly take the man seriously? I could, and did. I knew his language: the language of Biblical fundamentalism, of the wrath of God, of Hell and damnation. I recognized ancestral voices prophesying war, and I knew their theological roots. Where my colleagues heard only the piping melodies of the flute bands, which followed him everywhere, I knew the words to their tunes:

> *There's power in the Blood,*
> *Power in the Blood!*

Paisley did not have a high opinion of the United Kingdom to which he pledged his loyalty. The *Protestant Telegraph* which he edited (motto: "The Truth Shall Set You Free") described sixties England as hell–bent. Its mini–skirts were "the cause of the serious population explosion" facing Britain. The BBC was "that vehicle of corruption", and Independent Television (including Granada) was "noted for its drunkenness, lewdness, immorality and Popery". The Church of England was "a spiritual brothel, harbouring theological prostitutes and ecumenical pimps". The Roman Catholic Church, of course, came in for even more rabid invective:

> Rome may paint her face and attire her hair like Jezebel of old, but I still recognize the murderous wrinkles on the brow of the old scarlet–robed hag. She may clothe herself in her finest attire, but beneath the gorgeous robes I see the leprous garments of her whoredom.

Catholics "breed like rabbits and multiply like vermin". They had infiltrated every British institution, not excluding the Brownies, where they were "engaged in spreading the dogmas of 'Holy Mother Church' in the pack. We believe that these Roman Catholic infiltrators are specially chosen and trained to do this job". The only British institution worthy of praise was my old friend Mary Whitehouse who was single–handedly combating "crime, illegitimacy, venereal disease, violence, infidelity, promiscuity and drinking". England itself "currently wallows – nay, revels – in filth, sin and evil of the most horrible forms. Abortion and sodomy are by law condoned, even encouraged. Divorce, adultery, fornication, sex perversion, rape, infanticide, murder and illegitimacy flourish". As for journalists, they were:

> ...the whirring multitudes of pestiferous scribbling rodents commonly known as Press reporters and newsmen. This gangrenous population, to be found in every rat hole in Fleet Street, however, are not as perilous as the typhus carriers, i.e. sub–editors and editors. These creatures are mentally flaccid, physically hairless, repulsive and repellant. They usually sport thick–lensed glasses, wear six pairs of ropey sandals, are homosexuals, kiss holy medals or carry secret membership cards of the Communist Party. Most of them are communistoids without the guts of a red–blooded Communist, or Roman Catholics without the effrontery of a Pope Pius XII. Sometimes these anonymous editorial writers are a mixture of the two. Spineless, brainless mongoloids, as maliciously perilous as vipers.

In several *World in Action* films over five or six years I chronicled Ulster's descent into hell, dogging first the IRA, then Paisley's rag–tag army. I met, interviewed and filmed the main protagonists on both sides, constantly running into trouble with our regulators, the Independent Broadcasting Authority, which frequently insisted on changes before transmission and twice banned my programmes on the IRA. Paisley became as baffled by me as I was by him. I don't think he had ever before met a reporter who could converse with him in his own Biblical language and could quote the good book back at him, chapter and verse.

On one occasion, when I was filming in his Martyrs' Memorial Church, his wife Eileen pointed to the long hair of my very sixties cameraman, Mike Dodds, and flicked through her Bible to present me with Paul's condemnation of unshorn locks: "Doth not even nature itself teach you, that, if a man have long hair, it is a shame unto him?" (1 Corinthians 11:14). When she had finished a voluble exposition of this verse, I took her Bible and showed her verse 34 of chapter 14, a page or two later: "Let your women keep silence in the churches: for it is not permitted unto them to speak... And if they will learn any thing, let them ask their husbands at home: for it is a shame for women to speak in the church". Eileen Paisley had the grace to smile. I'm not sure her husband would have done so.

A year or two later I supplemented my television reports from Northern Ireland with a book, *The UVF, 1966–73: An Anatomy of Loyalist Rebellion*, which documented Ian Paisley's previously hidden role in the formation and leadership of Ulster's Protestant private armies. I showed how his inflammatory rhetoric had directly influenced the men – Noel Doherty, Gusty Spence, John McKeague – who had brought Loyalist terror to the streets of Belfast and Londonderry while the IRA was still so disorganized that its initials were said bitterly in the beseiged Catholic ghettos to stand for "I Ran Away". The book sold 20,000 copies in Belfast alone within a month of publication. While it was still hot news, I bumped into Paisley in Belfast's Europa Hotel. "*David Boulton,*" he bellowed, in a voice which could surely be heard across the wide waters of Belfast Lough, "I am *wrestling* for your *soul!*" I could only thank him for his consideration.

Unlike most of my colleagues who hated the place and found its mix of religion, politics and terror too contemptible to waste time on, I was drawn to Northern Ireland and jumped at every opportunity to return with a film crew. I loved the gentle, green landscape, haunted and despoiled by a history of violence and hatred, and was introduced to the hidden mysteries of Lough Neagh by a young up–and–coming poet named Seamus Heaney, who gave me a memorable private tour of its secret places. I loved bombed and battered Belfast, its energy and resilience. I loved the people, the so–called "ordinary people" of both communities.

Among the very first films I made there with my colleagues Brian Armstrong and Brian Blake were two community portraits, one of the Protestant Shankill, the other of the Catholic Falls. We lived among them, welcome guests, learning their songs, listening to their stories, drinking endless cups of tea by day and downing endless cheap beers by night. The two films were denounced by former Attorney–General Sir Hartley Shawcross as "Marxist propaganda" because of their unspoken but unmistakable message that the two working–class communities that faced each other across the sectarian front line had far more in common with each other than either had with the middle–class Protestant Ascendancy which, from its comfortable redoubts in the leafy suburbs, divided and ruled them.

And in the early seventies it briefly seemed that the message might be getting through to some of the combatants themselves. Gusty Spence, the UVF leader, serving a life sentence in Crumlin Road jail for sectarian murder, made tentative moves towards a Shankill–Falls coalition based on working–class solidarity rather than religious tribalism, and even Paisley's new–look Democratic Unionist Party, which replaced his Protestant Unionists, began cautiously to emphasize class politics rather than overt sectarianism. This emphasis was rapidly abandoned, however, when escalating terror from the reorganized IRA polarized the communities, and Paisley's followers, thoroughly indoctrinated in their leader's rhetoric of power in the blood, made it clear that there would be no votes for any compromise with neighbours they saw as their ancient enemies, even if they did share a history of exploitation and oppression, slum housing and outdoor lavatories.

My love affair with Northern Ireland and its people was, like most love affairs, not without angst and self–questioning. From the start, my *political* sympathies were with the nationalist and Catholic communities, for generations the victims of gerrymandering, discrimination and denial of the most fundamental civil rights. My sympathy extended to the political ends of republicanism, though decidedly not to the IRA's bloody means to achieve those ends. But Catholicism as a *religious* culture was strange and uncongenial to me. I was repelled by its big black churches, its liturgical mumbo–jumbo, its plastic Madonnas and Jesuses, its bells, books and candles, its smells, its black–robed priests. The Church's historic insistence on segregated schooling seemed to me a tragic and reactionary mistake, and its fear of modernity marked it in my mind as some kind of odd medieval survival, an outpost of what was still, in the seventies, the fear–driven, priest–ridden society south of the border. But while I had no sympathy whatever for the *politics* of Protestant Loyalism, with its flag–waving jingoism and its comic armies of Orangemen, Apprentice Boys, Black Orders and such, its endlessly repeated slogans of "No Surender!", "Remember 1690" and "F... the Pope", and its dour determination at whatever cost to hold on to Protestant privilege and power, the *religious* culture of Paisleyism was very familiar to me from my Brethren and evangelical days. It was wired into my brain. I knew their hymns and choruses, their Bible references, the impassioned language of their cries for divine grace and favour. It was all very unsettling.

I was well aware, of course, that what was often simplistically misconstrued on the mainland as a "Holy War" was in fact the long and bitter coda to an ancient war of conquest, a war over land and the power that possession of the land conferred. Because the rival communities had rival religious cultures, and because their traditions embraced rival versions of the Christian religion, God had been conscripted by both sides (as has been his fate since time immemorial) to give moral legitimacy to a tribal power struggle. The IRA and its nationalist sympathizers were not fighting Protestants to assert religious doctrines like papal infallibility or the immaculate conception of the Virgin Mary, and the Loyalist paramilitaries were not striving to overthrow transubstantiation. This was straightforward power politics shamelessly enlisting the emotional and atavistic potency of religious language, religious symbols and religious loyalties. That's the trouble with God: he has proved all too easily appropriated to any special interest. But if what I saw on the streets of Belfast and Derry and in the villages of Fermanagh and Tyrone was not primarily a religious war, I knew the religious imperative that sanctioned the struggle for political ascendancy was nonetheless potent and powerful.

My colleagues were mistaken to see in Ian Paisley a tub–thumping politician cynically donning a mantle of piety. I knew that Paisley and many of those who packed his Martyrs' Memorial Church, marched with his Volunteers and yelled "No Surrender!" at his DUP rallies were genuine, sincere believers. That was the problem. Thomas McDowell, who killed himself while blowing up an electricity sub–station and trying to implicate the IRA, was a member of Paisley's Free Presbyterians and a born–again Christian. John McKeague, leader of the murderous Red Hand Commandos, told me how he had come to Jesus, even as he escorted me, blindfolded and at gunpoint, to meet Gusty Spence, another God–fearing convicted sectarian murderer who was on the run after being sprung from custody by the UVF. Paisley himself was a man of prayer, a man of the Bible, a man who genuinely believed himself a humble servant of the Lord. I knew, because I too had been there.

While Northern Ireland was for some years my special patch, it was far from being the only area I covered for *World in Action*. On the domestic front we investigated and exposed police corruption, the Poulsen local government scandal (with its ramifications all the way up to Conservative Home Secretary Reginald Maudling, whose career we brought to an ignominious halt), and abuses of power wherever we could find the hard evidence that would stand up in a libel court. In the United States, I documented the worldwide Lockheed bribery scandal, exposing the corrupt practices of trans– and multi–national companies. The series became a book, *The Lockheed Papers* in Britain, *The Grease Machine* in the States, published in five languages and serialized in the newspapers of eleven countries. Further afield, we smuggled our cameras into countries under right and left wing dictatorships, documenting human rights abuses, giving dissidents a voice, and exposing judicial torture. I was thrown out of Greece, Uganda and Czechoslovakia, and denied entry to white Southern Rhodesia when I tried to sneak in to make a film about what we hoped would be the country's last white Christmas. Later, in the nineties, I met again some of the dissidents I had filmed in the seventies: Vaclav Havel, whom I had interviewed while he was under house arrest, and was now President of the Czech Republic; Alexander Dubcek, the deposed leader of the "Prague Spring" and its push for "socialism with a human face", about whom I had written and produced a drama–documentary, *Invasion*, and who had re–emerged as the hero of the Czech "Velvet Revolution" of 1990. When the Communist regimes collapsed, my former contacts opened doors for me and I found myself helping first the Czech and then the Hungarian and Russian governments reorganize their broadcasting systems in line with democratic values – rather more convincingly in the Czech Republic than in Russia or Hungary.

Our crusades were not always successful. When Ted Heath was challenged for the leadership of the Conservative Party by Margaret Thatcher, then best known for withdrawing the free milk which had long been supplied as a health supplement to junior schoolchildren (she was dubbed "Maggie Thatcher, milk snatcher!"), we decided that here was a fine opportunity to lampoon this over–ambitious lady. We had only to put a camera crew with her for a week of self–serving campaigning, we thought, for her to make a fool of herself without any help from us. We knew, however, that the Tories had little time for *World in Action*, which had a reputation for being rather less respectful to politicians in general, and Conservative politicians in particular, than they thought was their due. It would be difficult to persuade her that what we had in mind would further her ambitions. Co–producer Linda McDougall (whose idea it was) and I met her at the House of Commons, prepared for a tough bargaining session, but found her at her most charming and reasonable. Yes, we could follow her on all her engagements and in all situations, public and private, excluding only the bedroom and bathroom. And she was true to her word.

When, just over a week later, I sat in the darkened viewing theatre and watched the rushes – the twenty hours or so of raw, unedited film footage – I knew she had got the better of us. Every word she spoke in her cultivated cut–glass voice, every dainty step she took, was calculated to appeal to the three hundred (overwhelmingly male) Tory MPs who alone made up the electorate in this leadership contest. Whether waving the flag or relaxing at home with husband Denis, commanding photo–calls or playing the ordinary housewife at the kitchen sink, she sold herself – not to the country (that would come later) – but to a band of former public schoolboys in the House of Commons who fondly remembered their nursery nannies and the secret pleasure of being handbagged by a dominant woman experienced in giving compliant bottoms the smack of firm government. Our programme went out on the Monday night, and Heath's vote crumbled on the Tuesday. When the milk snatcher snatched a comfortable victory, Linda and I knew our clever wheeze had helped deliver Britain into the hands of the Philistines.

But if we had setbacks, we also had our triumphs. This was a golden age for investigative journalism in broadcasting, and we had no doubt that we were batting for Good against Evil, and making a small contribution to the better health of a faltering world which had begun to turn its back on the optimism of the sixties. When I moved on to wider responsibilities as head of news, current affairs, arts and religious programmes in the eighties, I suggested that *World in Action* might be recognized by the Independent Broadcasting Authority as a religious programme. This would have meant Granada would not have had to run so many tedious church services to fulfill its allotted God–slots.

Suspecting a brazen case of tongue in cheek, the Authority flatly turned me down. But if I failed to convince them, I came close to convincing myself. "Comforting the afflicted and afflicting the comfortable" seemed to me a good definition of doing what I had once seen as the Lord's work. Mary had praised God in that he had "scattered the proud in the imagination of their hearts, put down the mighty from their seats, exalted them of low degree, filled the hungry with good things, and sent the rich empty away". We had tried to follow much the same programme. I told myself this was religion true and undefiled, and this, if anywhere, was where whatever we might still wish to label "God" might still be found.

But the truth was that since my abandonment of fundamentalism (or fundamentalism's abandonment of me) I had been cutting God down to size, lopping off a hand here, a foot there. Now there was virtually nothing left of him. If I worshipped anything at all, it was a divine Cheshire cat, *sans* claws, *sans* teeth, *sans* virtually everything. Only the grin was left – or was it a wistful smile, or even a painful grimace?

CHAPTER 5

Words of God

Zounds! I never was so bethumped with words...
– William Shakespeare, *King John*

SEEKING TO MEND a broken world from the relatively well–paid and glamorous position of a television producer was no doubt a good deal less demanding and stressful than the work of priests, policemen and social workers in the inner cities. But producing *World in Action* did have its problems and challenges, such as the occasional confrontation with an enraged Londonderry mob, being chased through Prague by the Czech secret police, or the prospect of ending an assignment to Uganda in one of Idi Amin's stewpots. Even on more run–of–the–mill stories there were stresses, strains and always the tyranny of the deadline. We generally had two weeks to research a story, two weeks to film it, and two weeks to edit it into a polished programme – and then straight into the next subject. On big, highly topical stories, the six–week schedule might be telescoped into six days or even six hours. I could find myself frantically filming on a Saturday and editing without a break through Saturday and Sunday night and all day Monday for transmission that evening – and starting the next story on Tuesday. I needed a get–away, a place to escape to with Anthea and our two baby daughters whenever the pressure was temporarily eased. So in the summer of 1972 we started looking for a weekend holiday home in the Yorkshire Dales, a couple of hours' drive from Manchester.

Taking the high, narrow road from Ingleton over Kingsdale on a bright September day, we skirted the long whale–back of Whernside, the highest of Yorkshire's "three peaks", to reach the steep drop from Deepdale Head down into the valley of Dent. These were the Dales as Wordsworth pictured them in *Peter Bell*:

> *And he had trudged through Yorkshire dales,*
> *Among the rocks and winding scars,*
> *Where deep and low the hamlets lie*
> *Beneath their little patch of sky*
> *And little lot of stars...*

Far below us were tiny isolated farmhouses, each commanding a little patchwork of bright green fields, separated by irregular dry–stone walls. Behind each farmhouse was a neatly squared–off plot of rough fell or moorland, unenclosed common grazing until, in the mid–nineteenth century, each farm was allotted its own share, divided from its neighbours by long straight walls which climbed like dry–stone staircases to the mountain summit. "One of those would do very nicely!" we told each other, and laughed at the thought of townies like us attempting to live the good life of Yorkshire shepherds and dairy farmers.

Down in Dentdale, we found ourselves driving into what looked to be a farmyard *cul–de–sac*. Had we taken a wrong turning? No, this was "Dent Town", a tight semi–circle of terraced cottages on each side of a roughly cobbled street. You could get through the "town" in thirty seconds, and that was with slowing down to avoid being bounced out of your seat by an erratic cobble. We later learned that Hartley Coleridge, poet son of the more famous Samuel Taylor Coleridge, had had a similar shock when visiting Dent early in the nineteenth century:

There is a town, of little note or praise;
Narrow and winding are its rattling streets,
Where cart with cart in cumbrous conflict meets;
Hard straining up and backing down its ways
Where, insecure, the crawling infant plays...

We were to have plenty of experience of "hard straining up and backing down its ways" over the next thirty years, but the narrow, winding and rattling streets were new to us then. We drove slowly towards the head of the dale on a magical mystery tour till we came to Lea Yeat bridge over what the locals called "Big Beck" and the map more formally designated "River Dee". Alongside the bridge was a plain stone building with a headstone over the door announcing that it was a Quaker meetinghouse, built in 1702. We stopped and peered through the window. In the centre of the room was a full–sized billiards table, and the wall at the far end was lined with crates of beer. This was a new kind of Quakerism to me! I was subsequently disappointed to learn that Friends had sold it years ago and it was now the local "Institute" where farmers met not for silent worship but for the occasional evening's escape from what one politically incorrect local called "the bleating of sheep and womenfolk".

On the far side of the bridge was a gate, and attached to the gate was a sign saying "For Sale". Beyond the opening, a rough track curled across the meadow to disappear behind a steep bank. The track, we reasoned, must lead to a house: the house that was for sale. Leaving the car, we followed our own version of the yellow–brick road to a cobbled farmyard where a grey–stone, seventeenth–century farmhouse, looking its age, faced a shamble of derelict pig pens, hen houses and a well–built barn. It was called Hobsons, and something told me that a life–changing choice was about to face us. We knocked on the door.

A large, friendly woman invited us in and introduced us to a visiting neighbour. Both were elderly, well into their eighties. They crouched over a frugal fire, their shins covered in rolled newspaper to keep the sparks from striking at their bare skin. We looked around the house: one tiny brass tap in the kitchen, over a slop–stone sink; wallpaper hanging loosely from the walls, pushed away by rising or falling damp; windows running with condensation. A frog of a house awaiting the kiss of a prince. Just what we wanted! But there was one problem. We were looking to become country cottage–dwellers, not new recruits for the Country Landowners' Association; and this house was to be auctioned as part of a single lot that included 75 acres of farmland.

So we left, to continue the search elsewhere. Over the next few days we scoured the Lake District, only to discover that even a modest cottage in one of the less desirable areas, on a main road and with no garden, was beyond our budget. We couldn't get Hobsons out of our minds. One late October day we went back for a second look, knew that Hobsons was indeed our choice, and decided to make our bid. Mortgages were hard to come by in those days, particularly on second homes, but, as luck would have it, the manager of the local building society recognized me as the reporter he had seen interviewing prime minister Harold Wilson on TV only the week before. He decided I must be a "celebrity", and was eager to lend as much as we wanted. We wanted quite a lot.

The auction was held in Dent's Memorial Hall on the night of Thursday November 9, 1972. It was preceded by a week of torrential rain, the unrelenting kind which seems to have forgotten how to stop, and calls into question God's rainbow–signed promise that his death–by–drowning spectacular of Old Testament times would be a one–off.

Driving into the dale after dark, we found our way blocked by floods where Big Beck had burst its banks. Abandoning the car, we rolled up trousers and skirt and began to wade into the black waters, but they were too deep for us. By good fortune, Jim Middleton's tractor appeared and we were invited to jump up and hold tight. Dropped safely at the steps of the Memorial Hall, we prayed that the waters would close on any Egyptians bent on out–bidding us. Inside, we found half a dozen potential purchasers who had had the foresight to arrive a day early and book into the Sun Inn for the night, plus a score of locals from the right side of the flood waters, for whom property auctions always provided good free theatre. At a trestle table in the centre, Dick Harper, the auctioneer, was conferring with the owners and their solicitors, apparently discussing whether they could announce "rain stopped play" and postpone the proceedings to a better night and a fuller house. But the expectant audience soon made common cause to put paid to that notion: we hadn't braved the storm only to be denied our opportunity or entertainment. And the rival bidders, eyeing each other carefully to assess credit rating and courage under fire, were not going to stand for any postponement of death or glory.

So the bidding started. At first it rose quickly in thousands, and those who had come in hope of picking up a quick bargain soon dropped out. Within minutes there were three, then just two bidders left, raising each other in five hundreds, then two hundreds, then tight little hundreds, with never more than a raised eyebrow or a barely detectable nod. One dropped out with a shake of his head, the other looked to the auctioneer to perform the ritual of bringing the hammer down in his favour. It was now or never. I made my first bid: an extra fifty. Heads turned. My opponent nodded fifty more. I nodded back. Soon we were nodding like demented mascots in a car window. The auctioneer registered each little movement, and I caught a quick glimpse of Anthea at my side; she had forgotten to breathe for five minutes and was now an unbecoming shade of puce. Suddenly, my opponent stopped nodding and slowly shook his head. "Going for the first time," said Dick Harper, and the head continued shaking. "For the second time..." and no one moved. After what was surely the longest time–freeze since Joshua stopped the sun and moon in their tracks to give his armies time to mop up the Gibeonites, the hammer came down and Anthea and I were proud but awestruck owners of a 75–acre Dales farm.

For two or three years we did little more than use the unimproved shell of the house to camp out in whenever I could escape from *World in Action*. Later, we sold off part of the land to finance some sorely needed renovation. We spent our summer holidays helping get the hay in and trying to turn one field into a wildlife area – not easy, as wildlife in the form of deer and rabbits took a delight in destroying the wildlife in the form of newly planted trees and shrubs. For two hard–pressed adults and two young daughters, this became our little Eden, our republic of heaven.

I was always conscious that Hobsons, both house and farm, had been around much longer than I had. Our ownership was a short blip in its history. We were temporary stewards, and we had to respect what we were stewarding. It was impossible to sit in the farmhouse kitchen or walk the old tracks that criss–crossed the fields without wondering who had sat and walked there centuries ago. Who had settled here in the first place? Who had built the house, first in timber and thatch, and later proudly in stone? Who was Hobson? Who had enclosed the land and built these dry–stone walls? Who, long before mechanical help was available, had made the cutting from a spring on the hillside to bring water to the house? What connection, if any, did these our predecessors have to the old Quaker meetinghouse at our farm gate? Had families from Hobsons worshipped there in silence before the beer crates arrived?

My curiosity was heightened as we began to get used to visitors knocking on our door: visitors from the United States, Canada, Australia and New Zealand. They had all been bitten by the bug of family history and had traced this or that ancestor to Hobsons Farm, Dent. They wanted to see the old family homestead for themselves.

I was no historian, but I was a journalist and I knew how to locate sources and do disciplined research. Whenever I could spare time from my television work, I trawled the county and parish archives for references to Hobsons. I located wills and deeds which eventually enabled me to compile a fairly complete list of everyone who had lived in the house and worked the farm since Elizabethan times. But it is not possible to research one farm without continually coming across references to the neighbouring properties and their inhabitants So I found myself discovering the history not only of Hobsons but of most of the little farms in the upper dale. And what I discovered was that, from the seventeenth to the early nineteenth century, many of the farms and families were indeed linked to the Quaker movement.

George Fox, "first among equals" in the group that founded Quakerism after the English civil wars of the 1640s, had passed through upper Dentdale on his journey from Pendle to Swarthmoor in 1652, a missionary journey that had set the country alight and given the new movement lift off. He had held one of his earliest recorded meetings in Stone House, a farm just above Hobsons, and among his early converts or "convincements" were the Mason brothers who lived at Cowgill, just over the bridge. Neighbouring Huds House and Harbergill were early Quaker farms, and down the dale at Gate, Captain Alexander Hebblethwaite had abandoned the New Model Army for the new model "people of God". Meetings had been held at Lea Yeat, where the meetinghouse was built in 1702 – one of two in the dale – and John Haygarth of Hobsons was listed in the records as a trustee. Later, one of his relations ran a Quaker school from Hobsons. Reading the experiences of my former neighbours, often in their own spidery handwriting on flaking, damp–spotted paper and in language of Biblical formality and dignity, was an extraordinary experience. Against the grain, against the drift of my prejudices, I felt myself subtly reconnected to the Biblical imagery and word forms of my childhood.

The minute books, records, letters and loose documents I found in the archives told a stirring story of conscientious dissent and divine discontent. The men and women who scraped a living from these remote, unyielding uplands were far from the pious fundamentalists I had spent so much of my childhood among, but they spoke a related language in clear Biblical measures. They were radical republicans to a man and woman, glad to see the back of King Charles and looking to make a New Earth as well as a New Heaven. They went to jail for refusing to pay tithes or attend church. They demanded radical reform of poor laws and the courts. The aristocracy was to be abolished, its wealth distributed among the most needy. And although they scandalized their orthodox neighbours by insisting that the Bible was a record made by fallible men, rather than the very word of God himself, it was the Bible they quoted to authenticate their vision of a new Jerusalem in Yorkshire's green dales.

And they suffered for it. Alexander Hebblethwaite and Richard Harrison spent much of their long lives in and out of prison, first under Cromwell, then under the restored monarchy of Charles I. Thomas Wilkinson died in jail, and Thomas Salkeld's wife Ann and her two children fell ill and died when he too was jailed. Thomas Wilkinson's wife Agnes died when she was left to run the farm after his incarceration at York castle, "she being a sickly and weak woman very much: yet without being heard much to complain, endured affliction with much patience and at last finished in much sweet peace of conscience". When a group of Friends held an open–air meeting on the slopes of Rise Hill above Dent, "desiring that some lost sheep might be found and brought home to Christ Jesus", they were met with "very great abuse by a rude multitude, with stoning, clodding and abuses beside – scoffing, mocking, railing and the like, all which Friends endured with great patience which they had learned of Christ Jesus by minding his Light". Their meeting infiltrated by paid informers, Friends were arrested twenty at a time and marched across the hills to York. Meetings were broken up by the local militia. One in nearby Brigflatts was raided by Ensign Lawrence Hodgson leading the Dent trained band, "cursing and swearing and threatening that if Friends would not depart and disperse, he and they could kill and slay and what not, he holding out a pistol cocked, and also armed with a sword, and made himself very furious and terrible..." When Friends carried on their silent meeting as if nothing was happening, "they got furiously to be behind them, to drive the said people forth... till with harrying and thrusting and beating they were forced out". One undaunted Quaker matron demanded to be allowed to return to collect her hat!

Sometimes their non–Quaker neighbours, drafted in as bailiffs or constables, braved persecution themselves by daring to show sympathy. When the bailiffs called on Anthony Mason of Lea Yeat, by Hobsons gate, and confiscated all seven of his cows for non–payment of tithes, one of the bailiffs took pity on his wife and five small children and "quietly turned back one old cow to help give them a little milk". I often imagine I see that old cow making its way back to Anthony Mason's when I pass his house, as I do every day. Neighbours and relatives sometimes paid Friends' fines without their knowledge or approval. The in–bred fellow feeling of Dales folk often overrode religious and political rifts.

It was one thing to be aware that Quakers in general had been persecuted in the past, but quite another to read such vivid accounts of the persecution and suffering of the men, women and children who had lived in the houses and farmed the farms which I was coming to know so intimately. I felt the keenest solidarity with them. I could not share their faith in all its seventeenth–century particulars, but I could understand their aspirations for a kingdom not *of* this world yet very much *in* this world. One Sunday I went along to Brigflatts meeting for worship with my ten–year–old daughter Katy. We sat through the silence. On the way home I asked her what she thought of it. "Well, dad," she said after a pause, "it was OK, except that I was the youngest there, and you were the second youngest!".

In 1986 I published my little local researches in a book, *Early Friends in Dent: the English Revolution in a Dales Community*, dedicating it to Friends at the seventeenth–century Brigflatts meeting–house. "In silence, in that most beautiful of places," I wrote, "it isn't difficult to recall the generations of Sedbergh and Dent Friends who have met there week in week out for more than three hundred years. Their successors today oppose nuclear weapons where the pioneers opposed tithes, Third World poverty where their predecessors opposed the slave trade. Revolution has given way to liberal reformism, rebellion to respectability; where there were yeomen there are now teachers and retired civil servants. The kingdom of God has changed. God himself isn't what he was. But today's Quakers are a visible and recognizable remnant of the men and women who made the English revolution".

I was gently chided by one of the elders, when I showed him the first draft, for the bit about God himself not being what he was. Surely he was the same, yesterday, today and for ever, I was told.

> *Before the hills in order stood,*
> *Or earth received its frame,*
> *From everlasting, thou art God,*
> *To endless years the same...*

But I didn't change it. The God worshipped by educated, liberal twentieth–century Friends is a more liberal, more diverse God than the one Thomas Wilkinson the cart–maker, Agnes Wilkinson the farmer's wife and Ann Salkeld, mother of two, died for. That too is the trouble with God: he won't stand still, won't be pinned down. And it was clear that, though I now labelled myself a humanist, he wasn't going to leave me alone.

In the Orwellian year of 1984 I found my eyes glued to the rival BBC channel as it broadcast the ground–breaking television series *The Sea of Faith*, produced by Peter Armstrong and written and presented by the Dean of Emmanuel College, Cambridge, Don Cupitt. Most vividly and compellingly, Cupitt charted the decline of institutional Christianity, taking his cue and his title from Matthew Arnold's nineteenth century poem *Dover Beach*, with its haunting evocation of the receding tide of faith:

> *The Sea of Faith*
> *Was once, too, at the full, and round earth's shore*
> *Lay like the folds of a bright girdle furl'd.*
> *But now I only hear*
> *Its melancholy, long, withdrawing roar,*

Retreating, to the breath
Of the night–wind, down the vast edges drear
And naked shingles of the world...

Faith has retreated, said Cupitt, and our understanding of God as universal mastermind has retreated with it. Twenty years after Arnold's poem, Nietzsche was proclaiming the death of God. The long series of fundamental changes set in motion by Galileo, Descartes, Kant, Hegel and Freud had eroded cherished beliefs in a supernatural order. It was time to accept the blindingly obvious: that religion itself was a human creation, a product of human history, human language and human culture. Critically, Cupitt insisted, God himself was of our making, not we of his. There was no transcendental God "above the bright blue sky" – or anywhere. God could live on only as the supreme symbol and imagined personification of our highest and most cherished values: love, truth, beauty, integrity.

The television series and the book that went with it spoke to my condition. As Cupitt recognized, he was resuming the discussion of the nature of God begun twenty years earlier by Bishop John Robinson in *Honest to God*. Cupitt would subsequently take Robinson's ideas much further, but for the time being we were back with something like the Tillich–Bonhoeffer–Robinson model of God as "ground of our being" and "ultimate value". I had rejected this in the sixties as playing with words. Robinson, I had complained in *Tribune*, was "so stretching the meaning of words as to change their nature altogether and finally render them unserviceable. 'God' once meant something clear and definite. So did 'heaven' and 'prayer' and 'worship'. Was there any point," I had wondered, "in my continuing to use the same words but giving each of them a special, private meaning?" I had concluded then that there wasn't. "That is why I am no longer concerned to inject new meaning into the word 'God'. That is why I found my own attempt to be honest–to–God made me cease to apply to myself the label 'Christian'."

But two decades later, Cupitt was forcing me to rethink all that. Language didn't work as I had somewhat naively supposed. Words grew, changed, flowered. The God–word had no fixed static meaning. It shifted in nuance and reference, changing as we ourselves changed. It had meant one thing to me as a Brethren child, another as a social activist, yet another as an experimental Quaker humanist. This potent three–letter word had a history. God had a biography. It was time to make his acquaintance again.

CHAPTER 6

Dead but He Won't Lie Down

*The personality of God is nothing else than the
projection of the personhood we find in humankind...
Consciousness of God is human self–consciousness.*
– Ludwig Feuerbach, *The Essence of Christianity*

READERS WHO HAVE managed to get this far may by now be asking
whether this isn't more about God's trouble with me than mine with
him. But I have chosen to write from experience, and experience is
personal, so part of the trouble with God is that I can't write about it
without writing about me. And although experience is personal, it isn't
necessarily unique. Others who have lived through the same period –
the transition from late modernity to postmodernity, from the twilight
of the old gods to the secular age in which a personal God is dead but
won't lie down – will surely recognize something of my experience in
their own. We may not be all in the same boat, or even sailing the same
seas, but I'm pretty sure I am no lone yachtsman.

So let me summarize where I think I have got to, before
summarizing where I think I am going.

When I was a child, I spoke as a child, I understood as a child,
I thought as a child. I worshipped a child's God: an unseen companion,
a heavenly father, a shelter in the time of storm. He was my maker, my
helper, redeemer and friend. He kept his eye on me all the time, which
was rather disconcerting, but also comforting. He was pleased when I

was good, and sad but forgiving when I was bad. He ruled the world, even if the world didn't know it. He would soon be coming to claim his own, and I had no doubt that I was one of his own. This life, with its tiresome rounds of homework, its playground squabbles, its dark mysteries (what was the connection between germs and Germans? why did animals bite? how did girls pee?) was merely the prelude to a better life with God in Heaven, one which would go on for ever and answer all my questions. We are but strangers here: Heaven is our home.

I did not know it then, but my God was already something of a relic, a precious antique, a quaint survival from a pre–scientific age, hanging on by his fingertips. He was King of Kings, Lord of Lords and Heavenly Father in an age that had effectively given up on kingship (except as an accessory of the heritage and tourist industry), made lords a laughing stock, and was in the process of dismantling patriarchy. As first cause and creator, he simply wasn't needed any more: Darwin and Einstein had rewritten the creation story, and the new myth was not only more credible but also more awesome and mysterious, more profoundly beautiful and more life–enhancing and inspiring than the old. His churches were old, grey and smelly with damp and dry rot. The trouble with the God of my childhood was that he refused to grow up, and I refused not to grow up.

So he gave way to a more liberal God, a less defined and less personal God, the God who, according to James' epistle, wanted us to know that faith without works is dead. Here was a God who would have us march, not to Zion but to Aldermaston, the God whose "banners bright, gleaming in the light" were the banners of the poor in revolt against the rich, the powerless in hot and purposeful pursuit of the powerful. Here was a God we could call by new names – names that we were not sure we really understood, but that at least had a grown–up ring to them: "life force", "ground of being", "ultimate concern". But we soon had trouble with this God too. Like the Cheshire cat, there was too little of him. A grin wasn't enough. He didn't pluck at the heartstrings. He didn't fill the churches, or slow the pace at which they were emptying. And millions who had turned away from his predecessor, instead of transferring their faith to the new model, preferred to worship at the altars of quite different gods who came (at a price) in bottles or crystals or "mind, body and spirit" manuals. The trouble with the God made in the image of liberal theologians and radical activists was that he was good at promising but weak on delivery.

So we decided to manage without him. We pronounced him dead. Deceased. *De trop*. The late. The new hymns we sang ("No saviour from on high delivers" and, whenever we were about to be moved, "We shall not be moved") simply left him out. We devised new communion rituals that celebrated our humanity rather than his divinity. We worked to mend the world, but it was our world, not his. If we were aware of something greater than ourselves, that something was not what we would want to call God. If we knew in the depth of our being that there was another world to be won, we knew also that the other world was this one. Our old childhood God had first given way to our adult "ground of being" God, and had finally been banished to the basement where we kept all the old furniture we no longer had room for but couldn't quite bring ourselves to throw away.

But we had trouble with this God too – this absent God, this no–God. He wouldn't stay dead. He continued to haunt us, a holy ghost who wouldn't let us alone. How could we wholly banish a God who saturated the culture that had shaped us, the stories, mythologies, poetries, symphonies, songs, paintings that formed the framework of our understanding of ourselves and our world? How could we detach ourselves from the God who in the beginning was the word, the God who is embedded in the language that both creates us and, through us, makes the world conscious of itself? Just when I thought I had despatched God to the happy hunting–fields of my lost childhood, up he popped again in the faded records of an old farmhouse. And there he is still, in the tall tales of Moses the law–giver, the randy poems of Solomon's songs, the parables of that peasant genius Jesus, the madness of the mystics, the magic of medieval carols, the mythologies of Milton and Blake, the doubt and despair of Arnold, the head–scratching of Robinson and Cupitt, the passions of Bach, the masses and operas (yes, especially the operas) of Mozart, the secular oratorios of Michael Tippett, and in cinema, song lyrics, newspapers, television... To get God out of human culture is like getting metre and rhyme out of poetry: you can do it, but at the cost of destroying what you are trying to save. Our contemporary humanism is richer, fuller, deeper when it is content to make use of the words of our God mythology in the full knowledge that it *is* a mythology, a construct made in the context of human history by the human imagination.

In this first part of the book I have used my own biography to reflect on the trouble with God. In the second part I want to shift the focus from my biography to God's. I want to question the notion that he is the same yesterday, today and for ever, the one unchanging thing in an ever–changing universe. I hope to show how our human ideas of God have changed – and, since God *is* our human ideas of him, how he has grown, matured, and been born again.

Then in the final part I want to reflect on what it means to abandon the props of belief in a supernatural God while continuing to make use of our rich heritage of God–stories. I call this religious humanism and the quest for the republic of heaven. Be patient. We'll get there.

.

PART TWO

God's story

Nor is God virtue, nor light, nor he liveth, nor he is life, nor he is substance, nor age, nor time, nor there is any understandable touching of him, nor he is knowledge, nor truth, nor kingdom, nor wisdom, nor one, nor unity, nor Godhead, nor goodness, nor is he spirit as we understand spirit, nor sonhood, nor fatherhood, nor any other thing known by us or by any that be; nor is he anything of not–being things, nor anything of being–things; nor any of those that be, know him as he is, nor he knoweth those things that be as they be in themselves, but as they be in him.

– Anonymous 14th–century author of *Denis Hid Divinity*

CHAPTER 7

God's Ancestors

Before the gods that made the gods
Had seen their sunrise pass...
G K Chesterton, *The Ballad of the White Horse*

UNTIL RELATIVELY RECENTLY it would not have occurred to any believer that God has a life story and is a suitable subject for biography. The monotheistic traditions – Judaism, Christianity and Islam – developed a doctrine of the essentially unchanging nature of God. He made things happen, but things did not happen to him. He made history, but himself had no history. God had no infancy and no maturity. If he had a beard, he had always had a beard. He might seem merciful one day and judgmental the next, but mercy and judgment were permanent fixtures in his unchanging nature. Living as he did in an eternal present, he could have no history, because both *eternity* and *present* preclude development – without which there can be no life story, no biography.

But what did change – and it changed profoundly from age to age and culture to culture – was humanity's perception of the divine. So while theologians focused on their unchanging God, anthropologists turned the spotlight on the changing ways in which human beings perceived their divinities. What made it possible for theology and anthropology to co–exist for a time without conflict was the imagined distinction between *our* God – the god named God – and *other* gods with names like Zeus, Baal, Ra or Ganesh. Being "false" gods, mere human creations, these were proper material for anthropological or biographical investigation in the sense that they had a beginning, a middle and an end. They were born (at least in the human imagination), they were worshipped, they died. *Our* God, on the other hand, while he could of course be studied in relation to human history, was altogether above and beyond that kind of investigation. That is what made him God.

This blinkered perception could last only so long as we were either ignorant about other religious traditions, or unquestioning in our assumption that our God was *the* God and other gods were idols. As a fuller awareness of other traditions developed – that is, as air travel and electronic communication shrank our world – God began to seem less immune to biographical investigation. He had to take his place, though it was still a most exalted one, among the other gods whose comings and goings gave religion a history. Today, we no longer find it strange or arrogant when fine writers like Karen Armstrong and Jack Miles write God's life story (see Armstrong's *A History of God*, Heinemann, 1993; Miles' *God: a Biography*, Simon & Schuster, 1995; and in more mocking but very informative vein, Alexander Waugh's *God*, Review, 2002).

Gods are almost certainly as old as human language and consciousness. In *The Origin of Consciousness in the Breakdown of the Bicameral Mind*, Julian Jaynes argued persuasively that human consciousness springs from the two–chamber structure of our brains, an arrangement that gives us the ability to have an internal dialogue with ourselves. So, as civilization is born and cities grow, leadership and the internal voices are vested in divine beings, first on earth and then in heaven. Language is the mechanism for this amazing development. If you need internalized instructions about what to do in a new and unexpected situation when your leader is not at hand, you need to hear your leader's voice in your head – or, later in the development, the voice of your god. Religion, then, is a product of language. As this language–dependent facility for internal dialogue develops, we call it

consciousness. Human consciousness, then, is the birthplace of
the gods.

Jaynes' suggestion that it was the evolved structure of the
human brain which created the internal dialogue that gave birth to
consciousness and the idea of gods is not, of course, the only choice on
the menu. Wilhelm Schmidt, in *The Origin of the Idea of God*, first
published in 1912, proposed that prehistoric man began by creating one
God, the First Cause of all things and Ruler of heaven and earth. But
he proved too exalted and inaccessible, eventually becoming so
heaven–bound that he was of no earthly use. Men then created the more
attractive gods of the pagan pantheons: gods who fought great battles,
did great deeds, fell out among themselves as men do, and lusted after
goddesses or bestowed their favours on all–too–human virgin milkmaids.
True religion, in Schmidt's book, was the story of humanity's attempt to
rebuild a relationship with the lost High God. Karen Armstrong,
commenting on Schmidt's theory in her own *History of God*, reminds us
that belief in a lost High or Sky God "is still a feature of the religious
life in many indigenous African tribes. They yearn towards God in
prayer; believe that he is watching over them and will punish
wrongdoing. Yet he is strangely absent from their daily lives: he has no
special cult and is never depicted in effigy. The tribesmen say that he is
inexpressible and cannot be contaminated by the world of men. Some
people say that he has 'gone away'."

Another theory, less dependent on psychology, sees gods as the
cynical inventions of rulers and would–be rulers, called into being to
legitimize the power of warlords and tribal patriarchs through castes of
priests claiming a special status as intermediaries between the
mysterious and the mundane. Commandments had far greater
authority when they could be represented as written by the gods on
tablets of stone, and social control was more easily managed when those
who were to be socially controlled could be persuaded that things must
be this way because that's how the gods decreed it. Thus, not just in
Victorian England under Victoria's God, but throughout the world and

under all gods, it could be claimed by those who wanted to keep it that way that

> *The rich man in his castle,*
> *The poor man at his gate*

were in their respective positions not because of unjust human power relations, but because

> *God(s) made them, high and lowly,*
> *And ordered their estate...*

The social control theory, however, would seem to have more going for it as a theory of how the gods were managed by humans than an account of how they actually began. Rudolf Otto in *The Idea of the Holy* (1917) proposed that gods arose as expressions of early man's acute sense of being surrounded by the unseen and unknown, and that this predated any quest for explanations of the origin of the world or attempts to find a basis for ethical behaviour. Although Otto was not as explicit as Jaynes, he too seems to have located the birth of the gods in the development of human consciousness as expressed in language. It appears, then, that we are justified in picturing the parallel and interactive development of two vital capabilities: a communication system that evolved from primitive warning shouts and mating calls into the miraculously rich and complex set of grammatical languages unique to the human species, and simple consciousness of external events that came at last to recognize the mysteriousness of life and the world – of the sun, moon and stars, of night and day, spring and fall, of what was felt to be "holy" or "numinous". Karen Armstrong, commenting on Otto, draws attention to the difficulty we now have in relating imaginatively to the world of our ancestors:

Many of us no longer have the sense that we are surrounded by the unseen. Our scientific culture educates us to focus our attention on the physical and material world in front of us. This method of looking at the world has achieved great results. One of its consequences, however, is that we have, as it were, edited out the sense of the 'spiritual' or the 'holy' which pervades the lives of people in more traditional societies at every level and which was once an essential component of our human experience of the world. In the South Sea islands, they call this mysterious force *mana*; others experience it as a presence or spirit; sometimes it has been felt as an impersonal power, like a form of radioactivity or electricity. It was believed to reside in the tribal chief, in plants, rocks or animals. The Latins experienced *numina* (spirits) in sacred groves; Arabs felt that the landscape was populated by the *jinn*. Naturally people wanted to get in touch with this reality and make it work for them, but they also simply wanted to admire it. When they *personalized the unseen forces and made them gods,* associated with the wind, sun, sea and stars but possessing human characteristics, they were expressing their sense of affinity with the unseen and with the world around them *[my emphasis]*.

By assigning names to, and thus personifying the various manifestations of the numinous, men and women were able to establish with them a *relationship* that they could never have with abstract entitities or unfocused mysteries. Valour, love, fertility, the heat of the sun, could now be talked to, pleaded with, placated, and bribed with precious offerings, just like other walking talking beings.

William Blake, although no academic student of anthropology or the history of religion, wrote most presciently as early as 1790, in *The Marriage of Heaven and Hell*, of this process of personalizing the unseen forces, making them into gods – and then forgetting the process by which it had all happened, so that we come to think of our own creations as independent objective entities:

> The ancient Poets animated all sensible objects with Gods or Geniuses, calling them by the names and adorning them with the properties of woods, rivers, mountains, lakes, cities, nations, and whatever their enlarged and numerous senses could perceive. And particularly they studied the Genius of each city and country, placing it under its Mental Deity; Till a system was formed, which some took advantage of, and enslaved the vulgar by attempting to realize or abstract the Mental Deities from their objects – thus began Priesthood; Choosing forms of worship from poetic tales. And at length they pronounced that the Gods had ordered such things. Thus men forgot that All Deities reside in the Human breast.

The question that arises from this view – the view of Jaynes and Otto, of Blake and Armstrong that in the beginning humans created the gods – is whether the sense of the unseen and unknown, of the holy and numinous, was an inspired intuition of something objectively "real", or the product of a rapidly expanding human imagination. What were these gods and "geniuses", these good and evil spirits: were they intuitions, however imperfect, of an unseen reality which preceded and transcended humanity and was in essence independent of human consciousness, or were they poetic inventions, the *products* of human consciousness? It's a big question: perhaps the biggest theological question that can be asked. What are now sometimes called postmodern views of language offer an answer that is neither theist nor atheist in the traditional senses of these terms, but attempts to transcend these two poles.

Early cultures, then, produce gods and spirits attached to places – particularly important features like rivers and mountains – or to animals, trees, plants, or ancestors. These are not remote, unknown gods: indeed, humankind's whole intention in imagining them into being and naming them is to produce a better understanding of the world and how it works, since to understand it is to open up the possibility of manipulating it. So people talk to these gods, and in their bicameral minds they hear the gods talking back. What they hear is very human voices, speaking a specific human language (their own) and voicing very human needs and greeds. This river deity will keep the supply running only if certain sacrifices are made or the tribe's finest–wrought ceremonial spear is deposited in the river bed (to be dug up thousands of years later by puzzled archaeologists). This crop is more likely to yield a bumper harvest if the appropriate god is adequately appeased. The gods favour those who favour them. The secret of success is to find out the will of the gods, and perform it. Like lords and kings, the gods demand praise, adoration and unquestioning obedience. This, essentially, is how humanity must relate to the unseen and unknown, if it is to see more, know more, and prosper.

A world filled with spirits is a world aware of life and its essentials. The word *spirit* derives from the Latin word "to breathe", and early humanity was all too keenly aware that the essence of life was breath. To ex–*spire* was to die. To be in–*spired* was to be given new life. So a person's spirit was his or her life, or very essence. Once the idea of spirit as essence had taken root, the thought emerged that one's essence could survive death. The body might expire, but the essential spirit would survive, as soul, or incorporeal being. And if the "genius" of a well or a fruit tree was to be engaged, communicated with, related to, it too must have an essential spirit. So the perceived world thus filled with spirits became a spiritual realm existing in parallel to the realm of the body and matter. And because this spiritual realm was infinitely mysterious, unknown, dangerous and unpredictable, it became a superior realm – *more* "real", *more* essentially "true", than the material world, and entered only through magic, hallucinations and dreams, drugs and ritual sex, and the in–*spiration* of poets, priests and mediums.

Geographical separation meant that each of many different cultures gave its own spiritual realm a particular character. The spirit–gods of the Indus Valley produced a religious culture that evolved into the complex system that we now call Hinduism. Another set of spirit–stories, which seem also to have originated in India, produced the Celtic deities who populated much of Europe well into the Christian era. The African continent had its own gods and demons, and each of the native cultures – Europeans, North American "Indians", Pacific Aboriginal and Maori peoples – developed its own unique relationship to the local governing spirits of plants and place. Egyptians and Arabs, Chinese and Japanese, all created their own stories, songs and myths to live by. All made their own peace with the unseen and unknown, and imposed shape on chaos.

Did humanity make gods or gods make humanity? Human language and culture surely made both. And having made God, we discover that it's true, after all, that *God creates us*, for it is the gods we make for ourselves who make us what we are.

CHAPTER 8

The Making of a God

*God is the most perplexing and yet most compelling
figure in human history, revealed by a myriad of diverse
sources, to be mighty, jealous, rude, babyish, deluded,
omniscient, vicious, ratty, benign, merciful, duplicitous,
mysterious, wise, ignorant, grand, humorous, cruel,
loud, racist, just, unjust, both mutable and immutable,
visible and invisible, oafish, fragrant, anarchic...*
– Alexander Waugh, *God*

THE GOD WE call God was born in the Biblical land of Canaan in
the late Bronze or early Iron Age. He was not created from nothing. He
had a complex ancestry marked by close kin relationships between the
spirit–gods of the Middle East. Like his forefathers, he was made by
storytellers, poets and magicians, but also by warriors and conquerors.
He was a god of battles: battles fought then, as now, over land and
natural resources. As I write, today's newspapers and television screens
are filled with pictures of Israel's tanks securing their occupation of
conquered territory on the West Bank, including the little town of
Bethlehem, where once "the hopes and fears of all the years" were
expected to be met in the God of Israel. This, they say, is the land
promised to them by Yahweh, the God of Abraham. And this same
land, say the dispossessed, is the land of *their* fathers, won for them by
their God of Abraham, Allah.

Long before there was any tribe or group of tribes identifiable as the "children of Israel", the various peoples in the city states of the land of Canaan, on the eastern shores of the Mediterranean, had their own gods, the Elohim, a name that seems originally to have meant simply "the gods" (or "the higher order of gods"), much as the plural forms of cherub and seraph are cherubim and seraphim. For some tribes or nations it seems that either the Elohim became conflated into a single god, El, or El emerged as the High God or Sky God of the Elohim. Either way, there were gods a–plenty.

Much of what we know, or can deduce, about these gods and the people who lived under their spell comes from the discovery of texts found in the Late Bronze Age Canaanite (West Bank) city state of Ugarit, which preserve myths and legends of the religious cultures from which early Israelite religion evolved (see C R Driver, *Canaanite Myths and Legends*, 1956, and J Gray, *The Legacy of Canaan*, 1965). According to these ancient pre–Biblical Ugaritic texts, El was the son of a father–god, El'eb, who was assumed to be the creator of the world. El lived with his wife Asherah, mother of the gods, alongside other Canaanite or Semitic gods such as Baal, the god of thunder and rains and therefore of fertility, and Yamm, god of the untamed seas and rivers which continually flooded the land and threatened destruction of lives and crops. Asherah and Baal both make guest appearances in the Bible, Asherah as the god of the wicked Queen Jezebel and Baal as a local deity who lost a fire–making contest with the Israelites' god. Baal and Yamm continually fight each other in mythical re–enactment of the perpetual struggle between order and chaos, or birth, death and resurrection, with El, head of the council of gods (a model for Tolkien's Elrond?) trying to hold the ring.

When Baal's death in a violent struggle with a rival god, Mot, threatens the triumph of chaos and the end of fertility, his sister–lover Anat has her own way of putting things right. She tracks Mot down and slays him: "with a sword she split him, with a sieve she winnowed him, with a fire she burnt him, with millstones she ground him, in a field she scattered him and fed his flesh to the birds". This action of grinding Mot's body into corn and sowing it in the earth not only restores the harvest cycle, it also brings Baal back to life and at his second coming he is reinstated as Anat's lover. As Karen Armstrong comments, "This apotheosis of wholeness and harmony, symbolized by the union of the sexes, was celebrated by means of ritual sex in ancient Canaan. By imitating the gods in this way, men and women would share their struggle against sterility and ensure the creativity and fertility of the world. The death of a god, the quest of the goddess and the triumphant return to the divine sphere were constant religious themes in many cultures". They would reappear in our own familiar Christian tradition.

In attempting to chart the developing character of the god of Israel we face a number of problems. Our sources are primarily the Hebrew Scriptures which, on the face of it, tell a chronological story beginning with the creation of the world and ending shortly before the rise of Christianity. The early fathers of the Christian Church accepted the Jewish canon as their own "Old Testament", but changed the order of the books to make them climax in what they believed were prophecies of the coming of the Messiah. So the "Old Testament" is no longer chronological: it is as if a trendy theatre director were to stage Hamlet by changing the order of Shakespeare's acts to have the play end with Ophelia's suicide.

That problem may be dealt with simply by reverting to the original order, in so far as it can be ascertained. But there is a bigger problem: sorting the history from the mythology. There has been much scholarly contention over this for the past two hundred years, and in the last ten new research has sharpened the controversy. It seems that the people who understood themselves to be the "children of Israel" did not start compiling their story, at least in anything like the form in which we now have it, until after the destruction of their northern kingdom by the Assyrians in 721 BCE, when Hezekiah, who continued to reign in the south, had his scribes create a mythologized version of the birth of their nation and their god. The scribes drew on a variety of oral traditions that often conflicted with each other because they represented the different perspectives and experiences not only of the various tribes but of contending factions in court, the priesthood and popular religion. Their purpose was not to preserve an historical record as we would understand it, but to create a national, cultural mythology, a "true fiction", that would bind them together in the face of their enemies. It cannot be emphasized too strongly that the whole of the "Old Testament" was written or edited, not in the distant days of a mythical Moses, but very much later, when Israel's northern kingdom had been destroyed and a new myth of origins was urgently needed to forestall ethnic disintegration.

If our task here were to unravel the historical development of Israel's identity and religion, the sifting of historical from mythological data would be crucial. But we are not primarily interested here in the people of Israel: our focus is their god. So I propose to follow the path pioneered by Jack Miles in *God: a Biography*, taking at face value the *story* in which God is the principal protagonist in a vast epic of scriptural literature. Of course, we cannot altogether escape history this way, but we can make the history of a people play second fiddle to the biography of their god. What we are doing is taking what the eighth- and seventh-century BCE scribes put together and building our biography of their god (who became the Christian God) from their materials.

The story told by Hezekiah's scribes in what became the books of Genesis and Exodus has been interpreted in two different ways by modern scholars. There is the standard "immigration" theory and the more recent and radical "native" theory. Scholars preferring the immigration theory interpret Genesis and Exodus as describing two distinct waves of immigration by Semitic tribes into what would become the northern kingdom of Israel and the southern kingdom of Judah. The two waves were once assumed to have been separated by centuries, but some researchers now think they were more or less concurrent. However and whenever they occurred, these two phases of immigration were distinct from each other in the religious cultures they brought with them. In the first phase, possibly as early as 1850 BCE but probably nearer 1200 BCE, a people called Hebrews began settling in and around Hebron and later in Shechem, now Nablus, and the other "cities of the plain" in what was then called the land of Canaan. (Some scholars think these are the peoples known to the ancient Egyptians as the Habiru.)

Like every tribe and ethnic group, they (or those who wrote it all up later) had their own origin stories that were of crucial importance in defining their group identity. The stories of this first wave of migrants centred on a wandering chieftain called Abraham, who was said to have bought a plot of land at Hebron (purchase, rather than theft or conquest, emphasizing the legitimacy of his occupation). One of Abraham's grandsons, Jacob, was renamed Isra–El (probably "Strength of El", but some scholars suggest a compound of the Egyptian Isis and Ra with El)) and was honoured as the ancestor of the twelve tribes of Isra–El.

The stories told of an emigration to Egypt during years of famine and mythologized the incursions into Canaan as an escape from Egyptian slavery into a "promised land" reserved for them by their High God, El, whose name was perpetuated in place names like Beth–El (either "god of storms" or "temple of God") and, later, Isra–El itself. El's wife Asherah seems to have been written out of the developing narrative, except where the Bible hints that, as a fertility goddess of renowned sexuality, she has the bad habit of seducing promiscuous Hebrew communities away from the worship of her husband. But El himself acquired many names and titles: El Elyon, "God Most High"; El Olam, "Everlasting God"; El Shaddai, "God of the Mountain" or "God Almighty"; El Berit, "God of the Covenant".

The worshippers of El were by no means monotheists. They clearly believed in the existence of other gods such as Baal, Yamm and Anat, and older gods like Apsu, Tiamat and Mummu make fleeting appearances in their epic stories. Marduk, credited in Ugaritic texts with the creation of the first man out of the dust of the earth and the blood of a dead god, may be the prototype of Israel's later conception of the Creator God – an idea not initially associated with the Elohim. Meanwhile El ruled, if not as the one god, as head of his somewhat unruly council of gods, much as a tribal patriarch might rule over a council of quarrelsome rivals.

The second wave of Semitic immigration, according to the "migration" hypothesis, seems to have occupied the southern area that came to be known as Judah. Some historians place it around 1200 BCE, but, as noted, this influx may have been soon after or even at the same time as the first. This second wave introduced a different but closely related religious tradition. These people also claimed to be descended from a patriarch named Abraham and to have been held captive in Egypt, but they knew nothing of El and brought with them their own god, Yahweh – the "god without a name". Indeed, they insisted that Yahweh had always been their god, and that he, rather than the northerners' El, was the god of Abraham.

It was Yahweh, they said, who had commanded Abraham to leave his homeland and migrate to Canaan, Yahweh who had promised him that he would become the father of a great nation that would grow to be more numerous than the stars in the sky. Yahweh had also revealed himself to their leader, one of their own tribe bearing an Egyptian name, Moses, who had masterminded their escape from Egypt and given them Yahweh's law. (Some imaginative writers have suggested that Moses was a priest at the court of Akhenaton, the Egyptian king who tried to introduce monotheism. When this innovation was rejected, it is suggested, Moses led the defeated monotheistic remnant into exile. It's a good story – with not a shred of hard evidence to back it. Given the failure of repeated attempts to find convincing evidence of the

Israel–in–Egypt story, no scholars other than those committed to a literalist interpretation of the Bible believe that the Moses of bulrushes and burning bushes was an historical rather than a mythical figure.)

It seems that El and Yahweh co–existed for a time, perhaps as the gods of different Hebrew tribes, with some of the older gods of Canaan still lurking in the wings – particularly Baal, who attracted a following as a fertility god demanding regular ritual copulation. But between the eighth and fifth centuries BCE, as the tribes coalesced into a nation of Israel seeking a common identity in the face of internal revolts and external attack, there arose attempts to merge the different traditions into a single narrative. So El and Yahweh were conflated. The new story, which becomes the one we are familiar with in Genesis and Exodus, tells us that although Abraham had called his god El, this was because he did not know the name Yahweh (transliterated as Jehovah in English, and generally rendered as "the LORD" in the King James Version). The two gods are re–presented as one. So El stories and Yahweh/Jehovah stories sit side by side in what became the early Hebrew scriptures, with the more old–fashioned El being gradually phased out in favour of the far more awesome Yahweh, whose name by the third or fourth century BCE is so far above every name that it may no longer be written, except in the cryptic form YHWH, or spoken, except circumspectly as Adonai, "My Lord", or simply Ha–Shem, "the Name".

Though obscured by the English translations that render both El and Yahweh as "God" or "the Lord", the two traditions are still distinguishable in the Biblical record. El tends to be portrayed as a very mild deity who often appears in human form, as do the gods of the *Iliad* and the *Enuma Elish* (the pre–Biblical epic of the ancient gods). As Karen Armstrong comments, "El gives [Abraham, Isaac and Jacob] friendly advice, like any sheikh or chieftain: he guides their wanderings, tells them whom to marry and speaks to them in dreams". But Yahweh, even when back–projected as the real god of Abraham, is quite different. When he first makes contact with Moses on Mount Horeb he is not at all like the friendly familiar El. He does not let Moses see him, for no man can see Yahweh and live to tell the tale. Instead, he communicates via an intermediary spirit – "the angel of the Lord". Moreover, even this angel of Yahweh is too awesome to walk and talk with Moses as El had walked and talked with Abraham. Instead, he appears as a great fire in the midst of a bush, burning without consuming it. Moses turns to investigate, and Yahweh calls to him through the angel in the fire, telling him to keep away and take off his shoes, for he is standing on holy ground. Across the divide between the unapproachable burning bush and the place where Moses stands shoeless, Yahweh's voice from the bush proceeds to tell him of his destiny: to free those whom Yahweh calls "my people" from their bondage in Egypt. Moses knows the first question his countrymen will ask when he comes down from the mountain is "Who says so? By what authority are you telling us all this?", so he asks Yahweh his name. Yahweh's unhelpful response is that he is who he is and that's all Moses and the children of Israel need know: a reply that some have seen as God's first recorded attempt at light humour. But the poet–editors who put together the story are at pains to make plain that this god with a new name or no name, who simply is who he is, is the god of Abraham, Isaac and Jacob. He is not a confusing new rival to El but El in a dazzling new form, El writ large. Behind El's smiling providence Yahweh hides a frowning face.

Thereafter, many of the El stories are retold with Yahweh simply replacing the older model. Occasionally, both El and Yahweh versions survive side by side, to puzzle later generations of scholars and students, particularly those who want to understand them as history rather than myth, and inerrant history at that.

John Bowker's scholarly *God: A Brief History* (DK Publishing, 2002) offers some fascinating examples of the early scriptural spin–doctoring by which the El and Yahweh traditions were cunningly rewritten to bring them into apparent conformity with each other and with the new myth of one god for the one chosen people. The earliest–known version of Deuteronomy 32:8 has El dividing up human beings into a number of different nations, the number corresponding to the number of gods in his council, so that each nation would have its own god, and each god his own nation. Yahweh was assigned to the nation of Jacob, the children of Israel. But, says Bowker, the early editors of these first texts "were so shocked at the apparent recognition of other gods that they changed the words". Instead of the nations being divided "according to the number of gods", the doctored version, in Deuteronomy as we now know it, has them divided "according to the number of the children of Israel", whose god, Yahweh, is made to seem identical to El himself, just another name for the one true god.

Some of these inconvenient echoes of the older pluralist tradition seem to have evaded the spin–doctors, however. Psalm 82 has El in council, judging his lesser gods for failing in their duties, and sentencing them to die like mortals. Psalm 96:5, in the original, has a play on words: the "elohim" (gods) are written off by El as "elilim", meaning not–gods, nonentities. Although such references to gods in the plural have generally been interpreted as referring to false gods or idols, the Deuteronomy text could hardly be interpreted in this way, and therefore the scribes entrusted with the task of compiling an authorized version of early Jewish history took it upon themselves to rewrite it to make it fit the new mythology they were creating.

One or other versions of the "immigration" theory of Israel's origins held sway through the nineteenth and most of the twentieth century. But in the 1970s and over the next thirty years it was challenged by a more radical hypothesis – I have called it the "native" theory – which began to displace the "immigration" theory among many biblical historians and archaeologists. According to this view, the "children of Israel" did not (despite their own mythologies) conquer or migrate into Canaan from beyond its borders, either in one wave or two. Rather, their origins were indigenous. The Israelites were Canaanites. Or, to put it in contemporary but more provocative terms, the Israelites were Palestinians.

Two scholars, George Mendenhall ("The Hebrew Conquest of Canaan" in *Biblical Archaeologist Reader III*, eds. Campbell and Freeman, Doubleday, 1970) and Norman Gottwald (*The Tribes of Yahweh*, SCM Press, 1979) argued that groups of indigenous Canaanites, around 1200–1000 BCE, began to form a new social, political, ethnic and religious identity in Canaan's central hill country. A stele, or inscribed tablet, known as the Merneptah stele and dated to around 1207 BCE appears to give the first datable reference to "Israel", though it is not clear whether the reference is to a people, a territory or both. Some archaeologists have linked the emergence of this distinctive Canaanite group with an explosion of new small villages that emerged in the central hill country at that time, with new styles of domestic architecture. A fully argued case, not only for the "native" theory but for viewing virtually the whole of Israel's "history" as creative mythology (including the stories of David, Solomon and the United Monarchy) was made in 1999 in a ground–breaking book by Thomas L Thompson (*The Mythic Past: Biblical Archaeology and the Myth of Israel*, Basic Books, London). By then, even some conservative scholars such as William Deever, while resisting Thompson's wholesale demolition of David's city and David's line, had come to accept the "overwhelming archaeological evidence... of largely indigenous origins for early Israel" (*What Did The Biblical Writers Know And When Did They Know It?*, Erdmans, Grand Rapids, 2001).*

Whether they were conquerors of ancient Palestine, or native Palestinians themselves, the nomad–to–peasant warriors who forged a new identity for themselves in the Early Iron Age inherited a complex local religious mythology, including stories of bondage in Egypt and exodus into a promised land, in both El and Yahweh versions. Yahweh as protagonist of the Yahweh stories is a fearsome god. When he appears

---

*For a debate on Israel's origins between Thompson and Deever, see the *Biblical Archaeological Review*, July/August 1997. For my brief account of the native or indigenous theory I am indebted to David McCreery for his paper "The Search for the Historical Israel", delivered to the Westar Institute conference, Santa Rosa, California, on October 17 2002.

it is usually in earthquake, wind or fire, very much like his old rival, Baal. When he speaks, it is often through an underling, an "angel" or messenger, though as his intimacy with Moses grows he condescends to speak with him face to face, like a friendly El, and eventually develops an intimacy that allows Moses to grumble at and argue with him. Once, he tells Moses to hide his face as he passes: Moses may see his backside, but not his "glory", the glory of his face (and, scholars suggest, perhaps his genitals). He takes up residence in the "tabernacle", a special tent among the tents of a people on the move – Alexander Waugh wittily refers to it as God's mobile home – but the tabernacle is a terrifying place, a tent full of molten fire and holy smoke – the "fire and cloudy pillar" which today's hymn singers still look to to "lead us all our journey through". The newly united tribes of Israel have come to need a bigger god than El, who was merely chairman of the local council of gods. Yahweh fits the bill. He is the greatest and mightiest of gods, a wonder–worker above all wonder–workers. He is the Lord mighty in battle. He sees off Baal in an epic fire–raising contest. He tells the Israelites what they want to hear: that he will smite the Egyptians and break their hold, and will then lead his people into the land of the Canaanites, Hittites, Amorites, Perrizites, Hivites and Jebusites: a land "flowing with milk and honey", which will be theirs so long as he is properly honoured as their one true god. He is just the right god for an ambitious, expansionist confederation of warrior tribes: the one true god of Israel.

"The one true god", however, still does not mean the only god who exists. Yahweh is a jealous god: he has rivals, and from time to time his people turn to these "false" gods when Yahweh fails to deliver. They are false, not in their non–existence but in their legitimacy. "Thou shalt have no gods before me". Yahweh has struck a deal with Israel: worship me alone and I will take good care of you. Go whoring after my rivals and our covenant is broken – and you will live to regret it.

Yahweh, then, was the emblem under which the disparate Hebrew tribes had come together (ironically, under the old name

Isra–El). Yahweh was the nation's unity, its soul, its story, its meaning, its purpose, its destiny and promise. Yahweh was not a metaphysical First Cause, nor was he the best explanation the children of Israel could lay their hands on for such mysteries as why the sun rose and set, why the moon waxed and waned, what made thunder and lightning, and where we had all come from. Yaweh only gradually came to be seen as in some sense the universal creator god. The earliest Hebrew (or Jewish) account of creation, supposed by scholars to have been put together no earlier than the ninth century BCE by a scribe known as J (because he represents the Jehovah/Yahweh rather than the El tradition) is the one eventually included in Genesis 2:4–7. Here the god diplomatically named Yahweh–Elohim is mentioned in a quite perfunctory manner as the creator of an earth that was at first a wilderness because there was no–one to till the ground, and as the one who made a man out of dust and breathed into his nostrils to bring him to life as God's own gardener and farm worker.

The much fuller, richer story of a seven–day creation, beginning with the invention of light (via language: the word "light" preceded light itself) and proceeding through the division of dry land from sea to the creation of grass, herbs and fruit, followed by sun, moon and stars, then fish and fowl, then cattle, beasts and creeping things, then man "made in the image of God", and finally woman made from man's spare rib – all this was a late development, no earlier than the seventh century and possibly as late as the fifth or fourth centuries, when what are now the first five books of the Bible (the Torah) began to take something like their final shape. The poet who so majestically and imaginatively expanded the earlier brief creation story, and whose work is given pride of place as the opening chapter of Genesis, evidently felt free to draw on a wide range of sources, including Egyptian mythology as well as the El traditions and the Babylonian creation myths of the *Enuma Elish*, both of which were by then in written form.

The creation sequence here echoes that of the *Enuma Elish*, and the story of the temptation, fall and expulsion from Paradise seems to belong to the Elohim tradition – particularly when the serpent tells Adam and Eve that God's worry is that if they eat of the Tree of Knowledge they "shall be as gods [note the plural], knowing good and evil". Indeed, the very first recorded conversation in this version of the creation story is not between God and Adam but between the gods themselves: "Let *us* make man in *our* image, after *our* likeness". While this could conceivably be the royal we, as in Queen Victoria's "We are not amused" and Margaret Thatcher's "We are a grandmother" – neither of which anyone would take to indicate a plurality of Victorias or Thatchers – it seems far more likely that this is a survival from the plural–Elohim tradition. However that may be, God, by whatever name, has become a complicated being: creator of all things, including all humankind, yet jealous that this final part of his creation may themselves become godlike, sharing his divine knowledge and immortal nature. But while still very much the god of his chosen people Israel, this more complex Yahweh–Elohim, who tries to deter Adam from disobedience by telling him that a single bite of forbidden fruit will kill him ("in the day that thou eatest thereof, thou shalt surely die"), was also coming to be seen as in some sense the *only* god, or at least the Lord High God, the creator of *all* tribes and nations, claiming for himself the right to tell his creation how it must behave. We begin to recognize the infant version of the Almighty God of the Christian tradition, though he clearly has a lot of growing up ahead of him.

Early Yahweh has much of the capriciousness of an infant. He is not well behaved. He lies to Adam and Eve in telling them that eating the forbidden fruit will kill them on the spot (later in Genesis 6:3 commuting their death sentence to 120 years, though he is fairly flexible even about that, as Methuselah's 969 years attest). And he drives them from Paradise when they listen to his rival, the serpent. His wish that they remain ignorant of "good and evil" clearly refers to the "shame" (theirs or his?) of sexual awareness, yet it is he who has commanded them to increase and multiply. His own "sons" (we are back with the Elohim here) fancy the daughters of men and "come into" them (Genesis 6:4), producing giants and men of great renown who are half man, half god. Women are particularly badly treated, made subject to their menfolk and sentenced to agonizing pains at childbirth. Men are sentenced to hard labour in the fields – perhaps a mythologized rationalization of the historic transition from what seemed in retrospect a golden age of hunting/gathering to the harsher life of farming in what could be a cruel and unpredictable climate. When his human creations use their free will in ways he does not like, this god repents of having made them and drowns all but Noah, his family and some lucky animal couples in what is perhaps mythology's most barbaric fit of pique. When Israel does his will, he rewards it with the spoils of war. When Israel fails to give him his due, it is punished with the vengeful rage of a criminal psychopath.

Yahweh uses famine, pestilence, disease and earthquakes to discipline his people, but his ultimate weapon is man's inhumanity to man. Disobedient Israel is smitten by its enemies, under Yahweh's instructions. At his instigation powerful enemies ravage disobedient Israel, and those enemies are in turn smitten when Yahweh chooses to fulfil his obligations under the covenant he has made with his chosen people. Playing out his role as Shaw's "omnipotent Bogey Man", Yahweh's own morality is not subtle. He "keepeth covenant and mercy with them that love him and keep his commandments", and he "repayeth them that hate him to their face, to destroy them: he will not be slack to him that hateth him, he will repay him to his face" (Deuteronomy 7: 9–10). His punishments for disobedience include:

> a consumption... a fever... an inflammation... an extreme burning... the sword... blasting... mildew... the botch of Egypt... the emerods (piles)... the scab... the itch whereof thou canst not be healed... madness... blindness... astonishment of heart... Thou shalt betroth a wife, and another man shall lie with her;

> thou shalt build an house, and thou shalt not dwell
> therein... thine ox shall be slain... thine ass shall be
> violently taken away... thy sheep shall be given unto
> thine enemies... The Lord shall smite thee in the
> knees, and in the legs, with a sore botch... And every
> sickness and every plague, which is not written in the
> book of this law, them will the Lord bring upon thee,
> until thou be destroyed... (Deuteronomy 28:22–61).

So there! "An eye for an eye and a tooth for a tooth" seems, by
comparison, mere wimpish liberalism.

Perhaps the most chilling of the many startling stories of
Yahweh's wrath is that recording his instructions to Israel as to how they
must deal with the occupants of the promised land once they have taken
possession of it. The epic story of the Exodus, the flight from slavery to
freedom, has inspired every captive people throughout history, not least
in recent centuries and our own times, when slaves imported from
Africa to America, the Inca, Tupac and Amaru peoples of South
America, the Sandanistas of Nicaragua, the Kurds of northern Iraq and
Turkey, have echoed captive Israel's cry, "Let my people go!" But the
archetypal *liberation* story is also an archetypal *liquidation* story, that of
a divinely inspired fanaticism which commands ethnic cleansing,
extermination and genocide. What is happening in the "Holy Land"
today, as I write, looks like an enactment of the mythical
commandment of Yahweh in Deuteronomy 7:

> When the Lord thy God shall bring thee into the land
> whither thou goest to possess it, and hath cast out
> many nations before thee, the Hittites and the
> Girgashites, and the Amorites, and the Canaanites,
> and the Perizzites, and the Hivites, and the Jebusites,
> seven nations greater and mightier than thou; And
> when the Lord thy God shall deliver them before thee;

thou shalt smite them, and utterly destroy them [some modern translations say "exterminate them"]; thou shalt make no covenant with them, nor shew mercy unto them...: ye shall destroy their altars, and break down their images, and cut down their groves, and burn their graven images with fire...: And thou shalt consume all the people which the Lord thy God shall deliver thee: thine eye shall have no pity upon them...

There is much, much more. Even before the entry into the promised land, Yahweh's servant Moses orders the extermination of the Midianites and is furious when only the Midianite men are killed and the women and children are kept as booty. Moses orders the killing of all except 32,000 virgins, who are to be retained as sex slaves, and the married women and boys follow their menfolk to the death camps. Such stories are told without qualms. How else, the authors might ask, should we expect the Lord God of Battles, the god of Israel, to behave?

This warrior–god's religious rules and regulations seem no less bizarre to modern readers. He was no respecter of political correctness, unashamedly embracing racism, sexism and contempt for lesser breeds without the law. He had a particular horror of the blind, the broken and the blemished, insisting that the ritual sacrifices of burnt offerings which he demanded as his due must not be offered by "whatsoever man he be that hath a blemish... a blind man, or a lame, or he that hath a flat nose, or anything superfluous, or a man that is broken–footed, or broken–handed, or crookbackt, or a dwarf, or he that hath a blemish in his eye, or be scurvy, or scabbed, or hath his balls broken... " (Leviticus 21:18–20). Add to this sad collection the whole of womankind, blemished or not, and we begin to appreciate just how cruel, arbitrary and discriminatory the Lord Yahweh was in his laddish youth.

Hezekiah's scribes may have "made up" the tales of enslavement in Egypt, the epic Exodus and the triumphant conquest of the "promised land" as a potent origin myth to assert their distinct identity and indestructibility when threatened first with Assyrian and Babylonian and then Greek and Roman assimilation. But whether constructed from history or mystery, mythology or creative fiction, it is the epic literature of the Bible which gives us our picture of the untamed and wilful deity who would grow up to become the mature God of Judaism, Christianity and Islam. By a series of sea changes we see how this God, the subject of our biography, slowly matures, repents of his laddish misdeeds and begins to grow in grace. His growing up is what we turn to next.

CHAPTER 9

God Grows Up

*If a faithful account was rendered of Man's ideas upon
Divinity, he would be obliged to acknowledge that for
the most the word 'gods' has been used to express the
concealed, remote, unknown causes of the effects he
witnessed... He solves the difficulty, terminates his
research, by ascribing it to his gods... When, therefore, he
ascribes to his gods the production of some phenomenon...
does he, in fact, do anything more than substitute for the
darkness of his own mind, a sound to which he has been
accustomed to listen with reverential awe?*
– Paul Heinrich Dietrich, Baron von Holbach,
Systeme de la Nature

THE FIRST CHANGE in the life of the Israelites to produce a
corresponding change in the nature of God himself was the one we have
been looking at: the slow but remorseless syncretism by which other
gods were absorbed into the one person of Yahweh. The second was the
series of revolutions, reflected in a mythic account that may bear little
resemblance to what we would call history, by which an Israel initially
ruled by chieftains and warlords became first a confederation under
"judges" and then a united nation under anointed kings. The third and
fourth were the occupation of northern Israel by the Assyrians in 721
BCE and the destruction of the southern kingdom of Judah in 586 BCE.

The latter, by scattering the children of Israel, created the need for a divinely sanctioned law and order, a powerfully cohesive god–force that could bind the separated tribes together.

The net effect of these changes was that the primitive Yahweh of Moses matured into a more complex god for an increasingly complex society. By the seventh century BCE he exhibits a new persona: he has become a civilizing law–giver, a god who tells his people how to behave, the ultimate authority on personal and social morality. Although the exhaustively detailed moral codes that begin with Leviticus and Deuteronomy, including the Ten Commandments, have been retrospectively assigned to the legendary age of Moses, textual critics tell us that their final formulation belongs to a much later age, probably no earlier than the seventh or eighth centuries BCE. The earlier tribes of Canaan and Israel no doubt had laws and conventions, as all human societies must, but attributing these rules and customs – including dietary and sexual taboos – to the nation's god was an innovation. It no doubt strengthened the hand of the human rulers of Israel, but it also changed the nature and character of the God portrayed in the scriptures.

He remained "Yahweh Sabaoth", Lord of Hosts or armies, but he continued to acquire new and more attractive characteristics. When Hannah (the source of whose story in 1 Samuel 2 could belong anywhere between the eleventh and sixth centuries) prays for a child, she is addressing a very different Yahweh from the god so high and mighty that he wouldn't let Moses see even his angel in the burning bush. Hannah's god emerges for the first time as a god of the underdog. In Hannah's words, he breaks the bows of the mighty and gives strength to those that stumble; takes food from the well–satisfied and gives it to the hungry; makes the barren woman fruitful and leaves the mother of many forlorn; deals death and gives life. He "raiseth up the poor out of the dust, and lifteth up the beggar from the dunghill, to set them among princes, and to make them inherit the throne of glory... for by strength shall no man prevail". This doesn't sound at all like the unpleasant little god who wouldn't let the lame, the blind and the "broken–balled" or impotent anywhere near him at sacrifice time. As Jack Miles reminds us in *God: a Biography*,

> What is particularly interesting about Hannah's prayer, apart from its blending of divine character traits, is the first ever mention of concern on the Lord's part for the poor, the feeble, and the needy as well as the barren. Lowliness (to use that as a summary word) has not constituted, earlier in the Bible, any special claim on the Lord. When the Israelites groaned in bondage in Egypt, it was not principally because they were in bondage but principally because they were his covenant partner, that God noticed their groaning. And when Hannah speaks about the poor and needy, we are to understand the Israelite poor and needy. Nonethless, there is a distinct new emphasis here; and when God accepts Hannah's thanks, he also accepts, tacitly, her characterization of him.

The god of the powerful has come to show an unexpected and unprecedented interest in the powerless. But this is only the start. The god who lorded it over the tribal lords and was thus the Lord of lords, and who judged the judges and was thus the Judge of judges, becomes with the establishment of the monarchy (attributed to around the ninth century, but recorded later) the King of kings. Does this contradict his claim to be god of the powerless? It would seem so, until he makes a new promise to the new King David, foretelling the role of David's son Solomon: "And when thy days be fulfilled, and thou shalt sleep with thy fathers, I will set up thy seed after thee, which shall proceed out of thy bowels, and I will establish his kingdom. He shall build an house for my name, and I will stablish the throne of his kingdom for ever". And then, out of the blue, the promise of a quite new relationship: *"I will be his father and he shall be my son"* (2 Samuel 7:12–14).

This is the first time God has been perceived as a father: God the Father. And the father–son relationship is quite different from that of king and subject or lord and vassal. "Fatherhood" comments Jack Miles,

> is an absolute, not a conditional state. The father of a son cannot, in the nature of things, cease to be such. If the father disinherits the son, he is the father of a disinherited son. If he slays him, he is the father of a slain son. If he denies him, he is the father of a denied son. Even if he aborts him, he is the father of an aborted son. Functionally, it is this about fatherhood that commended the image to the Lord and to the biblical writer. But once in the Lord's mouth, once on the page, fatherhood, one of the very richest natural symbols in human experience, inevitably begins to take on a life of its own. Unconditionality is just one among its innumerable possibilities. There is an enormous difference between the God of our fathers and God our father.

There was no suggestion in the tradition that El had fathered human children, even the "children of Isra–El" (though his wife Asherah had many offspring by consorting with different partners, human and divine). In the Genesis story, the shadowy "sons" of Yahweh–Elohim, the demi–gods who were half human, half divine, had helped themselves to the daughters of men and produced giants, but before his promise to David, the Lord in whatever shape and form had never described himself as God the father. In other mythologies, gods had fathered the world. In ancient Egypt, the sun god, with both male and female attributes, had fathered/mothered other creatures by an awkward form of masturbation which involved having oral sex with himself/herself, and swallowing the seeds of life to sow them in his/her own belly. But Yahweh promised a very different fatherhood, and it signalled both a transformed relationship with Israel and a transformed perception by Israel of who their god was.

Never anything less than the Lord of Hosts, never diminished in his Almightiness, God's relationship to his chosen people nevertheless now became not only the unconditional, irrevocable one which is intrinsic to fatherhood, but it assumed a parental *tenderness* and *compassion*. Love has not hitherto been absent in the relationship: God has made it clear that he loves, and that he demands love in return ("with all your heart and with all your soul and with all your strength"). But until now it has been a matter of "love me – or else...!" Moreover, the "love" he has hitherto demanded is not what we understand by the word today, with its connotation of a strong and caring emotional relationship, but something more akin to reverence, or even fear. Now the god revealed in Hannah's prayer as having a hitherto hidden concern for the poor and powerless, and by his promise to David as having a concern for justice, begins to take on the outlines of a loving father exercising a tender care over his family. God is growing in emotional maturity. He is growing up.

And in the prophets who continue to call Israel to repentance before, during and immediately after their exile in Babylon, we begin to detect hints that the family could be an extended one. In the prophecies of Micah and Isaiah it is not only the children of Israel who are to be gathered under the fatherhood of God, but "many nations". A wider world will say of the Lord, "he will teach us of his ways, and we will walk in his paths". It is not Israel but the "strong nations afar off" who will "beat their swords into ploughshares and their spears into pruning–hooks:

> Nation shall not lift up a sword against nation, neither
> shall they learn war any more. But they shall sit every
> man under his vine and his fig tree; and none shall make
> them afraid... For all people will walk every one in the name
> of his god, and we will walk in the name of the Lord our
> God for ever and ever. (Micah 4:3–5 and Isaiah 2:4).

Of course, Micah and Isaiah are prophesying a time – "the last days" – when the "many nations", Israel's enemies, will see the error of their ways and choose to "go up to the mountain of the Lord, and to the house of the God of Jacob", and put themselves under God's judgment. They prophecy the final victory of Israel, when even gentiles will come to acknowledge the supremacy of Israel's very own Lord of Hosts. But even a triumphalist interpretation of this prophetic vision must acknowledge a dawning recognition that God the Father is ultimately the father of all, not just the children of Israel. And he is a father who will apparently tolerate some diversity within the family, as his children will be free to "walk every one in the name of his [own] god".

Yahweh–Elohim (for it is still he) has developed a capacity for compassion, even a social conscience. He has condescended to argue with his human family (with Abraham, Moses, and especially Job) and listen to the pleas of the poor and weak as well as the rich and strong. Though still apoplectic when his children wantonly disobey, this wrathful god has begun to mature into something resembling a god of love. And indeed it is as a most ardent lover that he appears in the final act – one of the last books to be written and incorporated into the canon of Jewish scriptures: the *Song of Songs*.

A dazzling collection of erotic poetry, it is not surprising that when the *Song* reached its final edited form around 400 BCE it was attributed to the legendary Solomon. Tradition told that Solomon had three hundred wives and seven hundred concubines, a statistic that presumably established him as something of an expert on erotic love (though how he had enough energy left over to supervise the building of the Temple must remain a matter of scholarly conjecture). The collection makes no mention whatever of God or the gods, and few modern interpreters see it as anything other than a wholly secular fantasy of love and lust in wonderfully expressive and exotic language. That, indeed, was how many Jewish scholars saw it until the first century CE, when it was finally decided which ancient books would be included in the Hebrew canon. But some scholars at that time, led by the hugely influential teacher Akiva, argued passionately that the *Song* should be included as an allegory of the love between God and his people (his people being Israel to Akiva, but the Church to later generations of Christians). "He who trills his voice in the chanting of the *Song of Songs* in the banquet–halls and makes it a secular song," said Akiva, "has no share in the world to come". All scriptures were holy, but the *Song* was "the Holy of Holies".

The maiden (God's beloved) speaks first:

> *Let him kiss me with the kisses of his mouth:*
> *For thy love is better than wine...*
> *Therefore do the virgins love thee.*
> *Draw me,*
> *We will run after thee...*

God the lover answers:

> *Thy cheeks are comely with rows of jewels,*
> *Thy neck with chains of gold.*
> *We will make thee borders of gold*
> *With studs of silver...*

The beloved responds, more passionately:

> *A bundle of myrrh is my well–beloved unto me;*
> *He shall lie all night betwixt my breasts...*
> *Behold, thou art fair, my love;*
> *Behold, thou art fair;*
> *Thou hast doves' eyes;*
> *Behold, thou art fair, my beloved...*
> *Our bed is green.*

The lover:

> *As the lily among thorns,*
> *So is my love among the daughters.*

The beloved:

> *As the apple tree among the trees of the wood,*
> *So is my beloved among the sons.*
> *I sat down under his shadow with great delight,*
> *And his fruit was sweet to my taste.*
> *He brought me to the banqueting house,*
> *And his banner over me was love.*
> *Stay me with flagons, comfort me with apples:*
> *For I am sick of love.*
> *His left hand is under my head,*
> *And his right hand doth embrace me...*

And fully aroused now, her lover answers:

> *Rise up, my love, my fair one,*
> *And come away.*
> *For, lo, the winter is past,*
> *The rain is over and gone;*
> *The flowers appear on the earth,*
> *The time of the singing of birds is come,*
> *And the voice of the turtle is heard in our land...*
> *Arise, my love, my fair one,*
> *And come away...*

Or, in William Tyndale's exquisite sixteenth–century translation:

> *Up and haste my love, my dove, my bewtifull and come,*
> *For now is wynter gone and rayne departed and past...*
> *Up haste my love, my dove,*
> *In the holes of the rocke and secret places of the walles...*

They love, but there are lovers' insecurities. "By night on my bed I sought him whom my soul loveth: I sought him, but I found him not". So she goes in search of him, "about the city in the streets and in the broad ways". And "I found him whom my soul loveth: I held him, and would not let him go, until I had brought him into my mother's house, and into the chamber of her that conceived me".

Whether this is a secular love story or an allegory of the love between God and his people is surely not a matter on which scholars can make definitive pronouncements (though many purport to have done so). The point is that Akiva and his school *believed* it to be the holiest of all expressions of their relationship with their lord and their god. They *chose* to interpret it that way, and in doing so they changed the nature of their god by giving him a passionate love life. And they did so at the very moment when a new Jewish sect, soon to be known as Christians, was claiming that this same God had so loved his human creation that he had become one flesh with it. A new chapter in God's biography was about to be written.

CHAPTER 10

Father and Son

Three–in–one! Eases, lubricates, protects working parts!
– advertisement for a proprietary oil

WHEN HEROD THE Great set about spectacularly enlarging the
Temple in Jerusalem towards the end of the first century BCE, restoring
it to its legendary glory under Solomon, he was providing a home fit for
the God of Abraham, Isaac and Jacob, the God of Israel who had grown
up over the centuries. Once a tribal deity who promised protection in
return for worship, he had become in time the creator god, the author
and guardian of personal and social morality, comforter of the poor and
weak, father of his children, and lover of his chosen spouse: the one true
God, still recognizable in our hymn–books two thousand years later as
"the Ancient of Days, pavilioned in splendour and girded with praise".
Herod would have recognized this God. But he could not have guessed
what he would become in a new tradition to which Judaism was about
to give birth.

First century BCE Judah was a vassal state under the Romans.
Its kings and governors were Roman appointees, either collaborationist
Jews or Roman administrators. Corruption was rife, and sects
multiplied as some of the more zealous and fiercely nationalist Jews
broke with court and Temple to pursue a purified form of Yahweh
worship, often in the deserts and mountains. The Essene communities

are examples of one such sect. Most Essenes were celibate. They paid particular attention to cleanliness and ritual purity. Their leader was a shadowy and unnamed "Teacher of Righteousness", who emphasized the importance of an ethical life – justification by works as well as faith – and who prophesied that one day "All the nations shall acknowledge Thy truth, and all the people Thy glory". The Essenes were only one of many thorns in the flesh of Jewish and Roman authorities. We happen to know about them because their writings survived, not least among the Dead Sea Scrolls, and because several contemporary authors, including the historian Josephus, wrote about them. Josephus makes clear that there were many such sects, many such teachers, and many who looked to the coming of a messiah, a saviour and liberator, as promised by Yahweh's prophets. And, says Josephus, such troublemakers were routinely crucified by the occupying power.

The common notion of the Israel of those years is that of a small nation living in Roman–occupied Palestine, just as we picture the Gauls as a people living in Roman–occupied Gaul and the British a people living in Roman–occupied Britain. But in the first century BCE the Jewish people were by no means restricted to Palestine. Their communities were to be found far beyond the borders of the old kingdoms of Judah and Israel, in Asia Minor, Syria, Egypt, Greece and Rome. These Jews–in–exile, this "Diaspora", generally paid lip–service to Jerusalem and the Temple as their spiritual home, but their isolation made them particularly vulnerable to the customs, cultures and religious ideas of their largely Hellenized host communities. Hellenism was the prevailing culture and intellectual world–view of the Roman Empire as moulded by the Greek philosophers. So, while Jews in the land of Judah emphasized their Jewish identity either by ostentatious observance of their Temple customs and rituals in the face of their foreign overlord or by sectarian revolt, their growing satellite communities around the shores of the Mediterranean, cut off from the centre, tended to become gradually more Romanized and Hellenized.

What did this do to their God? We can best answer by looking at the influential writings of Philo, a Jewish theologian–philosopher who was born about twenty years before the date traditionally assigned to Jesus' birth and who died in 50 CE, some twenty years after the supposed date of Jesus' crucifixion. Philo lived in Alexandria, Egypt, where some scholars believe the Jewish community of around 100,000 was larger than the population of Jerusalem. (There were probably a million Jews living in Egypt). His writings, preserved by later Christian communities that were profoundly influenced by them (though they make no mention of Jesus or a Jesus movement), show that his philosophy was clearly derived from Greek Stoicism and Platonism, and his Yahweh was a very different god from the angry, ever–threatening tribal Yahweh of the old, old stories. He writes of "the divine Plato" – a startlingly un–Jewish notion – and describes God in Platonic terms as "transcending virtue, transcending knowledge, transcending the good itself and the beautiful itself". For Philo, God is no longer the god of the Jews alone but a god for all men, one who has laid down the moral law for the good of all mankind, not just the good of Israel. God is Wisdom, which existed before the creation of the world. He is ultimate reality and ultimate truth, the principle of reason governing the universe. God is transcendent. He has grown a metaphysical dimension, and as pure Being he belongs to no one race.

Philo wrote very favourably of the Essenes, devoting almost an entire book to them (*Quod omnis probus liber sit*, or "That every good man is free"). Although he himself came from a rich family, he championed the poor and the "poor in spirit". Like his possible contemporary James, he demanded works as well as faith. His familiarity with the teachings of the Essenes indicates that he was fully in touch with "non–conformist" tendencies within Palestinian Judaism, and it is clear that some strands of Palestinian Judaism were not entirely ignorant of or unsympathetic to Hellenized versions of their faith. In short, Jewish religion and culture, whether under the direct occupation in Palestine or under Hellenistic influence in the Diaspora, was in a highly unstable and volatile condition at the dawn of the Common Era.

Before the middle of the first century CE, another dissident sect was becoming visible. Unlike the case of Philo's school of theologian–philosophers and that of the Essenes, we possess not a single *contemporary* document or reference of any kind to the activities of the first groups constituting the Jesus movement or to the sayings and doings of its charismatic leader. For our information on both the man and the movement we are wholly reliant on accounts written at least a generation or two later, by which time there were already contending versions of what had happened, and rival interpretations of what it all meant. If by faith we were to grant to some accounts the status of Holy Scripture and divine inspiration, there would be no problem in ascertaining what was actually said and what actually happened. If, on the other hand, we place our faith in respectful but critical study of these documents, accepting that they were written, as were all texts, by fallible human beings for polemical purposes, we have a tangled web to disentangle. New Testament scholars have been disentangling away for more than two centuries now, and the lay student is still likely to be baffled by their fierce disagreements and evident uncertainties.

Some of the uncertainties centre on the dating of documents. All originals have long since perished, and what we have is copies of copies of copies, or fragments of copies, none that have been found (so far, i.e. 2005) dating earlier than 120 to 150 CE. As a starting point, then, the gospels and epistles which came to be collected in the New Testament could have been written any time between the end of the first half of the first century and some time in the first third of the second century. Only by a "critical" reading of each text in the original language, in all its variant forms, and considered in relation to what can be discovered about the historical context, can theologically disinterested (which is very different from uninterested) scholars begin to come to provisional conclusions about what was written when, what it may mean, and whether whatever "truth" it contains is the truth of history or the truth of myth, and the fact of the matter is that scholarly controversy continues to abound. Those of us who can read only the translations and have no specialized expertise must look for consensus where it is to be found, and remain open–minded where it is not.

These matters are crucial to the construction of an accurate historical account of the beginnings of the early church, but we need to remind ourselves once again that that is not our primary concern here. We are concerned with God and his biographical development. But the biographical development we are examining is the one whereby, in what is to become the Christian tradition, God the Father is transformed into God the Son and God the Holy Spirit: that is, the process by which the One becomes a Trinity. And central to that profoundly un–Jewish notion is the person of Jesus as perceived by his followers.

There is now strong support among scholars, though not of course unanimity, for the view that the first New Testament book to be written was not a book at all but a letter: the so–called First Epistle to the Thessalonians, written by the most important of all the early church missionaries, Paul, to an "assembly" or church he had recently established in the Greek city now called Salonica. If this is so, then the earliest known reference to Jesus in any written document is that in 1 Thessalonians 1:1 where Paul greets his readers with grace and peace "from God our Father and the Lord Jesus Christ". In verse five we have the first known reference to "the Holy Ghost", and in verse ten Jesus is described as God's "Son from heaven, whom he raised from the dead, even Jesus, which delivered us from the wrath to come". A major theme of the letter is the promise of the imminent return of Jesus, who "died and rose again", and it is this passage (4:14 – 5:11) which inspired the "Rapture" theology which so influenced my own boyhood and which remains a strong component of fundamentalist Christianity: "For the Lord himself [i.e. Jesus] shall descend from heaven with a shout, with the voice of the archangel, and with the trump of God: and the dead in Christ shall rise first: Then we which are alive and remain shall be caught up together with them in the clouds, to meet the Lord in the air: and so shall we ever be with the Lord". Thus the first recorded mention of Jesus is not as a wandering healer/preacher but as a god from heaven. The early church did not elevate a man to divinity: it transformed a heavenly spirit into a flesh and blood man. First came Christ, followed by Jesus.

This first letter to the Thessalonian Christians (who were probably largely, perhaps wholly, gentile rather than part of the Jewish Diaspora) is believed to have been written from Corinth in or about 51 CE. Some scholars put it slightly later and argue for the precedence of another of Paul's letters, that to the gentile churches in the Roman province of Galatia, in central Asia Minor, which may have been written a year earlier (though the weight of opinion seems to have shifted in favour of a date around 56 CE). Whether Galatians did precede 1 Thessalonians is of little consequence to our argument, as it too begins with a blessing in the name of God the Father and "our Lord Jesus Christ, who gave himself for our sins" and had been revealed by God as "his Son". Both letters indicate that by the fifties the executed teacher named Jesus (meaning "saviour") and hailed as the "messiah" in Hebrew or the "Christ" (anointed one) in Greek was regarded at least by Paul and probably most infant churches as in some sense the "son" of God, to be addressed as Lord (as was Yahweh): a supernatural figure.

Another contender for the first–ever mention of Jesus is yet another letter, this time not one of Paul's but attributed to James, said by Paul (but not by James himself) to be the brother of Jesus and described in a later narrative, the Acts of the Apostles, as the leader of the church in Jerusalem. Some scholars (but they are a minority) suggest that James's letter could be as early as 40 CE. The evidence is textual. It is addressed not to particular churches, like Paul's letters, nor indeed to churches in general, but to "the twelve tribes which are scattered abroad": that is, to the Jewish Diaspora. It makes only two passing references to "the Lord Jesus Christ, the Lord of glory", and does not refer to him as God's son. It reads like a letter addressed to scattered Jewish groups before followers of Jesus had separated themselves from mainstream Judaism and developed any settled conviction that Jesus was divine. It is strongly ethical in its famous and still moving insistence that "Pure religion and undefiled before God and the Father is this, To visit the fatherless and widows in their affliction, and to keep himself unspotted from the world". James urges his readers to be no respecters of the well–connected and well–dressed, and his message to the wealthy is blunt: "Go to now, ye rich men, weep and howl for your miseries that shall come upon you". Deeds, not words, bring salvation. "What doth it profit, my brethren, though a man say he hath faith, and hath not works? Can faith save him?" Faith without works is dead. This doctrine so startlingly contradicts Paul's insistence that justification *is* by faith alone and *not* by works that it has persuaded many scholars that it must be part of a later Paul–James argument. From the days of the early church fathers to Luther and beyond it has been argued that James' epistle should have no place in the canon of orthodox works. But the alternative to this interpretation of the letter as a later riposte to Paul is that it offers a glimpse of the early orthodoxy of the Jerusalem church led by James before Paul's dominance and his subsequent wholesale revision of Christian theology.

If Paul's or James' letters mark the first entry of the name Jesus into history, what of the gospel narratives? We return to near–unanimous scholarly territory in citing Mark as the earliest of the four accounts, but there is less unanimity in the dating. Few experts still argue for a date earlier than the 50s, and most favour the 70s, thus putting it two decades later than Paul's first letters. The opening verse of the most familiar version of Mark reads, "The beginning of the gospel of Jesus Christ, the Son of God", but the absence of "the Son of God" from some early texts has led to scholarly debate as to whether this was in the original but left out by some copyists, or not in the original and inserted to strengthen the sonship theology that developed later. We do not know. A little later in the first chapter Mark does have God declare "Thou art my beloved Son, in whom I am well pleased", but we cannot be sure that we are meant to understand this as a divine declaration of *unique* sonship. There is, of course, a *very weak* sense in which we are all seen by the Biblical writers as sons (or daughters) of a God who is father of all; a *weak* sense in which all *believers* are sons of

God (as in John's Gospel 1:12, where those who "received him" and "believed on his name" are given "power to become the sons of God"); and the *strong* sense in which Jesus alone is God the Son. (And it should not be forgotten that the capitalization marking a distinction between Son and son in our Authorized Version, which I am quoting, is a theological gloss by the seventeenth–century translators and has no equivalent in the original texts). The overall impression we are left with is that Mark does not emphasize the status of Jesus as Son of God, using the term only once (when, in a text of disputed authenticity, he reports a Roman soldier at the crucifixion as using these words). His Jesus is very modest about his own status, sometimes calling himself "Son of man" but refusing (11:33) to reveal by what authority he was saying what he was saying and doing what he was doing. Mark would appear to have been written before the strong sense of Jesus as unique Son of God had fully taken hold, though Paul and perhaps other leaders of the dispersed and diverse Jesus movement were evidently emphasizing the doctrine in its strong sense by this time.

The Gospels of Matthew and Luke are usually dated to a few years later, probably the mid–80s or a little later. They are both believed to have drawn on Mark's narrative and on an early collection of Jesus' sayings now lost but referred to by scholars as "Q" (from the German *quelle*, "source"). Both are much more positive about Jesus' divine status. Although Matthew gives him a genealogy beginning with Adam and running through David and Solomon to "Joseph the husband of Mary", he makes it clear that Jesus' conception was arranged by "the Holy Ghost" in what appear to be miraculous circumstances. His primary purpose is to preach Jesus as the Messiah prophesied in the Jewish scriptures, but his Jesus claims "All power is given unto me in heaven and in earth". His followers are to be baptized "in the name of the Father, and of the Son, and of the Holy Ghost", and he promises "lo, I am with you always, even unto the end of the world" (28:19–20). This Jesus is God. Luke is similarly unequivocal. His fabulous birth story is quite different from Matthew's, as is his genealogy, but the angel of the Lord tells the virgin Mary, who pleads that she "knows not a man", that it is the Holy Ghost who shall come upon her, the "power of the Highest" that shall "overshadow" her: "therefore also that holy thing which shall be born of thee shall be called the Son of God".

But the fourth Gospel, attributed to John, makes Jesus not just an epiphany, an appearance of God, but very God himself. John is usually dated to the last decade of the first century. John Robinson's highly original arguments for "the priority of John" (in a book of that name) have not found acceptance in the wider scholarly community, nor have theories ascribing authorship to John the son of Zebedee, who is named by Matthew as one of Jesus' inner circle of disciples. But the John who did write it, or the man who wrote in John's name, was clearly familiar with and strongly influenced by the Hellenised Judaism of Philo and his circle. In his majestic prologue he proclaims that in the beginning of time there was the *logos*, the Greek philosophers' term for the principle of reason and wisdom, the "word" or language by which chaos is ordered and made intelligible. The *logos* was "with God"; it "*was* God". It/he was the creator of all things. He was life, and this life was "the light of men": a light no darkness could ever put out. John proceeds to tell how a preacher named John the Baptist had been sent to bear witness to this light, Jesus, "the true Light which lighteth every man that cometh into the world" – a world he himself had made, but which did not know him. This principle of reason and wisdom, this *logos*, this Word, this creator of all things, had entered the world as one of his own creations, and had not been recognized. But those who had come to recognize him and had acknowledged him for what he was had been given the power to be "sons of God", living a new life which began not with conception and birth but with their new relationship with "the Word... made flesh", full of grace, truth and "the glory as of the only begotten of the Father". Here is Philo's metaphysical God, and John says this metaphysical God walked the world as a man named Jesus. We are as far from Yahweh Lord of Hosts as theology and philosophy in their wildest throes of fancy could conceivably bring us.

The transformation had taken perhaps half a century. Whether an historical, mythological or literary figure, the itinerant teacher/healer Jesus of the early decades of the century had made no such claims for himself. No such claims had been made by his brother James, head of the Jesus movement after Jesus' squalid execution. By the 50s, there were currents within the new "assemblies" or churches that did envision Jesus as in some sense the "son of God", without any clarity or unanimity as to what that meant. The missionary Paul, who antagonized Peter and James of Jerusalem by insisting that the salvation Jesus offered was open to all, whether Jewish or gentile, circumcised or uncircumcised, strongly urged the divinity of Jesus. Matthew and Luke produced biographies of Jesus which added to Mark's more reticent narrative, emphasizing both Jesus' humanity and his divinity. And finally John accorded Jesus the kind of divinity that the Hellenic world beyond the narrow confines of Judaism could understand. As Paul ingeniously tried to tell the Athenians (though they wouldn't wear it), Jesus was the unknown god of their own philosophers.

This God was everything the old god of Israel had been: creator, lawgiver, father, advocate of the poor and ardent lover of his bride (now redefined as the Jesus movement, the "new Israel"). But he was more. Where Yahweh and the old tribal gods had demanded blood sacrifice, the Christians' new–model God had made *himself* the sacrificial Lamb whose blood atoned for all sins. Jesus had been crucified, and something as extraordinary as the crucifixion of the Word made flesh required explanation. The blood sacrifice tradition provided that explanation. The Father–God had so loved the world that he had sent his Son to die as the ultimate redemptive sacrifice: one that would give those who accepted the sacrifice "everlasting life". And the belief, the conviction, that Jesus had risen from the dead, was taken as proof that sacrifice, the ritual taking of one life to preserve life in general, really worked. So the new–model God, who was in some mysterious sense Father, Son and Holy Spirit rolled into one, was one who could and did confer the gift of immortality on those who believed in him.

Belief in immortality, "everlasting life", was a development hastened by the Hellenisation of Judaism. Yahweh had promised much and threatened much, but never everlasting life. Indeed, from the start, according to the story, he had denied to Adam and his children the immortality that the gods enjoyed. During the two centuries before the start of the Common Era, some Jewish teachers had begun to argue that the special relationship Yahweh had built with Abraham and the prophets might be continued beyond death, and this received reinforcement from those who had received a Greek or Hellenistic education. The Greeks postulated the existence of an immortal soul, of which the mortal body was a mere temporary appendage. By the first century CE and the beginnings of the Jesus movement, the question of immortality was hotly contested within Judaism. The traditionalist party known as the Sadducees were the principal opponents on the ground that there was no clear warrant for it in the Jewish scriptures, and the newer, less tradition–bound Pharisees encouraged a Greek–influenced hope in the resurrection of the dead. Despite the poor press the Pharisees receive from the New Testament writers, Jesus is thought by many to have had much more in common with their party. Certainly the belief that he had himself risen from the dead proved beyond doubt to his followers that death had been robbed of its sting, and the grave of its victory.

There were still to come many long years of argument among Christian factions as to how God as Father, Jesus as Son and the Holy Spirit as an independent expression of both could be reconciled with the doctrine of one God. God as Trinity was a long time in the making. The question is often but mistakenly assumed to have been settled at the Council of Nicaea in 325 (on May 20th), but it is now recognized that the formulation known as the Nicene Creed came later, possibly not before the fifth century when it first began to be used in eastern churches as part of the Eucharist. The Roman church did not adopt it till 1014. The creed elaborates the foreword of John's Gospel to speak of

Jesus as "one Lord... the only Son of God, eternally begotten of the Father, God from God, Light from Light, true God from true God, begotten not made, of one being with the Father", himself the creator made incarnate as man through a virgin birth, who had died, risen, and would come again in glory to judge the living and the dead and to inaugurate a kingdom which would have no end. The Holy Spirit is also "the Lord", who "proceeds from the Father". (Not till centuries later did the western church decide that the Holy Spirit also proceeded from the Son, adding a late rider to that effect). The Nicene Creed, in its often tortuous and arcane formulations and revisions, shows all the scars of bitter theological infighting, resolved only by forms of words that still remained open to rival interpretations in other forms of words. But it completes the process in God's biography whereby he becomes the Triune God: God in his prime. What room is there, we may wonder at this point, for any further personal growth in the complex hero of our story?

CHAPTER 11

Sweet Reason

In the beginning of time the great creator, Reasonmade
the earth to be a common treasury.
– Gerrard Winstanley

WHAT ROOM IS there for further development in the biography of
God after his life story has climaxed in the Christian tradition with his
mature three–fold nature? The answer is, a great deal – not least because
Christianity was never the only show in town. Within mainstream
Judaism Yahweh remained firmly unitary, but that didn't mean that the
ancestral God of the Jews stood still. Judaism found new directions in
which to grow after the destruction of the Temple and the development
of rabbinical organization, and the God of the Jews grew with them. As
we have seen, the Christian church took several centuries to agree what
eventually became its orthodox Trinitarian view, along the way fighting
off not only Unitarian challenges but also the Gnostic factions that
wanted to divide God into two, a Supreme Being (largely derived from
Platonism) who was wholly spirit, and an inferior creator–god, the
"demiurge", whose particular responsibility was the material world with
all its imperfections. And no sooner had the church fathers resolved
these matters to their satisfaction (largely at the insistence of secular
power–brokers who were more interested in political stability than in
religious uniformity) than the prophet Muhammad in Mecca planted

his own landmark in history by creating a new tradition which swept away both the Trinitarian God and his pagan rivals in favour of one God of all peoples, not unlike the God of the late Jewish prophets except that he spoke Arabic. The Christian, Jewish and Muslim versions of God were all given a pedigree back to Abraham, but rival traditions constructed rival biographies. It is with the Christian biography that I am now primarily concerned.

Once God had been defined by credal formulae in the catholic and orthodox traditions of west and east, heresy (from the Greek word for "choice") became a dangerous business, tending, as it did, to lead to the rack or the stake. God was God as defined by the church, which meant that God was God as defined by the men who wielded power in the church. Indeed, their authority to wield such power was, they claimed, derived from the very God they had defined as the one who had given them the keys of the kingdom and a monopoly of interpretation of his word and will. They alone claimed the right to write his authorized biography. For over a thousand years the result was a mixed heritage of magnificent art, architecture and music overlaid by a squalid history of conquest and persecution, bigotry, repression, superstition, corruption and reaction. God was held captive by those who claimed to be his faithful servants, rather as Yahweh's fire and thunder had been domesticated by tribal leaders who had put the divine power into a box called the ark and triumphantly carried it around with them in a tabernacle–tent, God's closely guarded mobile home.

From time to time new heresies and offbeat mysticisms added a chapter here and a footnote there, and the growing cult of the Virgin Mary softened the relentless masculinity of the story's divine protagonist. But it wasn't until the protestant reformation of the sixteenth century that the Catholic version was substantially challenged. As the mediation of the Church began to be rejected in favour of a priesthood of all believers, and as the authority of the hierarchy gave way to the authority of Scripture, the way was opened for new, unofficial biographies, offering new slants and new insights. God's life story began to enter a fresh, creative phase, in which he himself was re–formed, along with the worshipping communities that kept him alive.

Different historical circumstances in different parts of Europe meant that the process of "reformation" differed from country to country. In Britain, the defining thrust came not from Henry VIII's loins but from the deposition and execution of Charles I and the abolition of church censorship, which directly precipitated what has been called "the radical reformation". During two extraordinary decades of revolutionary word and action, God was recast variously as the indwelling spirit of nature, as an inner or inward light of conscience, as Reason, and as a "bugbear" – a figment of the imagination. The dethronement of the king led inexorably to the dethronement of the King of kings; and although the restoration of the King of England in 1660 also rehabilitated the King of Heaven and his very own Church of England, things would never again be quite the same with God or his Church, both of which had been given the fright of their lives.

God's life story is usually told either from a philosopher's or a theologian's perspective, where the markers are Descartes, Spinoza, Hume, Kant and so on. Readers of Don Cupitt's magnificent *The Sea of Faith* or A N Wilson's excellent *God's Funeral* might be forgiven for supposing that only professional thinkers were involved in the constant process of modifying and modernizing God. The "poor bloody infantry" get scarcely a mention. But in mid–seventeenth–century England, the "vulgar sort" took the initiative and left their theologizing, philosophizing betters far behind.

The causes of the civil war which broke out in 1642 were hugely complex and do not concern us here; but in an age when religion and politics were inextricably mixed, God was never absent from the battlefield. The question that divided the nation was, who had the authority to rule, and whence was that authority derived. Since both sides at least agreed that all human authority was ultimately derived from God, it became an urgent question as to what kind of God he was, and who was to act in his name. Until the 1640s the established doctrine of the divine right of kings, upheld by the kings' courts and the kings' bishops, made God the ultimate royalist. "No bishops, no king" James I had warned those who proposed importing Edinburgh's Presbyterianism to London, and the bishops understood only too well that if there were no king there would be no bishops. Their implied warning, then, was "No king, no God". God sat on a *throne*. He *ruled* heaven and earth. Since Yarweh of old, he was King of kings and Lord of lords. To dethrone the king was to dethrone God. Regicide was deicide. This was understood by the leaders of both sides in the conflict, which is why the parliamentary forces opposing the royalist army at first claimed to be fighting for "king and parliament" against those who fought for king and court. Both sides stood, they said, for God and the king. The revolutionary English republic of the 1650s was made less by republican ideologues than by royalist incompetents.

What had underpinned the power of royalist state and Church before the 1640s was a draconian censorship. It was a punishable offence to print or circulate not only religious matter critical of the church but also any political news. No religious pamphlets, no newspapers. The mass medium of communication was the pulpit, and the only media magnate was Archbishop Laud. In 1637, by decree of Star Chamber, all but twenty authorized printers in London had their presses confiscated. No book imported from the continent was allowed on the market before it had been vetted by the bishops. When John Lilburne, later the Leveller leader and later still a Quaker, defied this regulation he was flogged within an inch of his life through the streets of London. John Bastwick, judicially mutilated for defying the censors, said from his pillory: "Were the press open to us we would scatter [Antichrist's] kingdom" (the institutional Church and royalist state). A year or two later it was, and they did.

In 1641, with the course set for open civil war, Parliament abolished the censorship and it was as if a vast dam had been breached, to flood the nation with news and speculation, free speech and opinion, Biblical criticism, anti-clericalism and heresies old and new. Presses were reassembled, newspapers produced and distributed, and the war of pamphlets was hardly less bitter and bloody than that on the battlefields. In the twenty years of relative freedom which ensued before a restored monarch and restored church hierarchy reintroduced full censorship, God was re–envisioned in ways that would change his life for ever.

The central conviction common to the many diverse strands of the radical reformation was that God was not the property of the institutional church. The Church in all its traditional forms – Catholic, Anglican and Presbyterian – had forfeited any claim to an exclusive right to speak for God, lay down his law, interpret his Scriptures or prescribe how he should be worshipped. Far from being the means by which the layman and woman might obtain access to divine grace, it had become a barrier between man and his God, much as it was believed that a corrupt court had come between loyal subject and the crown. Once the abolition of censorship was followed by the abolition of the Episcopal system and the breakdown of centralized ecclesiastical control, those who had long resented the dictatorship of the primates and their parish priests began to meet together informally to study the Bible without benefit of clergy. They saw themselves as liberated Christians making a new relationship with a God who was himself newly liberated from the clutches of his discredited church.

Hungry for information and inspiration, they devoured the books and pamphlets that were pouring off the newly established presses. These included reprints of works that had long circulated underground in defiance of the censorship, as well as English translations of continental works of protestant mysticism and radical speculation. The civil war itself provided an apocalyptic background to the new liberation theology: a sense that God was working out his purpose, that the day of the Lord was at hand. But what kind of Lord? What did God look like when stripped of the trappings laid on him by sixteen hundred years of church polity and piety?

Jacob Bauthumley was a Leicestershire shoemaker, recruited into Cromwell's New Model Army where radical ideas flourished in the late forties. In 1650 he published *The Light and Dark Sides of God* which put forward a pantheistic view common among groups known as Ranters:

> All the creatures in the world... are but one entire being... Not the least flower or herb in the field but there is the divine being by which it is that which it is; and as that departs out of it, so it comes to nothing, and so it is today clothed by God, and tomorrow cast into the oven... God as really and substantially dwells in the flesh of other men and creatures as well as in the man Christ, [and in] man and beast, fish and fowl, and every green thing, from the highest cedar to the ivy on the wall... [He is] in dog, cat, chair, stool... in this tobacco pipe... he is me and I am him.

A similar view of God as diffused throughout creation was advanced by the former minister Richard Coppin in *Divine Teachings*, a book recommended to the Levellers in their newspaper (cleverly titled *The Moderate*). "God is all in one, and so is in everyone," wrote Coppin. "The same all which is in me, is in thee; the same God which dwells in one dwells in another, even in all; and in the same fullness as he is in one, he is in everyone". Such views scandalized the orthodox and hastened the return of a limited censorship. Bauthumley had his tongue bored through, and Coppin was lucky to get away with six months in jail. But their pantheistic view of God or the divine, with its explicit rejection of any distinction between creator and creation and its understanding of God as integral to our humanity – indeed to all life – rather than over and above it, has profoundly influenced succeeding generations. It can be detected in early Quakerism, by which route it was an influence on Barach Spinoza in Amsterdam, the father of modern pantheism. It lives on in some current forms of "creation spirituality" and new age paganism. Its god is more a flower–power hippy than a baton–wielding police chief, it's slogan "make love, not war" rather than a litany of "thou shalt nots".

Scandalized churchmen argued that Ranter pantheism was only one short step from atheism, and they were right: it proved to be a step which some Ranters were happy to take. A Ranter "Christmas carol" mocked believers in these terms:

> *They prate of God; believe it, fellow–creatures,*
> *There's no such bugbear; all was made by Nature.*
> *We know all came of nothing, and shall pass*
> *Into the same condition once it was,*
> *By Nature's power; and that they grossly lie*
> *That say there's hope of immortality.*
> *Let them but tell us what a soul is, then*
> *We will adhere to these mad brain–sick men.*

Yet the God who was thus abandoned was the High God of the Church, rejected in favour of a God made in the image of man. Ranters continued to hold religious services, albeit in taverns, which they called "the house of God", and continued to sing songs of praise to the tunes of metrical psalms, albeit songs which the pious considered blasphemous, praising not God in heaven but the joy of living here and now. They even continued sacraments, of a sort. According to one hostile report, recounted by Christopher Hill in *The World Turned Upside Down*, "one of [the company] tore off a piece of beef, saying 'This is the flesh of Christ, take and eat'. Another threw a cup of ale into the chimney corner, saying 'There is the blood of Christ'". Ranters said they believed in heaven and hell, but heaven and hell on earth. Life continued after death only as the water of a stream continued after it had run into the ocean. Since God was all and in all, there was no act that could be condemned as contrary to God's will and therefore sinful. To the pure, all things were pure. Lawrence Clarkson, a former Baptist preacher who became known as "Captain of the Rant", taught that "there is no such act as drunkenness, adultery and theft in God... Sin hath its conception only in the imagination... What act so–ever is done by thee in light and love is light and lovely, though it be that act called adultery". Clarkson practised what he preached, sending his wife maintenance while travelling the country in the company of a Mrs Star. At one Ranters' meeting, he tells how "Dr Paget's maid stripped herself naked and skipped" – but on this occasion, he claimed, he had resisted the temptation to demonstrate that adultery was no sin. "All the world now is in the Ranting humour", complained one despairing puritan in 1651, but in truth Ranting was a short–lived phenomenon, both because it was cruelly punished under the 1650 Blasphemy Act and because most Ranters, having demonstrated to their fellows and to themselves their total rejection of the God of the churches, went on to seek a less nihilistic God within, many finding it in Quakerism.

More stable, if less radical than the Ranter groups, were those known as Seekers. The label was widely applied, not only to nonconforming communities in general but also to major public figures like John Milton, William Walwyn, and even Cromwell himself. Some Seekers were attracted by Ranter–type pantheism, but for most, their quarrel was not with the church's God but with the church itself. It was the churches and sects, in their view, that had deserted God, not God who had let down his church. Seeker groups were marked by a resigned withdrawal from sectarian controversy and a rejection of all denominational organization. A number of "shattered" Baptist and Independent congregations became Seeker groups, and in some of the more remote parishes in Yorkshire, Westmorland and Cumberland, Seeker networks were well established by 1652. William Erbery, a former parish minister and a chaplain in the New Model Army who was described in 1646 as "the champion of the Seekers", argued that Christians should "sit still, in submission and silence, waiting for the Lord to come and reveal himself to them". "And at last, yea within a little, we shall be led forth out of this confusion and Babylon, where we yet are, not clearly knowing truth nor error, day nor night: but in the evening there shall be light". Seekers met in silence, waiting for the Lord to speak to their condition: they were sometimes known as Waiters. Rejecting ordination, tithes and centralized control, their theology embraced the new emphasis on immanence, God within, without wholly rejecting transcendence, God without or beyond. Describing the typical Seeker as "bewildernessed as a wayfaring man", Erbery wrote: "Let him look upward and within at once, and a highway... is found in Christ in us, God in our flesh". Upward *and* within.

The "True Leveller" or "Digger" leader, Gerrard Winstanley, was neither a Seeker nor a Ranter (though, like many Seekers and Ranters, he ended up with the Quakers). For Winstanley, both God and the devil were internalized. "What you call the devil is within you"*. It is the devil that "leads men to imagine God in a place of glory beyond the skies". Winstanley's God is neither an external being nor a deified historical Jesus. Christ is "not a single man at a distance from you but the indwelling power of reason". "You are not to be saved by believing that a man lived and died long ago at Jerusalem, but by the power of the spirit within you treading down the unrighteousness of the flesh. Neither are you to look for God in a place of glory beyond the sun, but within yourself and within every man... He that looks for a God outside himself, and worships God at a distance, worships he knows not what, but is... deceived by the imagination of his own heart". But "he that looks for a God within himself... is made subject to and hath community with the spirit that made all flesh, that dwells in all flesh and in every creature in the globe". As God and the devil are not real persons, so heaven and hell are not real places. "Every saint is a true heaven, because God dwells in him and he in God, and the communion of saints is a true heaven". Angels too are "the sparks of glory or heavenly principles set in men". The Day of Judgment is a metaphor, as is the resurrection of the dead.

---

*This and the Winstanley quotations which follow are from Winstanley's works as quoted in *Gerrard Winstanley and the Republic of Heaven* by David Boulton, Dales Historical Monographs, Dent, England, 1999.

God understood as "the power of reason" was Winstanley's most striking contribution to the radical reformation's rewriting of God's biography. He preferred the word Reason to God, he said, because the latter word had become a stumbling–block to honest Christians. "In the beginning of time the great creator, Reason, made the earth to be a common treasury". "The spirit of right understanding has taken up his dwelling in this flesh, and from hence man is called a reasonable creature, which is a name given to no other creature but man, because the spirit of reason acts in him". The "powers of the heart" must "submit to the light of reason" if there is to be "love between all creatures". "The Spirit or Father is pure reason, and when flesh becomes subject to the reason within it, it can never act unrighteously or trespass against others, but it does as it would be done by". "Let Reason rule the man, and he dares not trespass against his fellow creature, but will do as he would be done unto. For Reason tells him, Is thy neighbour hungry and naked today, do thou feed and clothe him; it may be thy case tomorrow, and then he will be ready to help thee". Reason "knits every creature together into a oneness, making every creature to be an upholder of his fellow". Today, three and a half centuries later, it remains a most striking insight (though we do well to remember Shaw's revision of the "Golden Rule": "Do not unto others as you would they should do unto you; their tastes may not be the same"!).

Winstanley's Reason (or reason: sometimes he capitalizes the word, sometimes not, and there is no significance either way) looks at first sight like an astonishing anticipation of the quality which would give the next century its designation as the Age of Reason. But there is nothing smacking of mathematical logic or cold intellectualization in Winstanley's writings in the 1640s. I doubt that Winstanley would feel at home in the Rationalist Press Association. Sometimes Reason is love, sometimes community. "In the beginning of Time, the Spirit of Universal Love appeared, to be the father of all things: the Creation of Fire, Water, Earth and Air came out of him, and is his clothing. Love is the Word". Winstanley's Reason is what we might call "sweet reason": a principle of harmony and sweet reasonableness, which he sees as a cosmic power permeating the whole of "creation". It is the *logos* of John and Philo, the Word. But it is also common sense and enlightened self–interest: Reason dictates that we do unto others as we would be done by, so that others will do by us as they would themselves be done unto. For Winstanley, of course, this had the most profound social consequences. Sweet reason, love, harmony and do–as–you–would–be–done–by led to the conclusion that "The poorest man hath as true a title and just right to the land as the richest man", and that led to Winstanley's Digger experiments in Christian communism. "Action," he wrote, "is the life of all", and Winstanley's God, his Word of Reason, was a true, living God only in so far as he could be discerned and incarnated, tried and tested, in human action.

By 1651, however, Winstanley's fledgling communes had been broken up and dispersed, the Ranters had been put to flight by the Blasphemy Act, the Seekers were still seeking and the Waiters waiting. The high hopes entertained by the Levellers and their radical allies, especially after the execution of the king and the declaration of a republic, had been dashed by Cromwell's unwillingness or inability either to push the democratic revolution forward or rebuild a national church on the open model favoured by Independents and sectaries. In that same year, however, a young man named George Fox was released from Derby jail after serving a long sentence for blasphemously claiming that he was the son of God. Fox travelled through the north of England in 1652 and gathered a following, largely from local Seeker groups, which became the basis of the Quaker movement. By 1654 its missionaries were in London and Bristol, by the end of the decade it had spread throughout the British Isles and was knocking on the doors of America and Europe, and before Fox's death in 1691 it was by some accounts larger than all the other nonconformist denominations in England put together.

Quakerism, particularly in its earliest phase, synthesized much of the radical theology of the Ranters, "shattered" Baptists, Winstanley, and especially the Seekers. From the Ranters it took a fierce anticlericalism; from the break–away Baptists the image of God as the inward or inner "light of conscience"; from Winstanley an emphasis on non–violence and the "Spirit of Love" (though never called Reason by Quakers) and a social radicalism (but not communism); and from Seekers the ritual of silent worship, waiting on God. The Quakers' God was closest to that of the "champion of the Seekers", William Erbery, when he urged men to "look upward and within at once" – a God whose transcendence was not repudiated, but whose immanence was emphasized, even to the point of Fox insisting that there was "that of God" in everyone.

Quakers almost alone among the radical reformation groupings survived the collapse of the republic and the restoration of king and Church in 1660. That they managed to do so, despite harsh persecution, was largely due to the charismatic spiritual leadership, combined with organizing genius, of Fox. Much of their early radicalism, both social and theological, eventually wilted under the onslaughts of respectability and the attractions of quietism. But Fox and Friends ensured that God, perceived primarily as in us rather than outside us, speaking as the "light of conscience" rather than through the instruction of church or scripture, and manifested in deeds rather than creeds, survived beyond the turmoil of the seventeenth century to infiltrate his way into mainstream theology – and sow the seeds of the atheology of the future.

Winstanley and Fox taught that the ultimate authority in religious matters was *experience*. "This I knew experimentally" (or experientially) was a common refrain for both of them. Indeed, if neither the word of the church nor the word of scripture could be trusted as infallible, all that was left was the knowledge, wisdom or intuition derived from personal experience (interpreted through Reason for Winstanley, through "the Spirit" for Fox). In the seventeenth century, the verb "to experience" most commonly meant "to try out, to put to the test, to experiment", and "experience" itself meant "a trial, an experiment", rather than some vague subjective feeling. The new emphasis on experimental religion was no accident. What would later become the Royal Society of London for Improving Natural Knowledge was founded in 1645, at the height of the civil wars, to promote "experimental philosophy" and "experimental learning". "Experimental philosophy", or science, was to re-fashion God in ways very different from those envisaged by the radicals who had picked up the new jargon–word to promote experimental religion.

A leading light and early president of the Royal Society was Isaac Newton, who argued from his own experiments that the universe was governed by mechanistic laws, and thereby ushered in a new age of science and Enlightenment. Although Newton himself remained fervently religious, it was soon pointed out by his peers that his discoveries seemed to leave little room for a God, or even a cosmic Reason who steered history for his own purposes, intervening with the occasional miracle or providential answer to prayer. On the other hand, even a mechanistic universe required a creator, a first cause. Enter, then, a new slant on God: one that acknowledged him as the necessary initiator of the universe and its laws, but thereafter an absentee deity. "Deism", as this was called in the eighteenth century, proposed a God who, having got the world going, immediately lost interest and took early retirement. (Oddly, this absentee divinity was resurrected in 2004 by the veteran atheist philosopher Anthony Flew, who managed to alienate both religious and irreligious by arguing that the emergence of living from lifeless matter required an ultimate intelligence, but not the interventionist deity of the churches). Honour and worship were due to the Deists' God as first cause, and the practice of religion was useful in so far as it taught folk to know their place and honour their betters; but of Yahweh the architect of history, or Christ as Redeemer, or Winstanley's cosmic leveller, or Fox's inner light, there remained barely a trace in the received wisdom of the Age of Reason and Enlightenment, and in the new–fashioned deity of the philosophers.

But if new models of God were coming thick and fast, in response to new discoveries and new challenges, the older models were not entirely discarded. The Church of England, restored to power and influence in 1660, reinstated the King of kings in every parish, whatever the scientists, philosophers and the vulgar sort were saying. And the immanent God–within of the radical reformation, though reviled by new rationalist and old churchman alike as the product of vulgar "enthusiasm", survived to stage a second coming in the Romantic movement. For William Blake, God was no scientific abstraction, no absentee architect of Newtonian physics, but the crowning glory of the human imagination, the incarnation of "mercy, pity, peace and love", the "virtues of delight" which clothe "the human form divine":

> For Mercy, Pity, Peace, and Love
> Is God, our Father dear,
> And Mercy, Pity, Peace, and Love
> Is man, His child and care.
>
> For Mercy has a human heart,
> Pity a human face,
> And Love, the human form divine,
> And Peace, the human dress.
>
> Then every man, of every clime,
> Who prays in his distress,
> Prays to the human form divine,
> Love, Mercy, Pity, Peace.

Blake's poem – *The Divine Image* in *Songs of Innocence* – invokes Winstanley's religious humanism, and William Wordsworth's *Lines Composed a few miles above Tintern Abbey* reminds us of Bauthumley's pantheist God embedded both in Nature and "the mind of man":

...For I have learned
To look on nature, not as in the hour
Of thoughtless youth; but hearing oftentimes
The still, sad music of humanity,
Nor harsh nor grating, though of ample power
To chasten and subdue. And I have felt
A presence that disturbs me with the joy
Of elevated thoughts; a sense sublime
Of something far more deeply interfused,
Whose dwelling is the light of setting suns,
And the round ocean and the living air,
And the blue sky, and in the mind of man:
A motion and a spirit, that impels
All thinking things, all objects of all thought,
And rolls through all things...

The Ranters in their taverns, the Diggers in their communes, the Quakers in their meeting–houses and the poets in their imagination had given God a new face for new times. The theologians were left far behind. They had a lot of catching up to do.

CHAPTER 12

The Twilight of God

To the lexicographer, 'God' is simply the word that
comes next to 'go–cart'.
– Samuel Butler

IF, AS SOME of the most influential thinkers in the Age of Reason supposed, God was no more than a First Cause who had set Newton's universe in motion and then sat back, content to be a disinterested spectator of its joys and griefs, humanity evidently had no alternative but to set about working out its own salvation. The popular radicals of the seventeenth century had begun the process; the cool philosophers who followed them had rejected their "enthusiasm" and sought a rational faith; the masses, pressed by the industrial revolution into the service of new masters in their dark satanic mills, were turning their backs on all gods and all churches; and the Romantic poets were re–visioning God as the ultimate symbol of human love and compassion (Blake), as the elemental force rolling through all things (Wordsworth), as "the Archetype" of all living creatures made manifest in language (Coleridge), or as one big mistake (Shelley). Where were the professional religious in all this? The mainstream churches, it seemed, were the one place where nothing new was being said or thought about the nature of God. Their leaders preached a dated gospel to slowly dwindling congregations, defending the battered castle of faith by pulling up the drawbridge and hurling empty anathemas against a faithless age. Only "with faltering steps and slow" did theology begin to catch up with life as it was coming to be lived in the real world.

The theologies that best kept pace with the Enlightenment were those that had long kept their distance from traditional church structures, those that had had to fight for their own freedom from doctrinal and liturgical control and which most confidently embraced new light. The ejection of 1,700 ministers from the Church of England as a consequence of the Act of Uniformity of 1662 had created a new layer of nonconformity, alongside that of "Old Dissent" – the Quakers and what were left of the Commonwealth sects. Nonconformity was soon characterized by diversity, and within that diversity a number of the more liberal and adventurous chapels gravitated towards a position they came to call Unitarianism – rejection of a God in three persons in favour of a single–person God to whom Jesus was related as prophet, messenger, the ideal man, but not as the incarnate God himself.

Anti–Trinitarian forms of Christianity had an established history, from Arius in the third century to Michael Servetus and Lelio Sozzini in the sixteenth. Servetus had been put to death by the Calvinists for his heresy, but the followers of Sozzini (Socinians) had influenced scientists like Newton and philosophers like Locke. This view of Jesus as wholly human rather than uniquely divine was arrived at by critical examination of the scriptures and the church's historical accretions of doctrine, and as it was precisely this process of rational criticism that drove the Enlightenment project, Unitarianism found it easier to co–existed with Deist rationalism than did more conservative theologies.

One of the most important architects of the entente between eighteenth–century rationalism and free–thinking Christianity was the scientist–philosopher Joseph Priestley who, as a scientific materialist, denied the duality of mind and spirit, the existence of the soul, the divinity of Christ and the doctrine of the atonement. Christianity, he said, was "less a system of opinions than a rule of life". When Priestley died in 1804 his followers in Britain and the United States were numerous enough to create an influential Unitarian connection marked by an open, enquiring attitude to religious matters and the God question. Always few in number, they made a wholly disproportionate contribution to intellectual life, scientific advancement and social radicalism, particularly through the Association of Civil Rights, founded in London in 1819. Influential journals like Jeremy Bentham's *Westminster Review*, condemned for its "atheism" by the orthodox, numbered leading Unitarians among its regular contributors, and Unitarian chapels were notable centres of radical dissent in Manchester, Liverpool and throughout the English midlands.

Priestley spent the last few years of his life in the United States, where Thomas Jefferson fell under his influence. Jefferson risked his illustrious political career by undertaking his own study of what Jesus had "really said", as distinct from what the gospel writers had said he'd said. America's founding father was probably the first Biblical scholar to compile his own proposed list of authentic Jesus sayings, which became known as the Jefferson Bible. It consisted of a harmonized gospel in seventeen chapters, beginning with a non–miraculous birth and ending abruptly in Jesus' burial. Miracles, exorcisms and supernatural events were all cut from the record. This scandalized Jefferson's opponents in the 1801 presidential election, who claimed that if he were elected he would substitute his new Bible for the old throughout America! Jefferson nevertheless fought off his critics and won a famous victory. Despite his power and popularity, it was the old Bible that survived and prospered, while Jefferson's dropped into obscurity. But the scaremongering was probably a factor in ensuring that the complete version of Jefferson's study, *The Life and Morals of Jesus of Nazareth, Extracted Textually from the Gospels in Greek, Latin, French and English*, was not published until 1904, some seventy–eight years after his death.

Back in England a young Coventry ribbon manufacturer, Charles Bray, proposed that God should not be worshipped or prayed to, on the very rational grounds that he "will always do what is right *without asking* and not *the more for asking*". His view was elaborated in a two–volume work, *The Philosophy of Necessity*, published in 1841. Bray was married to the sister of another Unitarian thinker, Charles Hennell, whose book *An Inquiry Concerning the Origins of Christianity* had come out in 1838. Hennell's work was the first in English to take a rational, critical look at the life of Jesus, aiming to separate historical fact from mythical accretion, fantasy and wishful thinking. Applying his critical method to each of the four gospels in turn, Hennell suggested there was no hard evidence to support the view that Jesus was born by supernatural means, that he considered himself uniquely divine, that he worked miracles in defiance of the laws of nature, that he rose from the dead or that he ascended into heaven. Jesus was "a noble–minded reformer and sage, martyred by crafty priests and brutal soldiers". For good measure, Hennell argued, as his brother–in–law Charles Bray did in his books, that there was no point in concentrating on the unknown and unknowable possibility of a future life after death, so our focus should be on the present, not on heaven above but on "this beautiful planet" below.

Hennell and Bray would probably be no more than brief footnotes in the story of God were it not for the entry into Coventry life of a young woman whose literary genius would ensure her a place in the town's history even more notable, if less sensational, than that of Lady Godiva. Mary Ann Evans, who would later adopt the pseudonym George Eliot, moved there in 1841 shortly after her twenty–first birthday, in search of a husband. She found instead a group of radical intellectuals who were busy questioning every article of religion, politics and received morality. Formerly a pious Evangelical who had refused to read novels because they were fictions, and therefore lies, Mary Ann joined Bray and Hennell in their Unitarianism, and stopped going to church. Three years later she embarked on her first literary project, a translation into English from the German of David Friedrich Strauss's monumental work *The Life of Jesus Critically Examined.*

Strauss was a Lutheran minister in Germany, hugely influenced by the "New Christianity" preached by the philosopher Georg Hegel. In *The Phenomenology of Spirit* (1807) Hegel had proposed that God, or "Spirit", was the product of human consciousness maturing in history. Science, art, philosophy and religion were the expressions of the Spirit, but it was primarily in the history of religions that God arrived at his own maturity, in and through people's ever–developing consciousness of him. Strauss tried preaching this new, enlightened and rational understanding but was warned off by his ecclesiastical superiors, not because his views were considered demonstrably false but because it was feared they might destroy the faith of the simple burgher in the Lutheran pew. Nevertheless, the 26–year–old pastor began work in 1834 on his 1,500–page, two–volume *Life* which, when published in 1835, would create a theological earthquake – and put an early end to a promising career.

Where Hennell had proposed what might be termed a liberal or "modernist" interpretation by which the events recorded in the gospels were not denied but interpreted rationally and naturalistically, Strauss put forward an essentially mythic account. The stories of Jesus were... stories. Jesus was a Jewish teacher, acclaimed by his followers as the messiah. After his death, the religious imagination of his followers clothed his life in mythical and supernatural colours. The gospels should be read, not as history but as religious symbolism. Jesus was wholly human – as the Unitarians and Enlightenment rationalists maintained.

Hennell may already have read Strauss when he started work on his own *Inquiry*. He and his circle were certainly aware of the furore the *Life* was provoking in Germany. They decided an English translation was needed and persuaded a Radical MP with Unitarian sympathies, Joseph Parkes, to finance the project. The young Mary Ann Evans was commissioned to undertake the work. She was unknown, untried – and she was a woman. Parkes got cold feet, and Evans found Strauss's plodding German hard going. But in 1846 her translation of *The Life of Jesus Critically Examined* was published. Only Strauss's name appeared on the title page, with no mention on any page of the translator, who was paid twenty pounds for her two years hard labour. W S Gilbert's "singular anomaly, the lady novelist" who "I'm sure will not be missed" evidently applied with double force to a lady translator of radical theology.

Even as Mary Ann worked on Strauss's *Life*, however, another theological explosion was detonated in Germany. Ludwig Feuerbach, like Strauss, was one of the "young Hegelians" who first followed then sought to transcend the work of the master philosopher. In 1841 he published *Das Wesen des Christentums* ("the essence of Christianity"), which effectively did for God what Strauss had done for Jesus. God was not so much Hegel's emergent Spirit created by religious history, but rather the expression of human needs and values projected, as it were, onto a cosmic screen. Blake had said that mercy, pity, peace and love *is* God; Feuerbach said that God *is* mercy, pity, peace, and especially love. As Kathryn Hughes writes in her biography *George Eliot*, Feuerbach's work was "an attempt to salvage the spirit of Christianity in an intellectual landscape for ever changed by Strauss... Feuerbach's Christianity was a warm and generous humanism, which saw acts of love between men [and women] as the building blocks of faith". Love, Feuerbach wrote, "is God himself, and apart from it there is no God". But all that the eye of orthodoxy could see was the replacement of God by man, a defiant and blasphemous reversal of the fundamental article of faith that God had made man in his own image.

Feuerbach was clear that, in talking about God, humanity was in fact talking about itself: in worshipping God, humanity worshipped a projection of its own needs and desires. *Theo*–logy, words about or the study of God, had become *anthropo*–logy, words about or the study of humanity. But Feuerbach repudiated the charge of atheism (an imputation that his follower Karl Marx was happy to accept). A proper atheist, said Feuerbach, was not one who denied a personal or objective God, but one who denied the predicates or attributes of God – love, compassion, wisdom, justice. Conversely, the true believer was not one who merely assented to propositions about a personal God as a metaphysical being, but one who dared put his trust in these attributes as the essence of all that the God metaphor represented.

Mary Ann Evans was commissioned to translate Feuerbach's book, and *The Essence of Christianity* was published in London in1854. "George Eliot" had yet to be born: not one of the great novels – *The Mill on the Floss, Middlemarch, Silas Marner* – had yet been conceived; but the unknown, anonymous young woman who would shortly rival Dickens as the greatest of English Victorian fiction writers had already changed the intellectual landscape by putting before English and American readers the two most challenging and revolutionary theological works of the century. (She later completed a theological hat trick by translating Spinoza's *Ethics* from the original Latin).

These were unsettling times. Revolutionary theology was only one of the spectres haunting the frock–coated men and bustled women who made up the rapidly expanding middle classes. Continental Europe came close to social revolution, and Britain was convulsed by Chartist agitation, which threatened to rob middle–class men of the monopoly right to vote which they had been granted in the 1832 Reform Act. America was charging headlong towards civil war. Steam engines on rails and steam ships on the seas, coupled with the penny post and the electric telegraph, were shrinking a vast globe into a measurable ball that might be circumnavigated in eighty days. The deep–cutting of canals, by revealing the stratification of the earth's surface, was creating a new geology that cast doubt on received ideas about the age of the planet, and new discoveries in cosmology were changing traditional conceptions of the heavens. Now even the Bible, the timeless truths of Christianity and the precious promise of life after death were considered fair game for critical scrutiny. Was not even that defender of the established faith, the Master of Oxford's Balliol College, Benjamin Jowett, admitting that the Bible should be read and analyzed "like any other book... in the same careful and impartial way that we ascertain the meaning of Sophocles or of Plato"? The Lord God of Hosts, the King of Kings, no longer sat secure in his heaven, all was not right with the old world.

Into this sea of doubt, in 1859, Charles Darwin dropped his *Origin of Species* bombshell, not merely arguing but demonstrating with the hard evidence acquired in a lifetime of patient observation that life on earth, including human life, had evolved by natural selection, apparently without any guiding hand. Evolution itself was not a new idea: Charles' own grandfather, Erasmus Darwin, was a noted evolutionist. In one form or another the notion had been around for a century, and Unitarian and liberal theologians had had little difficulty in accommodating it within a creationist framework: God could as easily and credibly have made all creatures great and small by supervising their evolution from protoplasmal primordial atomic globule to oak and elephant as by creating all species at a single stroke. Even Arthur Schopenhauer, who as early as 1818 had pictured the evolution of "living, knowing beings" from the "mouldy film" which had formed on the cooling crust of just one among the "countless luminous spheres" in the universe, had allowed a place for a divine guiding hand in the whole awesome process. But Darwin's mechanism for evolution was natural selection: something that looked perilously like blind chance. Though Darwin himself was reluctant to admit it publicly (he called himself an agnostic rather than an atheist), his theory of evolution made God an optional extra in the great scheme of things: at best the First Cause of the Deists, at worst a supernumary who could now be consigned, along with the Gorgon and the Minotaur, to ancient mythology. But what did that make humankind? The crowning glory of evolution, or W S Gilbert's caricature:

Darwinian man, though well behaved,
At best is only a monkey shaved...

The falling eventide and deepening darkness of faith was captured most expressively, however, not by philosophers, theologians, satirists or even lady novelists of genius, but by a poet. Matthew Arnold belonged to the generation of Victorian intellectuals whose faith had been profoundly shaken by the changes brought about by the French revolution, the industrial revolution in Britain, and, above all, the assault on traditional Christian dogma. In 1859 – the year Darwin published *Origin of Species* – Arnold took his new bride to honeymoon in Dover. As he sat at the open window at night, hearing the waves of the outgoing tide drag the pebbles down the shingle at the foot of the famous white cliffs out into the English Channel, it struck him as a powerful metaphor for the out–going tide of religious faith, and his haunting poem *Dover Beach* was born. I quoted from it in Part One, where it impacted on my own story. Though familiar to many, it is worth repeating here in full:

> *The sea is calm tonight.*
> *The tide is full, the moon lies fair*
> *Upon the Straits; – on the French coast, the light*
> *Gleams, and is gone; the cliffs of England stand,*
> *Glimmering and vast, out in the tranquil bay.*
> *Come to the window, sweet is the night–air!*
> *Only, from the long line of spray*
> *Where the sea meets the moon blanched sand,*
> *Listen! you hear the grating roar*
> *Of pebbles which the waves suck back, and fling,*
> *At their return, up the high strand,*
> *Begin, and cease, and then again begin,*
> *With tremulous cadence slow, and bring*
> *The eternal note of sadness in.*

Sophocles long ago
Heard it on the Aegean, and it brought
Into his mind the turbid ebb and flow
Of human misery; we
Find also in the sound a thought,
Hearing it by this distant northern sea.

The sea of faith
Was once, too, at the full, and round earth's shore
Lay like the folds of a bright girdle furled.
But now I only hear
Its melancholy, long, withdrawing roar,
Retreating, to the breath
Of the night–wind, down the vast edges drear
And naked shingles of the world.

Ah, love, let us be true
To one another! for the world, which seems
To lie before us like a land of dreams,
So various, so beautiful, so new,
Hath really neither joy, nor love, nor light,
Nor certitude, nor peace, nor help for pain;
And we are here as on a darkling plain
Swept with confused alarms of struggle and flight,
Where ignorant armies clash by night.

These bleak, final lines of the poem express with moving eloquence the death of Victorian faith in a slow but sure progression towards a world which had seemed "to lie before us like a land of dreams, so various, so beautiful, so new". As religious faith had been undermined, so the promised land of dreams had become a world devoid of joy, love, light, certitude, peace, and help from pain, a place of "confused alarms of struggle and flight, where ignorant armies clash by night". What then was left? "Ah, love, let us be true to one another!" Faith and hope had been sucked away in that long, withdrawing roar. What was left was love. Love was Blake's God, and Feuerbach's, and love was all that was left of God for Arnold as he turned from the window to his honeymoon bed.

Dover Beach was not published until 1867, in Arnold's last collection of poetry. Meanwhile, back in Germany, another poet–philosopher, Friedrich Nietzsche, was inching towards the abyss Arnold had merely glimpsed (and would ultimately step back from). Surveying human history, and particularly the confusions of the nineteenth century, Nietzsche concluded that life was full of delusions, and the greatest delusion was supernaturalist religion. All religions, but Christianity in particular, were narcotics designed to suppress fear of unknown forces. All religious explanations had been rendered redundant by the rise of science. Not only had religion died, but God was dead too. The "death of God" is proclaimed most dramatically in *The Gay Science* (1882), where he famously pictures a madman running through the market, crying "I seek God! I seek God!". The bystanders laugh at him. "Why, did he get lost? asked one. Did he lose his way like a child? demanded another. Or is he hiding? Is he afraid of us? Has he gone on a voyage? Or emigrated?" The madman replies:

> Whither is God? I shall tell you. We have killed him –
> you and I. All of us are his murderers. But how have
> we done this? How were we able to drink up the sea?
> Who gave us the sponge to wipe away the entire
> horizon? What did we do when we unchained this
> earth from its sun? Whither is it moving now?
> Whither are we moving now? Away from all suns? Are
> we not plunging continually, backward, sideward,
> forward, in all directions? Is there any up or down left?
> Are we not straying as through an infinite nothing?
> Do we not feel the breath of empty space? Has it not

become colder? Is not night and more night coming on all the while? Must not lanterns be lit in the morning? Do we not hear anything yet of the noise of the gravediggers who are burying God? Do we not smell anything yet of God's decomposition? Gods too decompose. God is dead. God remains dead. And we have killed him. How shall we, the murderers of all murderers, comfort ourselves? What was holiest and most powerful of all that the world has yet owned has bled to death under our knives. Who will wipe this blood off us? What water is there for us to clean ourselves? What festivals of atonement, what sacred games shall we have to invent? Is not the greatness of this deed too great for us? Must not we ourselves become gods simply to seem worthy of it? There has never been a greater deed; and whoever will be born after us, for the sake of this deed he will be part of a higher history than all history hitherto.

The madman falls silent. The crowd is also silent. Then the madman adds:

I come too early; my time has not yet come. This tremendous event is still on its way, still wandering. It has not yet reached the ears of man. Lightning and thunder require time, the light of the stars requires time, deeds require time even after they are done, before they can be seen and heard. This deed is still more distant from them than the most distant stars – and yet they have done it themselves.

Nietzsche did not, as some suppose, proclaim himself as the one who had brought about the death of God. But he saw that Christianity – indeed all of western religious culture – was entering its final apocalyptic crisis as it faced the total collapse of its foundations; and it was this crisis, this imminent collapse, which he called the death of God. He is customarily seen, particularly by orthodox Christians, as a deeply anti–Christian figure, but some radical theologians, Don Cupitt among them, see his perspective as intensely religious. He perceived an important and paradoxical truth: that it was the Christian *search for truth* that had undermined Christian dogma and killed the Christian God. "All great things perish of their own accord," he wrote, "by an act of self–cancellation... Thus Christianity as dogma perished by its own ethics, and in the same way Christianity as ethics must perish; we are standing on the threshold of this event. After drawing a whole series of conclusions, Christian truthfulness must now draw its strongest conclusion, the one by which it shall do away with itself." This was the "tremendous event": but note that it is a madman who proclaims the event, and the God who has been murdered is the "holiest and most powerful of all that the world has yet owned".

If God was dead he must be buried, and it fell to the poet Thomas Hardy to describe the macabre occasion. In *God's Funeral*, written around 1910 (and largely neglected till A N Wilson used it to preface his own 1999 book of the same name), Hardy pictures a graveyard procession to bury a mysterious blurred shape which was both "man–like" and "an amorphous cloud of marvellous size", a symbol of "potency vast and loving–kindness strong". And the poet overhears the funeral oration:

> *O man–projected Figure, of late*
> *Imaged as we, thy knell who shall survive?*
> *Whence came it we were tempted to create*
> *One whom we can no longer keep alive?*
>
> *Framing him jealous, fierce, at first,*
> *We gave him justice as the ages rolled,*
> *Will to bless those by circumstance accurst,*
> *And long suffering, and mercies manifold.*

And, tricked by our own early dream
And need of solace, we grew self–deceived,
Our making soon our maker did we deem,
And what we had imagined we believed.

Till, in Time's stayless stealthy swing,
Uncompromising rude reality
Mangled the Monarch of our fashioning,
Who quavered, sank, and now has ceased to be.

So, toward our myth's oblivion,
Darkling, and languid–lipped, we creep and grope,
Sadlier than those who wept in Babylon,
Whose Zion was a still abiding hope.

How sweet it was in years far hied
To start the wheels of day with trustful prayer,
To lie down liegely at the eventide
And feel a blessed assurance he was there!

And who or what shall fill his place?
Whither will wanderers turn distracted eyes
For some fixed star to stimulate their pace
Towards the goal of their enterprise?

Winstanley and Blake had dethroned God from the heavens and reincarnated him in humanity, Nietzsche had announced his death, and Hardy had witnessed his burial. But God had been through that before: the Elohim had died to make way for Yahweh, and God incarnate had been crucified and risen again. The American atheist H L Mencken held his own memorial service for the gods in 1923, listing over a hundred ancient deities who had "gone down the chute" after reigning supreme over generations of worshipful believers – defunct gods, most of them now known only to specialists in divine exhumation. But as he listens to God's funeral oration, Hardy observes something else:

> Some in the background then I saw,
> Sweet women, youths, men, all incredulous,
> Who chimed: 'This is a counterfeit of straw,
> This requiem mockery! Still he lives to us!'

There were many who refused to sing of their God *requiem in pace*, many for whom the God the intellectuals were burying was indeed a mere counterfeit of straw. God's biography was not concluded by his obituarists, be they poets or philosophers. If his body lay mouldering in Hardy's grave, his soul went marching on in the imagination of those "sweet women, youths, men" who insisted "Still he lives to us!" We'll follow them into the twentieth century.

CHAPTER 13

A Living Fiction

*In today's terminology the incarnation may be described
as the humanization of God, the secularization of the
divine, and the earthing of heaven.*
– Lloyd Geering, *Is Christianity Going Anywhere?*

GOD'S BIOGRAPHERS, like all biographers, storytellers, painters, photographers, must adopt a point of view. From that point of view, things are seen in a particular perspective. Change your vantage point and your perspectives change too. From here, God is dead: from there, he is the resurrection and the life.

Those who choose to celebrate a living rather than mourn a dying God will remind us that the Age of Reason, marking in its own terms God's terminal sickness, was followed by the age of Wesley and the Methodist revival, marking not only the resuscitation of a dying religion but the rebirth of a dying God. We need to remember that the age of skepticism – of Darwin, Marx and Nietzsche – was also the golden age of the evangelical awakening in both Britain and America. And if the twentieth century saw from one perspective the triumph of secularism and naturalism over religion and supernaturalism, it also saw from another (particularly in its latter postmodern phase) an explosion of interest in "spiritualities", New Age and old, which breathed fresh life into God's nostrils and made of him once again a living thing.

At the beginning of this twenty–first century, more than four out of ten Americans attend church regularly, and nine out of ten say they believe in God, even if the God they believe in is "my own personal idea of God", or Spirit, or just that vague and undefined Some Thing. Even in god–forsaken and supposedly god–forsaking Britain, where the churches have been deserted by nine out of ten, the best–selling tabloid daily will lead the nation in prayers for the healing of a footballer's broken metatarsal in time for England to prevail in soccer's own Rapture, the World Cup. And beyond the boundaries of the industrialized, developed world, the gods are still sitting tight on their thrones, untouched, it seems, by an Enlightenment rationalism which might look to them like nothing more than a blip on the radar screen of humanity's long, complicated story. As the world has become more complex and uncertain, the attractions of simplicity and certainty have been at least as potent as persecution in fanning the flames of religious fundamentalism. God is not easily done away with.

Indeed, the most striking thing about nineteenth–century predictions of the inevitable demise of religion and its gods, was just how wrong they proved to be. Science, psychology and secularism undermined the bedrock foundations of the Christian church, but it managed to settle surprisingly well into the underlying sands. Survival had much to do with the adoption of a strategy whereby critical or inconvenient data is simply sidelined. Churchgoers have become adept at living by reason from Monday to Saturday and by faith on Sunday. Faith and reason have become parallel universes, in each of which the modern believer claims to have a home. The issue of supernaturalism and naturalism is not for them either/or but both/and: a logical nonsense, but a proven survival tactic.

However, as I keep repeating, we are less concerned (from *our* particular vantage point) with the church of God than with the God of the church. Twentieth–century theologians found they had a lot of explaining to do as their God continued to be not only increasingly marginalized by science but also scandalously impotent in the face of world–wide warfare, mass destruction, genocide and holocaust – in all of which God's faithful followers played starring roles – and such natural disasters as floods, fire, pestilence, earthquakes and tectonic tsunamis which could hardly be put down to fallen humankind. Once again, as in the previous century, it was German theologians who set the pace in exploring what could be salvaged from the wreckage of God's reputation.

In *The Sea of Faith* Don Cupitt pinpoints Karl Barth, Rudolph Bultmann, Karl Rahner and Paul Tillich as among the principle representatives of mainline modern theology. Barth, the most traditional of the four, reacted against the tendency of Feuerbach and Strauss to "reduce" God to a mere human projection, insisting on his autonomy. Bultmann argued that the pre–scientific world view of the Bible writers, New as well as Old Testament, needed to be "demythologized" or decoded, to uncover an essential message, the "real" word of God (but is there a kernel at the centre when we have finished peeling the onion, or is the kernel in the peel, the mythology itself?). Rahner developed Feuerbach's elision of theology into anthropology, emphasizing that theology must begin at "the human end", with human experience rather than divinely revealed dogma. The most radical was Tillich, who rejected what he called "supranaturalism" and insisted that "God does not exist. He is being itself beyond essence and existence. Therefore to argue that God exists is to deny him". God is "the ground of everything personal", but he is "personal" in only a purely symbolic sense, and if he is "not a person" he is also "not less than personal".

Cupitt suggests that each of the diverse and mutually incompatible theologies produced by these thinkers is best understood as:

> an individual and more or less autonomous work of
> art that expresses a personal vision... Barth's way of
> talking about God is intelligible only internally and on
> Barth's own terms, and Bultmann's way of talking about

God is similarly intelligible only on Bultmann's own terms, and so on. So markedly internal are the criteria of meaning in each case that it no longer makes sense to assess them as realists; that is, as if they were offering recognizable portraits in slightly different styles of an objective Being with known lineaments who is independently established in the language. Barth's God is part of Barth's theology, and Bultmann's of Bultmann's, and that is that. In short, they are artist–theologians.

So God, in their hands, is an artistic creation, better understood, perhaps, not as the supernatural Almighty or Ancient of Days but as an expression of our own imaginative and creative faculties: less our Father which art in heaven, more our heaven which art in art.

Modern innovative artist–theologians, however, tended to be no better understood by the wider public than modern innovative painters and composers. Theirs was and is a highly technical language, as obscure to the man in the pew as to the woman who would never dream of entering a church except for a wedding, a funeral or an evening of merry yuletide carolling. The creative theologian tends to derive much of his language from the *philosophy* of religion, a discipline not much encouraged among lay men and women in the local churches. But a more fundamental reason why so much theology, including radical theology, is largely incomprehensible to the uninitiated has to do with the intrinsic difficulty of saying new things in old ways. God–language is an old language, born and matured in a pre–scientific, pre–secular age. What radical theologians like Bultmann and Tillich have to say would often be much clearer if said in purely secular terms. But would it then still be theology?

In March 1963, the Anglican Bishop of Woolwich, John Robinson, published *Honest to God* – the cheap paperback which, in the process of my reviewing it for *Tribune*, and contrary to the author's best intentions, catapulted me out of my youthful Christianity. Robinson took the theologies of Bultmann, Tillich and Dietrich Bonhoeffer ("religionless Christianity") by the scruff of the neck and translated them into plain English. As noted earlier, the book was an instant sensation. It was one thing for obscure German theologians to worry themselves witless over something they called the ontological problem, opining in impenetrable language that God was not really a person, was not really "up there" and was generally much misunderstood by those who claimed to be his followers; it was quite another for a bishop in Britain's established church to deliver the same message in plain English – and in cheap paperback, marketed for the masses. Even Robinson's publisher at SCM Press, David L Edwards, worried aloud (in his own introductory essay in *The Honest to God Debate*) that Robinson's clearly articulated and oft–repeated assertion that God does not exist as a person separate from the world "may look like atheism", and therefore he was "not sure that it should be said to people without any power of reflective thought": an unconscious but significant echo of the complaint that the contemporaneous unexpurgated *Lady Chatterley's Lover* was not suitable for servants, daughters and paperback readers.

Robinson's popular exposition of Tillich did indeed look like atheism, and not only to the unreflective masses. No–one would describe Alasdair MacIntyre, Fellow of University College, Oxford, as unreflective, but he began his august and lengthy review for *Encounter* magazine with the blunt observation that "What is striking about Dr Robinson's book is first and foremost that he is an atheist" – indeed, "a very conservative atheist". Another distinguished religious affairs writer, T E Utley, asked "What should happen to an Anglican bishop who does not believe in God?" Robinson's God, Utley complained, is no more than "a principle of harmony at work in the universe, as 'Love', or as 'What we take seriously without reservation'. As a person, however, he is simply abolished". The point was echoed by conservative churchmen across the land. No such fuss had followed Tillich's own insistence (in *The Courage to Be*, published as a Fontana paperback only the previous year) that theism was outmoded because a modern religious consciousness drives us "towards a God above the God of theism":

> The God above the God of theism is present, although hidden, in every divine–human encounter. Biblical religion as well as Protestant theology are aware of the paradoxical character of this encounter. They are aware that, if God encounters man, God is neither object nor subject and is therefore above the scheme into which theism has forced him. They are aware that personalism with respect to God is balanced by a trans–personal presence of the divine. They are aware that forgiveness can be accepted only if the power of acceptance is effective in man – biblically speaking, if the power of grace is effective in man. They are aware of the paradoxical nature of every prayer, of speaking to somebody to whom you cannot speak because he is not 'somebody', of asking somebody of whom you cannot ask anything because he gives or gives not before you ask, of saying 'thou' to someone who is nearer to the I than the I is to itself. Each of these paradoxes drives the religious consciousness towards a God above the God of theism.

But if this had stirred no commotion in the pews, let alone the pubs, it was because Paul Tillich was a foreign academic philosopher whose language was not that of the layman. John Robinson, on the other hand, was a bishop, no less, who made the effort to say the same things in the language of the man and woman in Woolwich high street. But the trouble with 1960s God–language is that it employed an idiom born in and shaped by pre–modern consciousness; however secular the translation, it could not be made to seem at home in a world on the cusp of postmodernity. The result was that Robinson's revolution shook the churches briefly, awakened lay interest even more briefly, then subsided and vanished. The churches resumed their trajectory of declining attendance, God returned to his retirement home, and John Robinson spent much of the rest of his life explaining that he hadn't quite meant what his "unreflective" readers had supposed (or hoped, or feared) he meant.

Robinson drew back from his own radicalism because its logic, the logic of where it seemed to be leading, was just too painful. Enter, then, in 1980, another church–theologian, the Dean of Emmanuel College, Cambridge, who was convinced that the pain must be faced, and faced down. Don Cupitt took the title of his first radical book, *Taking Leave of God*, from the medieval mystic Meister Eckhart, who had written that "Man's last and highest parting occurs when, for God's sake, he takes leave of God". Few of Cupitt's outraged critics noticed the qualification "for God's sake" – and those who did pointed out that it was absent from the title. The Dean of Emmanuel was waving God goodbye (while holding tight, his enemies sneered, to his priestly licence to preach God's gospel in God's name).

In truth, just as Robinson had reflected a 1960s modernism, so Cupitt reflected, and was increasingly influenced by, the new postmodernisms of the 1980s. He noted the impact of "internalization, the process by which all meaning, including religious meaning, has come to be seen not as built into reality, but as generated within ourselves". Robinson had written at a time when society, community, *we* rather than *I*, were high on the agenda. Cupitt's world was a world in reaction against the sixties, a world whose iconic mother–goddess had declared "there is no such thing as society". So to internalization he added "the demand for spiritual autonomy, the right of self–government, even in matters of religion", which dictated that "the law written on stone tablets must be changed for a law written directly in men's hearts". Thus "the conservative religion of the sort that sets God authoritatively over the believer has become an anachronism; it is spiritually behind the times". If this was a problem, the answer was obvious:

> A stage has come in mankind's spiritual and moral development when we need to abandon theological realism, for an objective metaphysical God is no longer either intellectually secure nor even morally satisfactory as a basis for spiritual life. Instead, faith in God must be understood as expressing an autonomous decision to pursue the religious ideal for its own sake.

Such a faith would be "free, agnostic and no longer motivated by external guarantees or sanctions". So was born the God of "non–realism", the "non–real God" who had no "real" existence other than as a human creation or projection. In effect, Cupitt endorsed the projection theory put forward by Ludwig Feuerbach in *The Essence of Christianity*, but he gave the nineteenth–century theologian's radically modernist interpretation a late twentieth–century radical postmodernist twist.

In his follow–up book, *The Sea of Faith*, published as a companion volume to his own BBC television series of the same name (taken, of course, from Arnold's *Dover Beach*), Cupitt charted the changes in science, historical thinking, philosophy and theology set in motion by thinkers like Galileo, Descartes, Kant, Hegel, Feuerbach, Strauss, Kierkegaard, Nietzsche and Jung. Slowly but surely, largely unnoticed by the churches, traditional dogmas had quietly dissolved away, leaving us all "with no resources but those we can muster from within ourselves". Cupitt had become explicitly anti–supernaturalist, anti–transcendentalist, anti–metaphysical. He had no quarrel with the view of the non–religious that religion is simply and wholly human – but, he insisted, it was none the worse for that. Music and politics are human creations, and not thereby deprived of meaning and value. And in his oft–quoted peroration he writes of God himself:

God simply *is* the ideal unity of all value, its claim upon us, and its creative power. (God is indeed the creator, for value indeed made the world.) But the Platonic notion of God as an objective being, out there in a higher world, does nothing to explain the way he functions as *our* God, chosen by us, our religious ideal, our life–aim and the inner meaning of our identity. Just as you should not think of justice and truth as independent beings, so you should not think of God as an objectively existing superperson. That is a mythological and a confusing way of thinking. The truth, we now see, is that the idea of God is imperative, not indicative. To speak of God is to speak about the moral and spiritual goals we ought to be aiming at, and about what we ought to become. The meaning of 'God' is religious, not metaphysical, even though unfortunately a deeply engrained habit of self–mystification leads most people, most of the time, radically to misconstrue the true meaning of religious language. The true God is not God as picturesque supernatural fact, but God as our religious ideal.

So has I AM THAT I AM become I AM THAT I AM NOT? No more than the Bishop of Woolwich is the Dean of Emmanuel willing to be seen as an atheist, and he has a clever answer to the obvious question: "Does this amount to saying that God is simply a humanly constructed ideal, such that when there are no human beings any longer there will be no God any longer?" His answer is that there cannot be an answer because there should not be such a question! The question is "improper". It is improper "because it is framed from the obsolete realist point of view". So if you take Cupitt's view you won't ask the question; and if you don't take Cupitt's view, your question is improper. Neat one. But read on:

> The suggestion that the idea of God is man–made
> would only seem startling if we could point by
> contrast to something that has *not* been made by men.
> [Note that Cupitt has yet to discover gender–inclusive
> language: he does so a book or three later]. But since
> our thought shapes all its objects, we cannot. In an
> innocuous sense, all our normative ideas have been
> posited by ourselves, including the truths of logic and
> mathematics as well as all our ideals and values. How
> else could we have acquired them? Thus God is
> man–made only in the non–startling sense that
> everything is.

The philosophical quibble aside, I take this to mean that yes, God in fact lacks any independent existence beyond and outside the human imagination in which he was created, community by community, culture by culture, language by language.

The traditional view, derived, says Cupitt, from Plato and absorbed into Christian theology, is *realist*. God exists independently of the ways we have of knowing about or observing the world. From a realist point of view, the statement "God exists" is either true or false. Statements made about God are like statements made about your dog: they either correspond to reality, the "facts", or they don't. But, says Cupitt, there's another way of looking at all this: a *non–realist* way. From this viewpoint, God is understood not as a real person, power or entity (an intelligence, an energy, a thing like a rock or a daisy) but as a *symbol* or an *idea*. God is a fiction, but a necessary, instrumental fiction.

A useful commentary on Cupitt's "radical theology" and the non–realism of *Taking Leave of God* appears in a textbook on the philosophy of religion, *Arguing for Atheism* by Robin Le Poidevin (Routledge, London, 1996). Le Poidevin sees non–realism as one of two possible responses to the breakdown of the old realism. There is of course the response of atheism: the view that, since the

Platonic/Christian view of a real God no longer bites, God and religion are best rejected altogether. It's all a load of outdated nonsense: let's have done with it and move on. The non–realist response, however, shares the atheists' rejection of the old "real" God but not their rejection of the old theistic language. Non–realism seeks to reinterpret religious and theistic language, not as statements of fact which may or may not correspond to "the truth", but as poetry. The *reinterpretation* of religious and theistic language is the project of radical theology.

Le Poidevin goes on, however, to draw attention to what he sees as "a crucial ambiguity in [Cupitt's] statement of the non–realist position", and does so by selecting seven statements about God from *Taking Leave of God*:

1. "God is a unifying symbol that eloquently personifies and represents to us everything that spirituality requires of us" (p.9).

2. "The Christian doctrine of God just is Christian spirituality in coded form" (p.14).

3. "We use the word 'God' as a comprehensive symbol that incorporates the way that the religious demand presents itself to us" (p.96).

4. "...the suffering of God... is merely the tears and the fellow feeling of humanity" (p.113).

5. "[The spiritual life] is orientated towards a *focus imaginarius*" (p.10).

6. "The only religiously adequate God cannot exist" (p.113).

7. "God is a myth we have to have" (p.166).

Le Poidevin sees a "crucial ambiguity" between the first four of these statements and the last three. The first four take what philosophers call a *positivist* point of view: that is, a discourse which *appears to be* about God, who doesn't really exist, *actually* addresses (albeit in symbolic language) such real matters as those that intimately concern our moral, spiritual and psychological lives. On this view, theistic language is really moral language in code: note "unifying symbol" in statement 1, and "coded form" in statement 2.

But, says Le Poidevin, the last three statements seem to imply a different approach – one that he links with the philosophical principle of *instrumentalism*. "Instrumentalism… takes theories to be fictions, adopted because they are useful, not because they are true descriptions of the world". Thus

> theological instrumentalism is the view that discourse about God is purely fictional. Not only hell, but heaven as well, are fables. The point of reflecting on stories about God is not, obviously, that we are thereby enabled to predict the behaviour of the cosmos, but rather that our lives will be transformed. By having an image of the goodness of God before us, we will be encouraged to lead a less selfish, and therefore more fulfilling, life. The *idea* of God, rather than God himself, is thus an instrument through which good can be realized.

And the last three statements quoted from *Taking Leave of God*, particularly those seeing God as a "*focus imaginarius*" and "a myth", are examples of this instrumentalist or fictive view.

Le Poidevin suggests the positivist and instrumentalist views are incompatible, or at least that there exists between them a tension that radical theology has yet to grapple with and resolve. He also sees problems with both. The positivist approach may be summarized as trying to reduce theistic statements to non–theistic ones and reveal their "true" meaning. Thus, "Thou shalt love the Lord thy God with all thy soul" really means "you must love human ideals such as mercy, pity, peace and love wholeheartedly". But in that case, why do we need the coded version? Why not say what we mean in a more direct and less misleading fashion? To go back to statement 2 ("The Christian doctrine of God just is Christian spirituality in coded form"), why do we need to bother with the Christian doctrine of God once we have broken the code and found a way of getting on with "Christian spirituality" without God? Christian realists have long criticized pantheist or Spinozan ideas equating God and nature on the ground that if God is nature, what real use is there for the word "God" when nature says it all? That's the problem with a theological–positivist version of non–realism.

That leaves the instrumentalist version. Le Poidevin prefers this, but sees a problem here, too. "If talk about God is purely fictional, how is it that it can exert an influence on our lives? If it is only fictionally true that God requires us to lead a certain life, why should we respond to that requirement?" He finds a partial answer in the notion that these particular fictions may be read as parables – that *all* religious discourse is a parable. The question that is still left hanging, however, is how this kind of non–realism, God as no less fictional than the Good Samaritan, religion as nothing but one kind of story telling (and story hearing), relates to religious *practice*: worship, prayer, confession, contemplation. "The radical theologian, therefore, needs to explain precisely what we are doing when we are engaged in religious activity that appears to be directed towards a deity. If the correct understanding of religious doctrine is an instrumentalist one, how is it that we can become emotionally involved in religious worship?"

It's a question radical theologians have often ignored, either because the problem defies an easy answer or because many practitioners of radical theology have themselves abandoned church going and acts of worship, along with the "real" God. But Le Poidevin offers his own answer to why we might participate in a ritual involving theistic terms if theism is not "really true": for much the same reason that we go to a play or read a novel.

Although we understand that fiction is not a true description of reality, we can nevertheless become emotionally involved with it, and, through this involvement, our lives in the real world can be transformed. There is an apparent paradox here, that of fearing, pitying or loving things we know not to exist, but, once we have resolved the paradox, we can present a coherent account of the benefits of religion in a community of non–believers. The superficial disanalogies between fiction and religion do not threaten this defence of religion without belief.

The radical theology project is still young, still confused, and still has far to go. Cupitt himself has moved on from the theological non–realism of *Taking Leave of God* and *The Sea of Faith* to a more thorough–going philosophical anti–realism expressed in a steady stream of books, of which the most explicit and uncompromisingly anti–realist is *The Last Philosophy* (SCM Press, 1995). In moving on, he has not always succeeded in carrying his early admirers with him. Many in the Sea of Faith networks that he inspired still cling to a pre–Cupittian sliver of realism, while others are only just catching up with the early non–realism of *Taking Leave of God*. The positivist *v.* instrumentalist tension is unresolved, as is that between those who see non–realism as a form of religious humanism and those who reject the term humanism because of its association with militant atheism. Cupitt frequently describes himself as a "radical religious humanist", but there is an inherent instability in any movement that tries to bridge the gap between religion and humanism, as we shall see in the remainder of this book; and whether the various Sea of Faith networks in Britain, Australia and New Zealand and their sister organizations in the United States and Canada can overcome that instability and disprove Yeats' assertion that "the centre cannot hold" is a matter awaiting a jury verdict.

Instabilities and paradoxes aside, however, Cupitt and his radical theologians may be said to have completed the work of Blake and Feuerbach. They have dethroned a transcendent God Almighty and installed a fictional God, a projection of what we see in ourselves (or of what we might be), a radically immanent, fictional God who resides in the human breast (or mind, or imagination). The monster tribal god Yahweh–Elohim has come a long, long way. He outgrew much of his youthful hooliganism and settled down as a respectable combination of lawmaker and social worker, and then a father and a lover. While never abandoning his claim to the crown, he became his people's suffering servant. Thousands died for him, and tens of thousands killed for him. An increasingly scientific and secular world slowly turned its back on him, until all that was left, for some of his faithful followers, was an instrumental fiction. We are back with the Cheshire cat, of which only the grin remains.

So it may seem. But instrumentalism offers a different or at least a parallel perspective. If God is a fiction, he is the protagonist of one of the greatest of all works of fiction, the Bible. As a fictional figure, the hero of the most influential book in our particular tradition, he remains what he always was – the vast, incomprehensible, smiting, saving, life–giving, death–dealing, heaven–promising, hell–threatening super–character who somehow encompasses our human fallibility and wickedness as well as our aspirations to some degree of worth and virtue; who is willing to "forgive our foolish ways" and "reclothe us in our rightful mind". Like all fictional characters, he has changed and developed. But if he is a fiction, we are his author as well as his reader. Human communities fashioned him, imagined him into being by story telling, as in some of the old traditions the world was sung into being by its fictional creators. We said "Let us now make God in our own image and likeness", and we breathed into his nostrils the breath of story telling, and God became a living fiction. Now we can no more write him out of our story than we can obliterate our own history. But it *is* a story, and God *is* no more, but no less, than what we have made him. Which brings us back to humanism – and forward to the republic of heaven.

PART THREE

SEEKING THE REPUBLIC

It's my proudest task to join Lord Asriel in setting up a world where there are no kingdoms at all. No kings, no bishops, no priests. The kingdom of heaven has been known by that name since the Authority first set himself above the rest of the angels. And we want no part of it. This world is different. We intend to be free citizens of the republic of heaven.

– Philip Pullman, *The Amber Spyglass*

CHAPTER 14

The H–word

Know then thyself, presume not God to scan,
The proper study of mankind is man.
Placed on this isthmus of a middle state,
A being darkly wise, and rudely great:
With too much knowledge for the sceptic side,
With too much weakness for the stoic's pride,
He hangs between; in doubt to act, or rest;
In doubt to deem himself a God, or beast;
In doubt his mind or body to prefer;
Born but to die, and reasoning but to err;
Alike in ignorance, his reason such,
Whether he thinks too little or too much:
Chaos of thought and passion, all confused;
Still by himself abused, or disabused;
Created half to rise and half to fall;
Great lord of all things, yet a prey to all;
Sole judge of truth, in endless error hurled:
The glory, jest, and riddle of the world!
– Alexander Pope, *An Essay on Man*

"HUMANISM" IS A prickly word. For some, especially in Europe, it carries positive connotations of *humanitarianism* or *humane* behaviour, a philosophy of being nice to each other. For others, especially in the

United States, it evokes a decidedly negative response suggesting aggressive rejection of religion, arrogantly putting humanity in the place that should properly belong only to God. "Religious humanism" is even more problematical, and for some – both among those who call themselves "humanists" and those who would still wish to describe themselves as "religious" – it is an oxymoron. So we have some sorting out to do, both historically and linguistically.

The best study of the history of the word humanism is a little book, *Humanism: What's in the Word*, by the late Nicolas Walter, published in London in 1997 by the Rationalist Press Association with the British Humanist Association and the Secular Society (G W Foote) Ltd. I have drawn on it freely in much of what immediately follows.

The words "humanism" and "humanist", along with "humanity", are obviously derived from Latin *humanus* (human), *homo* (man) and *homines* (mankind or humanity). It is a linguistic curiosity that although the Greeks preceded the Romans in making explicit the distinction between the human and the divine, it was the Latin word rather than the Greek equivalent, *anthropismos*, that won out in the battle for the survival of the fittest term. Some writers have pushed the claims of *anthropism*, but it hasn't stuck, and I haven't heard of anyone proudly proclaiming himself an *anthropist*. (Philanthropists and anthropologists have their place, but it isn't here.)

Some five centuries before the Christian or Common era, during what some scholars have labelled the Axial Age, religious and cultural traditions around the world seem to have undergone seismic changes. For the "children of Israel", the change produced a more universal, more grown up and better behaved Yahweh. For the Greeks, stories of the human and the divine, of men and gods, began to be more clearly distinguished. The Greeks had gods – a lot of them – and stories of how they behaved were an intrinsic part of their religious understanding. But by the fifth century BCE it was beginning to be understood by some writers that the gods were literary or imagined embodiments of human characteristics, which implied that humans in some sense made the gods, rather than the other way round. If the defining characteristic of radical theology is a view of God as a human creation, the Greeks were doing radical theology two and a half millennia ago, when Protagoras (according to Plato, who didn't agree with him) said that "Man is the measure of all things" – all things presumably including the whole pantheon of divinities who cut such impressive figures in human literature.

The Stoic philosophers, following Protagoras and anticipating Pope in the view that "the proper study of mankind is man", probably established the first tradition that taught a universal brotherhood. (Universal sisterhood lay far in the future). Humanity was distinguished not only from the unpredictable gods, whose ways were a mystery, but also from the animal world, which lacked any capacity for reason and understanding. To be thoroughly human was to be educated, cultivated, manly, virtuous. The educated man, wrote the Greek–educated Cicero in the first century, "should be perfect in every part of *humanitatis*". "Humanitatis", wrote the second century CE Aulus Gellius, meant not so much *philanthropia* ("a kind of amiability and benevolence towards all men indiscriminately"), but *paideia* ("education and learning in the fine arts"). "Those who pursued *humanitas* in this sense", writes Walter, "were 'most humanest'... It was called *humanitatis* because it was possessed only by human beings, and in theory it was available to all human beings; but in practice it was clearly restricted to an intellectual if not a social elite, and this is what it came to mean". It was also restricted almost entirely to men. As a woman you had to be very elite indeed to qualify for inclusion in "mankind".

Walter adds the interesting observation that at much the same time a similar notion of *humanitatis* appeared on the other side of the world. For fifth–century BCE Confucius and his fourth–century successor Mencius in ancient China, the cultural and moral ideal was *ren* (humanness, humanity). The Chinese for humanism is *ren–ben–zhu–yi*, devotion to human principles. It was in this sense of cultivated human intelligence or liberal education that concepts of humanism survived into the modern western world through the renewed interest in Greek and Roman civilization that marked the Renaissance. The word humanism itself first appears in manuscripts from the Italian universities of Bologna and Pisa, where *humanista* or *umanista* is listed as a category of learning alongside chemistry, the arts and law. Initially, this use of humanism – *studia humanitatis* – was restricted to the study of classical languages and literature, and to the human matters on which this literature concentrated. Such studies soon came to be distinguished from traditional *studia divinitatis*, where the subject matter was religious, scriptural and theological. By the end of the fifteenth century, specialists in *studia humanitatis* were called Humanists and their subject was the humanities. In the following century the word found its way to France, where it appeared in one of Montaigne's essays – "That fault of theologians writing too humanly is seen more often than that fault of humanists writing too un–theologically" – and it reached Spain in the early seventeenth century when Cervantes, in *Don Quixote* (1615), has a wandering scholar explain that "his profession was to be a humanist, his pursuits and studies to compose books".

Human*ist* makes its first appearance in English in 1589, when the preface to a translation of Virgil's *Georgics* contains an apology to "weake Grammatists" and "courtly Humanists". Walter tells us (and I wish he had told us more) that it next appears in the first published proposal for a water closet, *A New Discourse of a Stale Subject* by John Harrington (1596), where reference is made to a cleric who is "a good humanist" rather than "a good divine". By 1617 the word had broadened its meaning. Fynes Moryson's *Itinerary* was addressed to "the Humanist, I mean him that affects the knowledge of State affaires, Histories, Cosmography and the like": a learned man in a general sense. The word made it into Samuel Johnson's *Dictionary* in 1755 and Webster's *American Dictionary* in 1841. Johnson allowed only its narrow use: "a philologer; a grammarian", but Webster added "one versed in the knowledge of human nature". An even wider sense, embracing virtually everything of human interest, is found in a short–lived weekly paper called *The Humanist* published in London in 1757 by an Irish clergyman, Patrick Delany. "The title of *Humanist*", explained Delany in his first issue, was "calculated to recommend every thing that is amiable and beneficent in human nature". The paper would "interest itself in all the concerns of human nature... which means not only amusement... but likewise something more than mere amusement", being "calculated to convey some little useful and entertaining knowledge of various kinds, historical, classical, natural, moral, and now–and–then a little religion".

As understood from the Renaissance until well into the nineteenth century, then, humanism had little to do with antagonism towards or rejection of religion or the church. Nicolas Walter – himself a convinced and evangelical atheist – slaps down the atheist J A Symonds, who popularized humanism in the 1870s, for arguing that "the essence of [Renaissance] humanism consisted in a new and vital perception of the dignity of man as a rational being apart from theological determination", and was "partly a reaction against ecclesiastical despotism". This, says Walter, was an example of the word humanism being "applied retrospectively and indeed anachronistically and un–historically to the fifteenth century", and wrongly interpreted as referring to "doctrinal controversy between theistic and humanistic beliefs". All that came much later. From the fifteenth to the nineteenth century the meaning of humanism gradually widened until it could embrace not only most matters secular but even "now–and–then a little religion". Walter, whose own sympathies clearly lay with the secularist and rationalist traditions that contributed to modern humanism, nevertheless emphasized that *humanist* and *humanism* in the distinctive sense in which they are understood today played no part in the Renaissance, or the scientific and intellectual revolutions of the sixteenth and seventeenth centuries, or the Enlightenment of the eighteenth, or the social and political revolutions of the late eighteenth and nineteenth centuries. Deists and "Freethinkers" did not think to call themselves humanists. Thomas Paine referred to and Auguste Comte founded a "religion of humanity", but neither called himself a humanist or described his stance as humanism. Those who did so label themselves tended to look to the past rather than the future. The words had reactionary rather than progressive connotations. Early Humanists opposed the new invention of printing and preferred Latin and Greek to vernacular languages. Similarly, later Humanists mostly belonged to the non–scientific culture defined in C P Snow's Rede Lecture *Two Cultures and the Scientific Revolution* (1959). To trace the development of today's humanist movement we have to look beyond yesterday's humanism, to forward–looking or "progressive" movements that had their origins either in critical theism or avowed atheism. In the rest of this chapter we turn our attention first to atheism.

The first atheist, it is sometimes said, was "the fool" cited in Psalm 14 who "said in his heart, There is no God". But this particular fool was almost certainly a *practical* rather than a *theoretical* atheist, living a godless life rather than proclaiming a conviction that the gods, including the Psalmist's Yahweh, did not exist. Probably the earliest atheists proper are to be found among the Greek philosophers – particularly Lucretius and Epicurus. But antiquity more often took a line of least resistance, bypassing gods rather than trying to banish or abolish them altogether. Some modern humanist writers (notably the Canadian Pat Duffy Hutcheon, in *The Road to Reason*) claim the Buddha and Confucius as early humanists (but not atheists) because they demoted the gods to the margins and privileged what was specifically human. Full–blown atheism – the conviction that gods and spirits do not exist, and that the term "God" can no longer be held to have any useful meaning – is hard to find until the modern period. In "Christian" Britain and America in particular, most skeptical thinkers and critics of supernaturalist religion, such as Thomas Huxley in England and Robert Ingersoll in the USA, preferred Huxley's coinage *agnostic* rather than atheist. Huxley defined agnosticism (*a*–gnostic, without knowledge, following *a*–theist, without god) as the principle that "it is wrong for a man to say that he is certain of the objective truth of any proposition unless he can produce evidence which logically justifies the certainty. This is what Agnosticism asserts; and in my opinion, it is all that is essential to Agnosticism. That which Agnostics deny and repudiate as immoral is the contrary doctrine, that there are propositions which men ought to believe, without logically satisfactory evidence; and that reprobation ought to attach to the profession of disbelief in such inadequately supported propositions" (*Science and Christian Tradition*, 1900). The first two sentences describe a neutral agnosticism, but the third may be thought to imply atheism, since God, the supernatural and an afterlife must surely be among those propositions which men ought not to believe, as they clearly lack logically satisfactory evidence.

Shelley famously wrote an essay – not a very good one – espousing atheism, and it got him expelled from Oxford; but the first committed propagandist to attempt to start an atheist movement in England was George Jacob Holyoake, who preferred to call his "affirmative atheism" Secularism. The leading ideas of Secularism, he wrote in *The Principles of Secularism Briefly Explained* (1859), were "Humanism, Moralism, Utilitarian unity: humanism the physical perfection of this life – moralism founded on the laws of Nature as the guidance of this life – materialism as the means of Nature for the Secular improvement of this life – unity upon this three–fold ground of Positivism". Perhaps aware that his "brief explanation" was too brief (and clumsy) for clarity, he later defined the principles of "affirmative atheism" as "Positivism in Principle, Exactness in Profession of Opinion, Dispassionateness in Judgment, Humanism in Conception". Later still, he summarized it all as Rationalism (Holyoake was very fond of capital letters) and founded the Rationalist Press Association in 1899.

Holyoake's principal rival among the atheist "chatterati" was Charles Bradlaugh, a clearer thinker and writer with a surer populist touch. Bradlaugh, who described himself as a "Free thinker", edited a journal called *The National Reformer* which was prosecuted in 1868 for blasphemy and sedition. As an atheist, Bradlaugh was unable to take the oath on the Bible, and therefore not permitted to give evidence in his own defence in court. He made much of this misfortune, and gained widespread radical support for a change in the law. Subsequently, and famously, he won election to Parliament as MP for Northampton in 1880, but as an atheist he was refused leave to take the oath of allegiance and was unseated. Standing again the following year, he was re—elected and again ejected – a farce which continued until he was eventually allowed to swear the oath on a Bible whose authority he expressly disavowed, finally taking his seat in 1886. In radical working—class quarters Bradlaugh was a hero, and the National Secular Society, which he had founded in 1866, rivalled Holyoake's Rationalist Press Association. But neither organization was Humanist in the modern sense until well into the twentieth century.

No less important were the Ethical Societies, which were founded in Britain and America through the late nineteenth and early twentieth centuries. Felix Adler, the son of a German Jewish rabbi, who emigrated to the USA in 1857 and became a professor of Hebrew and Oriental literature at Cornell University, founded a "Union for the Higher Life" to promote "sex purity, the principle of devoting the surplus of one's income beyond that required for one's genuine needs to the elevation of the working classes, and, finally, intellectual development". To begin with, Adler and the Union took no stance on God or religion; but in 1877, with the Union (and its version of the High Life) apparently defunct, Adler founded a "Society for Ethical Culture" in New York, the first of several such societies that he described as providing "something to take the place of the consecrating influence of the old religions". The ethical societies held Sunday services without prayers or ritual, and mostly without explicit God—language, but with plenty of uplifting "hymns" and addresses on matters of personal and social morality. Adler demanded of an ethical speaker that "he shall give his whole life to the problems of ethical living, having no professional or business interests in competition with his dedication to these problems".

In 1886, Stanton Coit, one of Adler's New York members who had emigrated to Britain, introduced the idea of Ethical Societies to London, persuading an existing congregation that had been founded as a radical "Unitarian and Universalist" society as far back as 1793 to become the South Place Ethical Society in 1888. The English societies formed an Ethical Union in 1928, "to promote by all lawful means the study of ethical principles; to advocate a religion of human fellowship and service, based upon the principle that the supreme aim of religion is the love of goodness, and that moral ideas and the moral life are independent of beliefs as to the ultimate nature of things and a life after death; and, by purely human and natural means, to help men to love, know, and do the right in all relations of life". In 1952 the Ethical Unions of Britain and the USA, joined by smaller sympathetic societies in Europe, formed the International Humanist and Ethical Union (IHEU) to provide "an alternative to the religions which claim to be based on revelation on the one hand and to totalitarian systems on the other". A subsequent statement by the IHEU (1991) inched closer to an explicitly anti–religious stance by asserting that its version of humanism "is not theistic, and it does not accept supernatural views of reality". In 2002 it described humanism as "an alternative to dogmatic religion".

Until the formation of the international union, the Ethical Societies continued to describe themselves as "religious", albeit in increasingly non–theistic terms. For Adler, "ethicism" was the new religion, displacing his own Judaism and a degenerate Christianity. In Britain, Coit's societies advocated "a religion of human fellowship". Coit even continued to use the word God in a vague, undefined sense, and called his West London society the Ethical Church. South Place, sole survivor of the movement, continued to claim religious status until 1980 and took even longer to rid itself of a clause in its founding objectives which described as one of its aims "the cultivation of a rational religious sentiment", replacing "rational religious sentiment" with "rational and humane way of life". Even after "humanism" had triumphed over "secularism", "rationalism" and "ethicism" (and a host of other contending isms) as the umbrella term for a non–theistic and non–supernaturalist view of the human condition, many humanists continued to speak and write of their "humanist *faith*", if no longer of their humanist religion – and many still do so.

This is hardly surprising. The inspiration of men like Holyoake, Adler and Coit was intensely religious. Their atheism or agnosticism was based on rebellion not against the exacting demands of a good God, but against his blatant moral inadequacy. They were faithful to the Judeo–Christian obligation to pursue truth, and it was in the name of truth that they found the old religious traditions wanting. In particular, they rejected a God whom Christians claimed to be the same old monster–Yahweh of the early Old Testament, a God who perhaps no longer smote his enemies with boils and "the botch" but now threatened them with everlasting hell–fire, a God responsible for nature "red in tooth and claw", a God able but not always willing to alleviate suffering. They turned their back on a God who had simply failed to live up to the basic standards of decency expected of ordinary men, women and children, and they separated themselves from those who claimed to worship such a god, those who professed to be still in thrall to the monster. What they did not turn their back on was the religious respect for truth and virtue, which is why so many of the ethical societies and their humanist successor–organizations came to resemble the very churches they had rejected. An Ethical Sunday service was likely to contain the same denunciations of "sexual impurity", selfishness and greed as any chapel meeting, in elevated tones not very different from those to be heard in any Gospel Hall. The hymns were full of praise and adoration – if not of God, of an idealized or deified humanity:

These things shall be! A loftier race
Than e'er the world has known shall rise,
With flame of freedom in their soul
And light of science in their eyes!
They shall be gentle, brave and strong...

Visit one of the old–style ethical societies today and you may well be reminded of a Welsh chapel or a puritan meetinghouse. Attend a humanist/rationalist/secularist meeting and you risk encountering the same solemnity and earnestness, the same hint of moral superiority, the same understated but palpable male dominance, the same sense of certainty and the same condescension towards the unconverted that you remember from your church– or chapel–going days. Atheistic humanism found it easy to bury God but harder to escape his legacy.

CHAPTER 15

Facing Both Ways

The Humanists' religion is the religion of one who says
yea to life here and now... It is the religion of courage
and purpose and transforming energy.
– Roy Wood Sellars, *The Next Step in Religion (1918)*

IF THE IMPLICITLY atheistic strands of free–thought, rationalism and secularism that fed into modern humanism found it hard to throw off an inherited religious sensibility, it is no less true that the strands that continued to affirm a religious or even a specifically Christian identity had equal trouble in staving off atheism. The modern humanist movement that emerged after the second world war was the child of both atheological and theological ways of thinking, and we turn now to the tradition of religious humanism which became increasingly interwoven with the rival traditions springing from atheism.

The development of a specifically religious and primarily Christian humanism may be traced to two very different sources, both of which we have necessarily noticed in Part Two, where we charted the post–Enlightenment transformation of God from transcendence to immanence, and from entity to idea. The first was the largely German–led movement within the Lutheran church towards free biblical criticism and a rational interpretation of Christianity. The work of Strauss and Feuerbach, particularly in *The Life of Jesus Critically*

Examined and *The Essence of Christianity*, heavily underscored the intuitive interpretations of lay theologians such as the English seventeenth-century radicals and poets like Blake, who had preached "God in us" rather than "God out there". Feuerbach in particular had repositioned God as a wholly human projection, and while it was only one step from there to abolish the deity altogether – a step taken by Feuerbach's disciple Karl Marx – there were German, British and American Christians who saw in the projection theory a God–given rationale for strategically situating themselves as both religious and rational. While such modernisers did not call themselves humanists – the term was still primarily used in its old sense of scholars specializing in "the humanities" – their position clearly involved a radically new emphasis on the human and natural rather than the superhuman and supernatural. Thus, while dispersed in "liberal", "progressive" or "modernist" churches and still lacking a name of its own, Christian humanism became a movement in its own right.

Where it took strongest root was in the second of our two sources, the Unitarian movement. Unitarianism had begun as a critique of trinitarian doctrine and an affirmation of the single personality of God the Father. Traceable as a persistent heresy throughout the history of the Christian church, it had emerged from an underground existence after the Protestant Reformation, when it survived the martyrdom of its most outspoken exponent, Michael Servetus, who was put to death at the instigation of John Calvin in the sixteenth century for his denial of the divinity of Jesus. John Biddle organized unitarian meetings during the relatively tolerant years of the English republic (1649–60), and some of his followers are believed to have been among the 1,700 clergy who were ejected from their Church of England livings in 1662 after the restoration of king and church. Among the hundreds of ejected clergy who set up dissenting or "nonconformist" chapels, some were explicitly Unitarian, and although the Toleration Act of 1689 excluded Unitarians from its provisions, they survived persecution and won more dissenting chapels over to Unitarianism in the eighteenth century.

Unitarianism began to be characterized not only by rejection of the Trinity and by veneration of Jesus as a purely human teacher, but by its repudiation of all creeds, which meant there were few doctrinal barriers to the adoption by their ministers and congregations of freer and more tolerant forms of Christianity . Traditional doctrines such as "original sin", eternal punishment and atonement through Christ's blood sacrifice were either abandoned or regarded as inessential, as were set rituals and liturgies. By the end of the eighteenth century there were large and influential Unitarian congregations in London (Essex Street), Manchester (Chapel Street) and other centres, active in most aspects of cultural, intellectual and scientific as well as religious life. Unitarians were immediately receptive to nineteenth–century biblical criticism and the radical conclusions to which it seemed to lead. Under the influence of men like the scientist Joseph Priestley and the philosopher James Martineau, Unitarianism became a reasoned religion, finding its authority (as had the early Quakers) not in scripture or church hierarchy but in experience and conscience, and proving receptive to new thinking in both secular and religious fields. As we noted earlier, it was among the Coventry Unitarians that Mary Ann Evans (George Eliot) adopted the radical theology that would mark both her translations and her novels of genius.

If British Unitarianism was liberal and progressive, American Unitarianism was radical. It was more profoundly influenced by German idealism, and in the mid nineteenth century leaders like Ralph Waldo Emerson and Theodore Parker were explicitly denying the supernatural in Christianity and encouraging the sympathetic study of other religious traditions. By the end of the century Unitarianism in the United States had become, far more so than in Britain, a thoroughly rationalistic movement, with some congregations joining a Free Religious Association which treated God as something of an afterthought. Nicolas Walter summarizes developments at the turn of the century:

Many Unitarians, especially in the Mid–West, began to go further. Having discarded the second and third persons of the Trinity, they discarded the first person too, replacing supernaturalism and theism with naturalism and humanism. Although they ceased to believe in God, they continued to call themselves religious, and mostly to count themselves as Unitarians, but increasingly to adopt the term *Humanism*. Between the two world wars, about one–tenth of the Unitarian denomination became Humanists, and there was a danger of schism between "God Men" and "No God Men"; but first the Humanists began to leave, and then the "God Men" began to adopt Humanism as well.

The process accelerated with the publication by Unitarian minister Frank C Doan in 1909 of a book called *Religion and the Modern Mind*, in which he specifically defended "humanism". Controversy continued throughout the war years. In 1918 another Unitarian, Roy Wood Sellars, produced *The Next Step in Religion* – the "next step" being humanism. "The Humanist's religion", he wrote, "is the religion of one who says yea to life here and now, of one who is self–reliant, intelligent and creative... It is the religion of courage and purpose and transforming energy." In a later book, *Religion Coming of Age* (1928) he prophesied "Christianity will gradually be transformed" into "humanistic religion". In the same year there appeared a collection of *Humanist Sermons* by 18 Unitarian and other liberal ministers, in which E Burdette Backus concluded: "Humanity has struck its tents and is again on the march towards a new religious faith" – adding that he was "keenly aware that that which I call religion will seem to many earnest men and women not religion at all, but irreligion".

Unitarians began a Humanist Fellowship at Chicago University in 1927, publishing a paper called *New Humanist* and founding a Humanist Press Association modelled on Britain's Rationalist Press

Association. At much the same time the Unitarian Society of Hollywood published the *Hollywood Humanist*, and humanist societies were started in Los Angeles and Oakland. Even when Unitarians left the church for humanism, they continued to see it as a religion. "Humanism is not simply another denomination of Protestant Christianity", wrote former minister Charles F Potter in 1929, when he founded the First Humanist Society in New York, "it is not a creed, nor is it a cult. It is a new type of religion altogether". And he added: "If humanists were to make a creed, the first article would be – I believe in Man".

Inevitably, humanists did soon make, if not a creed, a manifesto – and it was clearly proclaimed as a *religious* humanist manifesto. Published in the USA in 1933, it was organized by Dr Edwin H Wilson, a pastor in the American Unitarian Universalist churches and subsequently founder of the Fellowship of Religious Humanists, and drafted mainly by Roy Wood Sellars. The manifesto was signed by thirty–four "leading thinkers" of the day, mainly Unitarians but also members of the Ethical Societies and Progressive Jews, and as it represents the religious humanism of the early twentieth century at the apex of its influence it is worth reproducing here in full.

RELIGIOUS HUMANIST MANIFESTO (1933)

The time has come for widespread recognition of the radical changes in religious beliefs throughout the modern world. The time is past for mere revision of traditional attitudes. Science and economic change have disrupted our old beliefs. Religions the world over are under the necessity of coming to terms with new conditions created by vastly increased knowledge and experience. In every field of human activity, the vital movement is now in the direction of candid and explicit humanism. In order that religious humanism may be better understood, we desire to make certain affirmations which we believe the facts of contemporary life demonstrate.

There is great danger of a final, and we believe fatal, identification of the word *religion* with doctrines and methods which have lost their significance and which are powerless to solve the problem of human living in the twentieth century. Religions have always been means for realizing the highest values of life. Their end has been accomplished through the interpretation of the total environing situation (theology or world view), the sense of values resulting therefrom (goal or ideal), and the technique (cult) established for realizing the satisfactory life. A change in any of these factors results in alteration of the outward forms of religion. This fact explains the changefulness of religions through the centuries. But through all changes religion itself remains constant in its quest for abiding values, an inseparable feature of human life.

Today man's larger understanding of the universe, his scientific achievements, and his deeper appreciation of brotherhood have created a situation which requires a new statement of the means and purposes of religion. Such a vital, fearless and frank religion capable of furnishing adequate social goals and personal satisfactions may appear to many people as a complete break with the past. While this age does owe a vast debt to traditional religions, it is nonetheless obvious that any religion that can hope to be a synthesizing and dynamic force for today must be shaped for the needs of this age. To establish such a religion is a major necessity of the present. It is a responsibility which rests upon this generation.

We therefore affirm the following:

FIRST: Religious humanists regard the universe as self–existing and not created.

SECOND: Humanism believes that man is a part of nature and that he has emerged as the result of a continuous process.

THIRD: Holding an organic view of life, humanists find that the traditional dualism of mind and body must be rejected.

FOURTH: Humanism recognizes that man's religious culture and civilization, as clearly depicted by anthropology and history, are the product of a gradual development due to his interaction with his natural environment and with his social heritage. The individual born into a particular culture is moulded to that culture.

FIFTH: Humanism asserts that the nature of the universe depicted by modern science makes unacceptable any supernatural or cosmic guarantees of human values. Obviously humanism does not deny the possibility of realities as yet undiscovered, but it does insist that the way to determine the existence and value of any and all realities is by means of intelligent inquiry and by the assessment of their relation to human needs. Religion must formulate its hopes and plans in the light of the scientific spirit and method.

SIXTH: We are convinced that the time has passed for theism, deism, modernism, and the several varieties of "new thought".

SEVENTH: Religion consists of those actions, purposes, and experiences which are humanly significant. Nothing human is alien to the religious. It includes labour, art, science, philosophy, love, friendship, recreation – all that is in its degree expressive of intelligently satisfying human living. The distinction between the sacred and the secular can no longer be maintained.

EIGHTH: Religious humanism considers the complete realization of human personality to be the end of man's life and seeks its development and fulfilment in the here and now. This is the explanation of the humanist's social passion.

NINTH: In place of the old attitudes involved in worship and prayer the humanist finds his religious emotions expressed in a heightened sense of personal life and in a co–operative effort to promote the social well–being.

TENTH: It follows that there will be no uniquely religious emotions and attitudes of the kind hitherto associated with belief in the supernatural.

ELEVENTH: Man will learn to face the crises of life in terms of his knowledge of their naturalness and probability. Reasonable and manly attitudes will be fostered by education and supported by custom. We assume that humanism will take the path of social and mental hygiene and discourage sentimental and unreal hopes and wishful thinking.

TWELFTH: Believing that religion must work increasingly for joy in living, religious humanists aim to foster the creative in man and to encourage achievements that add to the satisfactions of life.

THIRTEENTH: Religious humanism maintains that all associations and institutions exist for the fulfilment of human life. The intelligent evaluation, transformation, control, and direction of such associations and institutions with a view to the enhancement of human life is the purpose and programme of humanism. Certainly religious institutions, their ritualistic forms, ecclesiastical methods, and communal activities must be reconstituted as rapidly as experience allows, in order to function effectively in the modern world.

FOURTEENTH: The humanists are firmly convinced that existing acquisitive and profit–motivated society has shown itself to be inadequate and that a radical change in methods, controls and motives must be instituted. A socialized and co–operative economic order must be established to the end that the equitable distribution of the means of life be possible. The goal of humanism is a free and universal society in which people voluntarily and intelligently co–operate for the common good. Humanists demand a shared life in a shared world.

FIFTEENTH: We assert that humanism will: (a) affirm life rather than deny it; (b) seek to elicit the possibilities of life, not flee from them; and (c) endeavour to establish the conditions of a satisfactory life for all, not merely for the few. By this positive *morale* and intention humanism will be guided, and from this perspective and alignment the techniques and efforts of humanism will flow.

So stand the theses of religious humanism. Though we consider the religious forms and ideas of our fathers no longer adequate, the quest for the good life is still the central task for mankind. Man is at last becoming aware that he alone is responsible for the realization of the world of his dreams, that he has within himself the power of achievement. He must set intelligence and will to the task.

The 1933 manifesto is very much a document of its times: pre–holocaust, pre–Hiroshima, unfailingly optimistic, with a nineteenth–century faith in progress undented by either the first world war or the economic depression of the twenties and early thirties. Its prose is clunky, portentous, and often opaque. It mentions neither God nor women. But what perhaps strikes a modern reader most forcibly is that in straining to retain a place for religion in humanism, its version of religious humanism is actually coming apart at the seams.

For all its Unitarian parentage, the manifesto is thin and unconvincing in its half–hearted insistence that its humanism is *religious*. Most of what it says about religion is critical and negative: there is no creator, no soul, no supernatural world, no theism, no deism, no theological modernism; and all religious institutions, "ritualistic forms", "ecclesiastical methods" and "communal activities" must be "reconstituted". These are the traditions we might reasonably expect those who avow a humanist perspective to sweep away. But what kind of "religion" will take their place? It is here that the manifesto is at its most vague, taking refuge in high–flowing but empty rhetoric. Religion as the signatories to the manifesto wish to "establish" it involves "a complete break with the past"; it consists of "those actions, purposes, and experiences which are humanly significant"; it aims at "the complete realization of human personality"; it replaces prayer and worship with "a heightened sense of personal life"; it denies "uniquely religious emotions and attitudes"; its goals are "joy in living", "the creative in man", and "the satisfactions of life".

It is clear, however, that such vacuous language brutally underlines the inherent instability of *this kind* of religious humanism. It is the language of those for whom religion has effectively lost all meaning. If, as the manifesto suggests, religion is equated with "labour, art, science, philosophy, love, friendship, recreation – all that is in its degree expressive of intelligently satisfying human living", then *religion* is merely another term for *culture*, but a far less satisfactory term, since it carries generations of baggage of which the broader term *culture* is free. To cling to the word "religion" in this way begins to look suspiciously like a tactic rather than a principle. It lays itself wide open to the accusation that so–called religious humanists are people who have lost their faith and plugged the gap with humanism, but won't or can't face up to the fact – or, more cynically, won't abandon a term (religion) that still has valuable connotations of morality and respectability that they wish to continue to exploit. Less harshly, an alternative verdict is that the religious humanist is one who has abandoned religious faith in his head but not in his heart: one who no longer believes, but (as Walter delicately puts it) is "reluctant to abandon the psychological and sociological support of a religious background".

Such weaknesses were quickly perceived. After 1933, and especially after the second world war, religion of any kind faded fast from the American humanist movement. When the American Humanist Association was founded in 1973, Wilson again had a major hand in the drafting of what became known as the second Humanist manifesto. This was far more secular in tone and content, defining humanism as an alternative to religion rather than a new form of it. Unitarian Universalists – a diminishing band – and secular humanists now went each their own way, to the extent that secular humanism often seemed less concerned to espouse positive human values and more inclined to mount a sustained and often bitter critique of religion in all its forms.

The struggle in America between religious and non–religious or anti–religious strands of humanism was mirrored in Britain. Here the place of American Unitarianism was taken by the Ethical Societies, in competition with the heirs of Holyoake and Bradlaugh in the secularist and rationalist movements. Although not yet the overwhelmingly secular country it was to become by the end of the twentieth century, Britain had a much faster–diminishing church–going population than the United States, and British humanists were perhaps less concerned to pretend to religious credentials. But those who did choose to position their humanism or ethicism within a modern, progressive religious framework could not escape the inherent instabilities that marked religious humanism. The resolution of the conflict between secular and religious versions of British humanism in the gradual abandonment by the movement of any last sliver of religion may be traced in the voluminous writings of Harold Blackham, the single most influential figure in the making of a British humanist movement.

Blackham's first base was the Ethical Union, formed from the Ethical Societies in 1920. In 1927 the Ethical Union declared as one of its objects the advocacy of "a religion of human fellowship and service, based upon the principle that the supreme aim of religion is the love of goodness". Blackham succeeded Stanton Coit at the Ethical Church in 1935 and became secretary of the Ethical Union in 1945. The war profoundly affected Blackham's view of the task of the humanist movement, and he set about the task of uniting all the Freethinking, Rationalist, Secularist and Ethical organisations in a single body. With the support of such key figures as Julian Huxley, Gilbert Murray and Bertrand Russell, he argued for humanism as "a philosophy of civilisation" (1946) and, as the cold war began, "a Third Force between... Christianity and Marxism" (1948). By 1950 humanism was for him "a decision, a commitment, a faith, a concourse of believers compassed about with a great cloud of witnesses... a religion of progress" – but the religious language was balanced by a more secular discourse: humanism was also "secularism... the slow growth of secular self–confidence, freeing itself during centuries from tutelage and authority, nerved by science to break the enchantment of the incomparable classical past and turn to even more dazzling prospects in the open future" ("What We Mean by Humanism" in the Ethical Union's magazine *Plain View* – quoted, as are most of these excerpts, in Nicolas Walter's *Humanism: What's in a Word*).

If humanism was still a religion of sorts – a "religion of progress" – it was nevertheless no longer "a church, in the sense of a company of believers withdrawn from the world of action with their minds fixed on a hope which transcends the immediate here and now".

But it required of its adherents some of the qualities associated with church membership: "a self–dedication and self–discipline, an achieved temper and sentiment, which is a work of withdrawal, reflection, and renewal". It had also inherited something else characteristic of religion: "It claims to be the truth of human life and requires the adherence of all men" ("Humanist Thought and Action" in *News and Notes*, Feb–July 1950).

Four years later, in his 1954 exposition of *Essentials of Humanism*, Blackham began to develop a conception of humanism that bypassed the old controversies by avoiding any significant reference to either religion or secularism. Here, humanist ideas are "not primarily ideas about the ultimate nature of things; they are central convictions about reason and science, freedom and morality, ideals and values". Humanism was "a commitment to defend, revise, and develop the irreversible ideas and ideals which have made the modern world and are now challenged and threatened". It was "a call to all men, a vision of what is to be achieved". All that is left of Blackham's old Ethical Church religious humanism is the evangelical tone.

And sure enough, by the 1960s, Blackham's humanism was "not a religion" but "an alternative to religion, an entirely different way of taking and tackling the world... Humanism, then, as an alternative to religion is a permanent and genuine cause, a programme, a shared vision and activity, a broad social and educational reform movement or party". This was the version of humanism that came to be adopted by the new British Humanist Association, formed in 1963 by the Rationalist Press Association and the Ethical Union (though the RPA subsequently withdrew and resumed its separate identity), with Julian Huxley as president and Blackham as secretary. The BHA's humanism is "free from theistic or dogmatic beliefs and doctrines", as is that of the International Humanist and Ethical Union, founded in 1952, again with Huxley and Blackham as president and secretary. The IHEU did not mention religion at all in its founding *Declaration on Humanism*, except tangentially when that document declared that "Ethical Humanism unites all those who can no longer believe the various creeds and are willing to base their conviction on respect for man as a spiritual and moral being"; and in its 2002 revision it is only those forms of "dogmatic religion... [that] seek to impose their world–views on all humanity" that humanists are said to oppose. The same humanists who were earlier so reluctant to abandon the psychological and sociological support of their religious background were now equally determined to prove that they had overcome their former dependence, and did so by turning their backs on their old religious allegiances.

The older types of religious humanism nevertheless continue to survive somewhat uneasily on the margins of both religion and humanism. In America, the depleted Unitarians joined with the Universalist Church of America in 1961 to form the Unitarian Universalist Association, which included both theism and humanism in its statement of faith. A Fellowship of Religious Humanists was founded in 1963 and still exists as the Friends of Religious Humanism, publishing a journal, *Religious Humanism*. Closer to the Christian mainstream, the former Bishop of Newark, John Selby Spong, now declares himself a non–theist Christian, as do many of the Fellows and associates of the Westar Institute and its "Jesus Seminar". Having been abandoned by his British publisher, Don Cupitt is now published by Westar's Polebridge Press.

In the American Jewish tradition a Society for Humanistic Judaism was established in 1969 and now (2005) has more than forty congregations and chapters. Its object is "to provide a humanistic alternative in Jewish life" and it "mobilizes people to celebrate Jewish identity and culture consistent with a humanistic philosophy". The Society promotes the training of rabbis, leaders and teachers for Humanistic Jewish communities, and holds Sabbath services that adapt traditional Jewish rituals to a rigorously non–theistic version of the faith. It is affiliated with an International Federation of Secular Humanistic Jews that has a presence in Israel.

Britain has no avowedly religious humanist organization, but individual Unitarians, Quakers and a few members of mainstream Christian churches call themselves Christian humanists, or just humanists. Richard Holloway, former Bishop of Edinburgh and Primus of the Scottish Episcopal Church, has embraced non–realism, and his best–selling books articulate a post–religious humanism. Anthony Freeman, who was sacked as a parish priest for publishing his book *God in Us: A Case for Christian Humanism*, and now edits the *Journal of Consciousness Studies*, has argued that Christianity is Jesus–centred rather than God–centred, citing both the fifth century Athanasian Creed and the modern concept of "emergence" to argue that "God is not a supernatural agent external to humanity but an emergent property of human life itself. That is what I call Christian Humanism, [and it has] the potential to free the Gospel from supernaturalism and superstition without losing all that is still of positive value in the Christian religion" (*Sea of Faith* magazine, January 2001). Freeman is a member of the Sea of Faith Network (UK), which has sometimes used "religious humanist" as a description of itself, though some members have been uneasy about the term, either because they don't like "humanism", or don't like "religious", or don't like labels.

The growth of interest in Buddhism has also seen the development of something akin to a Buddhist humanism under the influence of Stephen Bachelor's book *Buddhism Without Beliefs*, which preaches a Buddhism shorn of supernaturalism and centred on disciplines which are ethical rather than religious in a traditional sense.

But despite these survivals and revivals, it is hard not to concede that *modernist* or *realist* religious humanism had whatever heyday it ever had in the nineteenth and the first half of the twentieth century, and its story since then has been one of slow decline or diversification. It is not my purpose to attempt to resurrect it in any of its pre–postmodern forms. But I do want to argue that there is a place in postmodernity for a new radical humanism which, while it continues remorselessly to draw attention to the evils inherent in outmoded religious belief and practice, also recognizes in the best of religious culture, and not least in its fictive gods that have given us so much trouble, the rich and strange inheritance of poets and painters, composers and cathedral builders, saints and sinners – a legacy that exemplifies human genius and the human imagination, and that is still capable of inspiring and transforming human lives. What I mean by a "new" and "postmodern" religious humanism will become clearer in the next chapter, before we shift focus to the republic of heaven.

CHAPTER 16

Only Human

The last stage in the historical evolution of religion is universal religious humanism, and the last ethic is humanitarianism.
– Don Cupitt, *Philosophy's Own Religion*

IN THE SUMMER of 1991, at a crowded Sea of Faith conference in Leicester, in midland Britain, two intellectual bruisers debated religion and humanism. One was Nicolas Walter: anarchist, peace activist and passionate rationalist, whose scholarly work on the historical development of modern humanism I have acknowledged and borrowed from. The other was Don Cupitt: elegant, Cambridge, deanish and donnish. Their debate was not the familiar one that had raged for a century, between humanism and Christianity. What was at issue was not humanism but the *kind* of humanism that might speak to the condition of a postmodern world at the scruff–end of two Christian millennia.

Walter was clear and evangelical about the kind of humanism he and the Rationalist Press Association espoused, and particularly about its attitude to religion:

> We reject the whole of religion, not just the difficult
> bits. We reject the whole of the Bible, not just the

supernatural bits. We reject Jesus the man just as much as Jesus the God. We reject the doctrines of all the scriptures, and the deeds of all the churches. We see religion not as a necessary stage in the evolution of humanity, but as a long mistake – rather as Communism and Fascism were short mistakes. We see the shift from religion to non–religion as a process not of progressive revelation of changing truths but of progressive realization of changing lies. We see not so much the loss of faith as the recovery of sanity. Whether we prefer a Hegelian or Marxist or Darwinian or Freudian or some other interpretation of religion, we think not just that it is wrong now but that it was always wrong.

To his humanist opponent, this unreconstructed Enlightenment humanism was old hat. Cupitt argued that in our own generation,

The various Enlightenment, liberal and Marxist versions of humanism have broken down no less dramatically than traditional religious belief. But the business of making meaning, of re–imagining ourselves, our values, our world, has to go on. In the past, it went on communally and unconsciously, and the result was what we call religion. But now we have become conscious of what we are up to; and because we do it consciously, it will be a sort of humanism; but because we know we still need communal myths and rituals it will also be religion. We shall be religious humanists, making believe... We urgently need a new, this–worldly religious humanism as our human way of first imagining new values and a better world, and then actually working to bring them about.

If this was not the old scrap between religious believers and non–believers, nor was it a return match between the warriors of secular humanism and the religious humanism of the Ethicists and Unitarians (or Nonitarians, as so many had become). Cupitt's religious humanism – *radical* religious humanism, as he called it – was something very different from the old bloodless, filleted, half–this–half–that, facing–both–ways stuff of the 1933 Religious Humanist Manifesto which had been routed on the field of battle by the oddly combined forces of rationalists and the noble army of mitres. Cupitt was not in the business of resurrecting the recently discarded "rational religious sentiment" of the South Place Ethical Society, aware as he was that the only reward you get for facing both ways is a chronic crick in the neck. Nicolas Walter, modern and progressive, was tilting at a windmill that had long since lost the wind in its sails and had ceased to grind. Cupitt, postmodern and very present tense, was proposing a new kind of religious humanism that was as post–humanist and post–rationalist as it was post–Christian.

Cupitt's humanism had begun where the humanism of the nineteenth and early twentieth centuries had ended, with the conviction that the God of the Christian church, objective, transcendent, supernatural and interventionist, was a fiction. God had no independent existence outside human consciousness: no ears to hear our prayers, no eyes to see our good and evil deeds, no tongue with which to praise or reproach us, no loving arms in which to enfold us, no plan, no purpose, no will. He just wasn't that kind of being. All the gods, not just *their* gods but also *our* god, the god of Anglican priest Don Cupitt, the god named God, were human creations, imagined into being by human communities trying to make sense of a complex and often terrifying world. Some of those human communities, urged on by Plato and his disciples, had come to think of their gods as *real*: more real than the "real" world. But belief in real gods now produced far more problems than it had ever solved. People no longer invoked God or a pantheon of spirits to explain why things happen as they do, or how they came to be what they are. The old proofs of God's objective existence now seemed pathetic: a bright twelve–year–old could demolish them. And the very idea of an omnipotent and omniscient being cracking his metaphysical whip, commanding this and forbidding that, rewarding here, punishing there, had come to seem terrifying or disgusting, neurotic and spiritually alienating.

So far, so religious–humanist in the old sense. The authors and signatories of the fifteen theses of 1933 would probably have said "Yes, exactly so! That is why we must abandon God! God is dead, and we must bury him, mourning his loss if we will, but taking leave of him, with or without ceremony. Nevertheless, while abandoning him, let us hold on to the truths he has given us, for they are *true* truths, and it behoves us to demonstrate that we remain good religious folk..."

Cupitt's developing and more radical version of religious humanism, however, was rooted in late twentieth century culture, and particularly late twentieth century philosophy – and these were not what they had been in Julian Huxley's and Bertrand Russell's day. Both had become radically modified by the "linguistic turn", involving a complex series of developing understandings of the central importance of language in shaping our understanding of ourselves, the universe and everything.

First, Ferdinand de Saussure had proposed an understanding of language as a complex system composed of relationships between signs, or words, rather than between words and things "out there", which had been the traditional and therefore "common sense" way of thinking. Saussure's *structuralism* was carried further by the *poststructuralists*, who argued that far from our creating language to describe our concrete experience of the world, language actually creates us, in the sense that a complex structure of codes, symbols and conventions precedes each of us and essentially predetermines what it is possible for us to do and even think. We are born into a language–made world. Post–structuralism was taken even further by Jacques Derrida and the *deconstructionists*, who sought to demonstrate that the meanings conveyed by language could never be fixed and absolute but must always be "ideological constructs" which attempt to make that which is the product of a particular culture or thought system seem natural, inevitable and objectively true. If all this gives you a pain in the brain, I tender my apologies now. The point is that Cupitt was strongly influenced by the linguistic turn, though never a captive of any particular version of it, and it was this that gave his own understanding of religious humanism a new and radical twist.

In scores of articles, lectures, and more than twenty books following *Taking Leave of God* (1980), Cupitt has argued that we are in transition from an ancient metaphysical and God–centred vision of the world and of life to a new "humanistic and *language–centered*" vision of life and its meaning. This involves the abandonment of the traditional conception of knowledge as a fixed canonical body of truth, communicated to us by tradition and ultimately by divine revelation, and its replacement with a conception of knowledge as created entirely by human beings, and therefore flexible, disputable, and always subject to change. The old absolutes and fixed points have simply disappeared. In the old world view to which the churches and mainstream religious institutions are still rigidly committed, Truth has a capital letter and exists "out there" in the eternal Divine Mind. Human beings simply have to tune in to a revelation of this ready–made divine order of things, and fit themselves into it.

> Under the old regime... God's function was to guarantee the objectivity of the world and of truth. In the new world picture, the chaos of experience is getting turned into an ordered world by us, now and all the time. Only we have a world. We are the only makers of our world. We are the only world–builders. The world is built by language; only we have language and we, therefore, make the world what it is. (Address to SnowStar Institute conference, Niagara Falls, Canada, March 2002, reported in *Axial* magazine, Spring/Summer 2002).

Again,

> A world with nobody whose world it is is hard to imagine. A world seems to need to be known. Somehow, everything is channelled through us, comes to a focus in us. We seem to be the only language–users, and so the only beings who have a complete world. In us [that is, in the human animal], the world becomes described, known, lit–up – in short, conscious of itself. (*Sea of Faith* magazine, January 2001).

I want to dwell for a page or two on this emphasis on language.

Did we create language, or did language create us? In a biological sense, virtually all animals have acquired in the process of evolution a capacity to communicate with each other: to signal danger or the desire to mate, to threaten or to reassure, perhaps to indicate the whereabouts of food. Only humans have developed the astoundingly complex system of sound signs and written signs which make up verbal language. Verbal language alone gives us the capacity to think complex thoughts, imagine complex constructions, make logical deductions, reason, reflect, be fully conscious and conscious of our consciousness; and it is primarily verbal language which enables us to communicate fairly precisely what we think to other humans. In this we are unique. It is one of the primary characteristics that make us human. In this sense, language makes us and precedes us – or at least precedes us as reflective, thinking, knowing beings. In the beginning was the word: the rest followed.

The idea that we, the world and everything are in this profound sense *language–created* is not as new as we might suppose. It was certainly not invented by Saussure, Derrida or Cupitt. It is implied in the Greek–influenced opening of John's gospel just quoted. It is there right at the beginning of the Bible, in the third verse of Genesis chapter one. God says "Let there be light", and *then* there is light: the word precedes the thing. Light is spoken into existence. Cupitt argues from this that "Only a nihilist can understand the use of 'God' correctly. He sees how, when confronted by pure chaos, God [in the Genesis myth] uses language to divide up the cosmos and form a world. He then invites Adam to join in, by naming the beasts" (*Sea of Faith* magazine, January 2001).

In Native American and Inuit tradition, the world was spoken, sung or chanted into existence. In Australian aboriginal mythology, in the beginning was the *alcheringa*, the "dream time", when trees and plants, mountains and plains, animals and people, were sung into being. In *The Silmarillion* (his vast mythology of which the massive *Lord of the Rings* is only a part) J R R Tolkien draws on these ancient traditions in the creation myth he invents for his imagined world that is created from thought and music. "Iluvatar, the One" who, at the "beginning of Days", is all there is, makes the Ainur, the Holy Ones, "of his thought":

> and they made a great Music before him. In this Music the World was begun; for Iluvatar made visible the song of the Ainur, and they beheld it as a light in the darkness. And many among them became enamoured of its beauty, and of its history which they saw beginning and unfolding as in a vision. Therefore Iluvatar gave to their vision Being, and set it amid the Void... And a sound arose of endless interchanging melodies woven in harmony that passed beyond hearing into the depths and into the heights, and the places of the dwelling of Iluvatar were filled to overflowing, and the music and the echo of the music went out into the Void, and it was not void.

In Tolkien's fantasy, evil too is sung into being by way of the deliberately discordant variations introduced by Melkor, Tolkien's Lucifer–figure, who "sought to increase the power and glory of the part assigned to himself". (Every chorister will be able to name a Melkor in his or her choir!).

A contemporary illustration of the extent to which we are made, moulded and shaped by language is the influence of the mass media. Acres of forest are consumed each day to supply the newsprint that supplies us with yesterday's stories. In Britain alone we watch 110 billion person–hours a year of television and listen to around 200 billion person–hours of radio. We find more time than we've ever found before to read new novels, see new films and go to new plays, and nearly half of us are finding yet more tales on the worldwide web. Somehow, between consuming all these stories we contrive to find odd moments in which to work for a living, eat, sleep and make love. But just as we are what we eat, so too are we what we read. The media shape our appetites, our aspirations, our politics.

Every single one of the stories we read, hear, see, changes us a little and makes us a slightly different person from the one we were before. But the stories that most clearly make us what we are are the great foundation stories of our culture: the origin myths, redemption stories and epic tales of love and death. Every man, woman and child on the Indian sub–continent has been formed and shaped by the word–signs that constitute the *Mahabharata* – whether or not they have actually read the great Hindi epic or had it read to them. Every Arab has been shaped by the Koran, every Jew by the Torah. And everyone in Christendom and post–Christendom is what he is, speaks as she speaks, lives as he or she lives, in ways shaped by the Bible and Shakespeare. These are our very foundations, their themes, their inflections and their nuances forming the bedrock of the culture – both "high" and popular – in which we live and move and have our being.

Of course there are stories and stories. When we assure our children that "it's only a story", we are telling them that the wolf didn't really make a meal of Little Red Riding Hood. There are tall stories (which may or may not be short stories) and any journalist will tell you there are "good stories" which may or may not be accurate. And, of course, there are true stories and false stories – whatever story the first–grade philosophy teachers may tell you. It is an essential part of growing up that we learn to tell the difference between this and that kind of story, to know when fact is fact and fiction is fiction. That's why there is a growing emphasis on "media literacy". We may understand that every story is a construct, every storyteller has an intention, and that no story tells the whole story: all good postmodern dicta. But we still need to know the difference between "There was a holocaust" and "There was no holocaust", between "I never had sex with that woman" and "I only messed her dress". And if these distinctions are important in the little stories, how much more so are they in the big ones. Are the creation stories of Genesis I and the resurrection stories of the gospels "true" or "false", history or mystery, factual report or pure poetry? If they are true, is it the truth of the police notebook recording the details of a road accident or the truth of "all the world's a stage" or "my love is like a red, red rose"? Are we talking about the objective truth of an up–to–date telephone directory or the sound of the bell that *rings* true? We need to know. If media literacy is important in helping us discern one kind of story from another, theological literacy is hardly less so in enabling us to discern a poetic from a prosaic truth.

Sorting out Biblical history from myth, what "really" happened from poetic licence, was the project of liberal modernist theology. It was and remains a useful project, up to a point. Some of it is easy, some difficult, and some impossible: it is easy to place the story of God talking through Balaam's ass (or more precisely, through the mouth of his ass – Numbers 22:28), and Jonah's adventures in the big fish, as fables which "ain't necessarily so"; harder to ascertain whether Moses and Abraham were historical figures and the Exodus an historical event; and impossible (despite the work of the Jesus Seminar) to be sure what Jesus actually said. But none of this is any longer of primary concern. The reasonably well–read, reflective reader has come to understand the Bible stories as *literature*, and essentially as *fictions*. Some of these fictions relate to historical events, places and people, as Hamlet relates to Denmark and one of its early kings: but Hamlet is a work of fiction, and so are the Bible "histories". Some Bible stories are parables: fictions within fictions. Others are myths, poems, fables, fantasies, or morality tales. All are human stories that have made us, as we have made them. The Bible's God is the grandest fiction of them all. Jesus too is a fiction. There was almost certainly a teacher named Jesus in first–century Galilee, but we have no sure way of relating the Jesus of the Jesus literature – the gospels – to the man. The only Jesus we can be sure of is the Jesus of the Jesus literature. Of this Jesus we can say confidently, as we cannot say of the historical Jesus, that he *did* change water into wine, *did* raise Lazarus from the dead, *did* teach that we should love our enemies, *was* crucified and buried, *did* descend into hell, *did* rise again, and *did* ascend into heaven. We can demonstrate that all these things really do happen in the story, just as we can show that Hamlet really does see his father's ghost, and Frodo Baggins really does succeed in destroying the ring in the Crack of Doom.

This is not cynicism, nor is it skepticism. It is realism (in the everyday, not the philosophical sense). And this kind of realistic approach to our foundation texts, our religious and cultural myths, has one great instrumental merit. Where the old liberal modernist approach lopped off a branch here, filleted out a bone there, thinned this out, cut that away, till little more than a dry skeleton of the story remained, our postmodern understanding of language, text and story enables us to reclaim the lot as Grand Fiction in all its preposterous, glorious profusion and confusion. God *did* make Eve out of Adam's spare rib! He *did* drown the world, except for the animals that went in two by two, hurrah! hurrah! The star *did* stop in the middle of the sky right over the stable, and Mary *was* a virgin mother! That's the story. And we can see that it is a *true* story, not because it all "really happened", but because the great themes of life and death, love and hate, good and evil, redemption and salvation, are wrestled with in ways that are true to our experience.

A humanism that fails to acknowledge or actively denies the richness and continuing instrumentality of myths generated by the religious imagination seems to me both an impoverished and an old–fashioned humanism, whether it calls itself secular in an atheist sense or religious in the pared–down sense of the 1933 manifesto. The history of religion, says Nicolas Walter, is the history of a "long mistake", of "changing lies": it is "wrong now" and "was always wrong". Thus are banished the age–long accumulations of religious writing, music, art, dance, architecture: the infinitely complex system of imaginative symbols by which human communities explored their own humanity in a mysterious, awesome, wonderful world; the long search for values that transcend the needs and desires of our own egos; the myths and legends, fables and fantasies, stories, songs, proverbs and exhortations of the Hebrew Bible and the "New Testament", the *Mahabharata*, Rumi and Hafiz, the "dream time", John Donne, William Blake, Gerard Manley Hopkins, T S Eliot, R S Thomas, Bach's passion music, Mozart's masses, Mahler's *Resurrection* symphony... One long mistake? Some mistake, surely!

Standard models of humanism – which suppose that only in the last century or two has the human species achieved liberation from a darkness which lasted from the year dot to the dawn of the Rationalist Press Association and the National Secular Society – are surely too thin and undernourished: the result is an *anorexic humanism*. For those who take a particular pride in the wholly human spirit to cut themselves off from some of the crowning achievements of human culture seems both tragic and absurd. It's like drinking non–alcoholic wine, or making love without taking your clothes off: nice up to a point, but nothing like the real thing. So long as mainstream humanism persists in cutting itself off from mainstream humanity in this way, for just so long will it seem to many a dry, arcane interest, as blind in one eye as the Plymouth Brethren are in the other.

So humanism needs to be more generous and imaginative in its response to the rich range of religious culture, ranking Blake's

Imagination no lower than Winstanley's Reason. It needs to catch up with postmodernity, if not with the proliferating variety of postmodern*isms*, in extending its radical skepticism towards religion to include a no less radical skepticism towards ideas of progress, science, and objective ethics. It needs to become *more* radically atheist in rejecting not just the deification of imagined gods but the equally dangerous deification of humanity and its works.

I do not mean by this that humanism should be less critical of the dangers, inanities, cruelties and hypocrisies of religion and its institutions. God forbid. Fanaticism, dogmatism, superstition and the kinds of mysticism that are better described as mystification need to be kept under constant criticism. They are too dangerous to be ignored in the name of tolerance. The rationalists are right to insist that to oppose reason is unreasonable, and the secularists are right to expose religious privilege in politics (such as the scandalous survival of automatic representation for bishops in the British parliament). But such critiques will have a stronger bite when they are seen to be based on a commitment to human culture in the round, and to values of generosity and inclusiveness.

In arguing that by recognizing them as fictions and myths we can press the old, old stories back into service, I do not wish to suggest that we take them all at face value. I have argued that just as we need media literacy to help us evaluate the stories in our newspapers and on our television screens, so we need theological or atheological literacy to evaluate those in our mythologies. Such stories never have only one meaning, if only because we ascribe meanings to them, and we the readers are different. The Genesis story of the role assigned to humankind in naming and tending the beasts of the field and the fruits of the garden may be read as a reminder of human responsibility, *or* as an encouragement of human domination. The resurrection story may mean that death is not the end of life, *or* that faith, hope and love cannot be killed. The story of the "promised land" means liberation to some, enslavement and genocide to others – and, as I write, death on the streets of Jerusalem every day. That millions of Christian fundamentalists in the United States and Zionist zealots in Israel read the story one way, and insist that it gives modern Israel more than three thousand years later the right to occupy the west bank of the Jordan, only reminds us what can happen when we mistake history for myth and a fictive God for a real one. That generations of black slaves in America took the story as their own song of freedom, hearing Moses, way down in Egypt–land, telling old Pharoah, "Let my people go!" reminds us how the same tale can be a very different story.

I have joined with Don Cupitt in referring to "radical religious humanism". Some readers may still doubt that "religious" is an appropriate qualification for the kind of humanism I am arguing for, and if so I invite them to propose a more suitable one. But what I am seeking to describe is a humanism that is secular (in the literal sense of belonging to this world and this age), rational, ethical and imaginative, and which feels free to draw on, to feast on, the best of our long, complex, diverse heritage of religious expression. Such a humanism will know all too well the madness, brutality and repressiveness of religion at its most inhumane; but this will not blind it to the glories it glimpses of religious inspiration at its best. We know there are bad people, but that does not make us anti people; bad politics, but that does not (or should not) make us anti political; bad art, but we are not philistine; bad science, but we are not anti scientific. And there is wretched religion all around us, but that is no good *reason* for *imagining* that we should base our humanist life stance on an undiscriminating war on anything and everything expressed in religious language and deriving from religious commitment.

Radical religious humanism is a humanism that makes free with the resources of religion in its richly diverse forms, as with the resources of the whole of human culture. We know that we made it all, so we can unmake it and remake it. If we call on God to help us, we know we are using a resonant figure of speech. If we seek God's will, we know that we are simply looking for the best course in the circumstances. If we pray, we know we are talking to ourselves – and why not? An internal dialogue can make a most effective conversation. If we ask forgiveness, and for the strength to follow the light of our conscience, we know we are expressing our desire to be better people, and doing so in metaphors. If we say we are working for the republic of heaven, we know we are talking about our own responsibility for making the world, and our little part of it, a better place.

This kind of radical religious humanism is not the last relic of Victorian doubt, or modernist Christianity's last desperate kick. It is something new. It rationalizes religion and enriches humanism. It dissolves ancient differences between sacred and secular, the human and the divine, the natural and the supernatural. It does not deify humanity but it understands that our values are human values, and could be no other. It offers change, growth, renewal. It is for those who look for a life on the ocean wave rather than a safe harbour. It is for the seeker rather than the finder, for those who would make their own meaning and purpose rather than buy them off the shelf. It demands faith, hope, charity, determination – and a well–developed sense of humour.

CHAPTER 17

Make Believe

Only make believe I love you,
Only make believe that you love me.
Others find peace of mind in pretending.
Couldn't you?
Couldn't I?
Couldn't we?
Oscar Hammerstein II, *Show Boat*

Will you be confined to one world as we are? [Lyra asked
the angel Xaphania].

> *"No; we have other ways of travelling."*
> *"Is it possible for us to learn?"*
> *"Yes... It uses the faculty of what you call*
> *imagination. But that does not mean* making things up.
> *It is a form of seeing."*
> *"Not* real *travelling, then," said Lyra. "Just*
> *pretend... "*
> *"No," said Xaphania, "nothing like pretend.*
> *Pretending is easy. This way is hard, but much truer."*
> Philip Pullman, *The Amber Spyglass (Part 3 of*
> *His Dark Materials)*

Even for those of us who choose to maintain a religious faith perspective within a wholly humanistic outlook, radical religious humanism raises a lot of questions. In this chapter I shall try to address three issues: the place of religious practice (church–going and worship, where there are no longer real gods to worship); the meaning of "spirituality" in a world from which the spirits have fled; and the search for new foundations of morality when the old absolutes have crumbled and dissolved away.

Can you be a thoroughgoing radical religious humanist and still go to church, synagogue, temple or Quaker meeting? Can you, with integrity, be a priest, a minister, a member of the church choir? Can you share, or appear to share, in the use of God–language when you know your own use – if indeed you continue to use it – is radically different from that of most of the rest of the congregation? Can you take Communion, or join in saying the creeds and the Lord's prayer? Can you, at the carol service, bring yourself to sing "Very God, begotten, not created" with head held high, or "Lo, He abhors not the Virgin's womb" without vomiting? If you can, is your position coherent and honest?

The kind of radical religious humanism I am talking about has begun to find clear expression in the Sea of Faith networks in Britain, Australia and New Zealand, and in their linked organizations elsewhere (the Westar Institute in the United States, the Snowstar Institute in Canada). The Sea of Faith networks was inspired by Don Cupitt's 1984 book and television series of that name, and Cupitt has consistently argued that "the last stage in the historical evolution of religion is universal religious humanism, and the last ethic is humanitarianism" (*Philosophy's Own Religion*, 2000). Moreover, Sea of Faith's first "martyr" was Anthony Freeman, whose sin against the holy ghost was the publication of a book subtitled "The Case for Christian Humanism". Despite these endorsements of humanism, by no means every member of what has turned into a lively and diverse group of networks has felt comfortable with the term (and, as I noted earlier, there are others who question "radical" and "religious"). Even some of those who would readily describe their own position as in some sense humanist have argued against labelling the networks as such, usually on the ground that the genius of the movement lies in its refusal to commit to any *ism* or anything resembling a fixed ideology. The British network's stated objectives of exploring and promoting "religious faith as a human creation" look pretty humanist to some (and not least to traditionalist critics), but the "mission statement" is sufficiently ambiguous and flexible to attract those, for instance, who understand religious *systems* as man–made but see them as aspects of a transcendent divinity or cosmic benevolence: a position they quite properly would not wish to be called humanist. But if this is one potential fault line, there is a point at which it intersects with another, and that is over the question of religious practice.

Those in Sea of Faith who avoid a "humanist" label tend, unsurprisingly, to be prominent among those members who choose to remain active participants in church or other institutional religious activity. But there are many on the humanist side of the divide who also remain committed church members or attenders, particularly among Anglicans, Quakers and Unitarians. Some are priests and ministers: the "Godless vicars" brigade, as the papers tagged them when Sea of Faith first began to make waves and get itself noticed. So what do "radical religious humanists" think they are doing in church, singing hymns to words they don't "really" believe, reciting creeds that no longer make sense, participating in prayers to a deaf, dead god, or (in a Quaker meeting) joining in silent worship of... what?

Many would answer that it is precisely the non–realist and instrumentalist approach to religion that makes such participation possible. The realist atheist and agnostic – and mainstream secular humanism is realist in its insistence on the objective truth that God does not exist or that his existence is unknowable – clearly cannot recite "I believe in one God, maker of heaven and earth", or ask the forgiveness of "Our Father which art in heaven" without doing violence to her convictions and laying herself open to the charge of hypocrisy or self–deception. But the theological instrumentalist, the non–realist, does not suppose that God and religion are objectively true or untrue, only that the concepts have instrumental value regardless of their objective truth–status. The instrumentalist understands God as a fiction, the protagonist in a fictional story or poetic epic, and religious practice as participation in a fictional drama. It is precisely her understanding of story and myth that can make such participation possible, emotionally meaningful, and intellectually coherent.

In Robin Le Poidevin's *Arguing for Atheism*, already cited, there is an illuminating passage on fiction and the emotions. Le Poidevin asks why it is that we become emotionally involved in what we know to be "not true"? Why do we find ourselves having to dash the tears from our eyes at the end of *Brief Encounter* when the woman who has just said her last goodbye to the man she has fallen in love with is left desolate in the waiting–room? Why are we reluctant to take a shower after watching *Psycho*? We know these are stories. We know the woman in the waiting room and the man who has knifed the woman in the shower are not real, never were real, are "made up" by storytellers. But...

Is it that, for one fleeting moment, reality is suspended and we *forget* that we are hearing, reading or watching pure fiction? Do we weep or gasp because for a second or two we really believe we are being presented with the truth? Surely not, for we do not act as we would do if we believed, even for a moment, that we were in a similar real–life situation, where our response to the shower attack would be to scream the place down and run for our life. We know it is all fiction, and we have not been fooled into supposing these things are really happening, even for a moment. But we still feel the emotion, and the emotion persists long after we have left the cinema or put the book back on its shelf.

Le Poidevin tries an alternative suggestion: perhaps fiction generates emotions by bringing to our attention broad truths, albeit by fictional means? Do we weep at the death of Little Nell not because we temporarily think of Little Nell as a real person, but because we are vividly reminded of the appalling conditions in which the poor lived in Victorian England – conditions that we know all too well persist in other parts of the world in our own time? Are we troubled by a fictional account of tangled family relationships, broken love affairs, jealousy, betrayal, because it sets us thinking about our own true experience of such things? Possibly, but Le Poidevin suggests that it is not the whole answer. It doesn't do justice to our actual experience of fiction, where the immediate object of our emotion surely *is* the fictional character as an imaginary person, not as a representative of social evils or historical themes. It is the lovers themselves we pity, who, after their brief encounter, part for ever out of loyalty to others. Our tears are not for lovers in general or broken hearts in the abstract, nor are we necessarily projecting disappointment or heartbreak onto our own lives.

Having disposed of two theories, Le Poidevin introduces a third, proposed by Kendall Walton, a philosopher who has written extensively on the nature of our relation to fiction (see "Fearing Fictions" in *Journal of Philosophy* 65, 1978, and "How Close are Fictional Worlds to the Real World?" in *Journal of Aesthetics and Art Criticism* 37, 1978). Walton, says Le Poidevin, "proposes that when we become involved in a fictional story we are engaging in a game of make–believe. Just as a child pretends that a group of chairs set in a line is a bus, or that when armed with a water pistol in hot pursuit of the child next door he is chasing after a villainous monster, so we in reading a novel make–believe that we are locating ourselves within the novel. We are there, witnessing the events. We may even assign ourselves a role, and imagine talking to the characters. It is our active participation in the fiction that explains why we become emotionally involved."

But although the physiological responses may be the same as those of real fear, pity, or whatever, there is a difference.

A child who make–believes that a child–devouring creature is after it will not, unless something is wrong, feel genuine fear, for otherwise the child would not want to participate in the game. But the emotion is close enough to real fear for us to call it *quasi*–fear. Similarly, we will experience *quasi*–anxiety when watching a thriller on television: if it were genuine anxiety we would probably switch it off.

Thus Walton's solution of the paradox that we can be emotionally involved in a fiction or a myth we know is objectively false is that we play a game of make–believe in which the fiction becomes reality, and part of the game is to feel *quasi*–emotions, if not real ones. Armed with this account, Le Poidevin suggests that a defence of non–realist or instrumentalist participation in worship, prayer and religious ritual may be found in comparing the effects of the kind of fiction we call religion to the beneficial effects of the novel, the film and the soap opera:

> To engage in religious practice, on this account, is to engage in a game of make–believe. We make–believe that there is a God, by reciting, in the context of the game, a statement of belief. We listen to what make–believedly are accounts of the activities of God and his people, and we pretend to worship and address prayers to that God. In Walton's terms, we locate ourselves in that fictional world, and in so doing we allow ourselves to become emotionally involved, to the extent that a religious service is capable of being an intense experience. The immediate object of our emotions is the fictional God, but there is a wider object, and that is the collection of real individuals in our lives. In the game of make–believe (for example, the Christian one), we are presented with a series of dramatic images: an all–powerful creator, who is able to judge our moral worth, to forgive us or to condemn, who appears on Earth in human form and who willingly allows himself to be put to death. *What remains, when the game of make–believe is over, is an awareness of our responsibilities for ourselves and others.* [My emphasis].

With painstaking thoroughness, Le Poidevin goes on to consider objections to this account – after all, his book is called *Arguments for Atheism*! – but he is not finally persuaded by them. He accepts that the radical theologian or radical religious humanist can coherently explain why it can be useful to talk in theistic terms and participate in theistic religious practice if theism is not really true, by reference to our emotional response to other forms of fiction. Although we understand that fiction, by definition, is not a true description of reality, we can nevertheless become emotionally involved with it in ways closely analogous to our response to the reality of our own direct experience.

This seems to me a telling insight into what may be happening when I, for instance, attend and thereby participate in a Quaker meeting for worship, or an Anglican or Catholic wedding or funeral service, or when I sing "Credo in unum deum" in a Dent village choir performance of a Mozart mass. The one word in the Le Poidevin/ Walton account I might quarrel with is "pretend", with its whiff of self–deception. I do not so much *pretend* to worship and address prayers to God as *act out* that role as I *make–believe* – rather as an actor acts out (rather than pretending to be) Hamlet, or as I act out my own emotional involvement in Hamlet's drama from the back seat in "the gods" – the top tier in the theatre. So, in theology as in other forms of poetry, we engage in a "willing suspension of disbelief".

Of course, not all non–realists or humanists who happily continue to attend church would necessarily recognize this explanation or interpretation of their preference. They may say they go to church because it is a way of participating in a community ritual and thereby strengthening community ties. They would as happily participate in a Hindu ceremony, if they were part of a Hindu community, as they do in Evensong in their village church. Some may do so for emotional or psychological rather than rational reasons; perhaps because it links them with their childhood, or with a particular tradition of radical dissent; or because they simply enjoy the aesthetic experience. I suspect that many of the backsides in pews on Sunday mornings are humanistic backsides whose owners would be horrified if they thought their presence might be interpreted by anyone as an indication that they actually believed, in any literal sense, the plainly outdated doctrines expressed in all that music and poetry. The same is no doubt true for many a backside in the pulpit.

For many religious humanists, though, religious practice is no longer an issue. Some have given up going to church, and some never went. For many, institutionalized religion is the enemy rather than the friend of honest thinking. Alex Wright, in *Why Bother with Theology?* (Darton, Longman and Todd, London, 2002), argues passionately that we should not bother – except with what he calls "secular theology" (an extension of Bonhoeffer's "religionless Christianity"). He tells us at the start of his book, "I am not a churchgoer". His non–practising stance and attitude of "questioning agnosticism" is typical of a growing number who read theology as poetry without going to church, much as we might choose to read Shakespeare or listen to a CD of Mahler's *Resurrection* without going to the theatre or concert hall.

Radical religious humanists are sometimes more comfortable with a concept of "spirituality" than "religion" – but only sometimes. Spirituality has strong negative as well as positive connotations, and for some the former outweigh the latter. Where the use of the term appears to refer to belief in disembodied spirits, or an objectively real Holy Spirit, or a spirit world beyond our own known world, it seems at best meaningless and at worst dangerous. We have noted the wide range of available spiritualities – misty–mystical, gaseous, aromatic, Eastern... but for humanists, religious or secular, transcendental spiritualities will have little appeal. For them spirituality is essentially a *human* quality, a predicate of the wholly human spirit.

The British Humanist Association has campaigned hard to win acceptance of spirituality in this sense. When the Education Reform Act of 1988 required British schools "to promote the spiritual, moral, cultural, mental and physical development of pupils", the BHA issued a statement saying it "wholeheartedly endorsed these ideals" and suggesting that despite different interpretations of the word, "all can agree that the 'spiritual' dimension comes from our deepest humanity. It finds expression in aspirations, moral sensibility, creativity, love and friendship, response to natural and human beauty, scientific and artistic endeavour, appreciation and wonder at the natural world, intellectual achievement and physical activity, surmounting suffering and persecution, selfless love, the quest for meaning and for values by which to live".

When the Department of Education issued guidance on this area of the schools curriculum, it recognized that spirituality encompassed both theistic and non–theistic positions, and provided two definitions of the term. One connected it with "a sense of God or of Gods", but the other declared that "the spiritual area is concerned with the awareness a person has of those elements in existence and experience which may be defined in terms of inner feelings and beliefs; they affect the way people see themselves and throw light on the purpose and meaning of life itself". A Religious Education Syllabus based on this guidance suggested that spirituality "can be evidenced by human aspirations such as love, hope, compassion, forgiveness, faith, self–giving, altruism, etc." When David Pascall, then Chairman of the National Curriculum Council, addressed the Religious Council of England and Wales in 1992, he said that spirituality "has to do with relationships with other people, and, for believers, with God. It is to do with the universal search for individual identity – with our response to the challenging experiences of life, such as death, suffering, beauty, and the rare encountering of real goodness – it is to do with the search for meaning in life and values by which to live".

Humanists on both sides of the Atlantic had long held this non–transcendentalist view of spirituality. Julian Huxley, first President of the British Humanist Association, had written, "The spiritual elements which are usually styled divine are part and parcel of human nature" (*Religion Without Revelation*, 1927). The American psychologist A H Maslow had written for the American Humanist Association, "The spiritual life is part of our biological life. It is the 'highest' part of it, but yet part of it. The spiritual life is part of the human essence. It is a defining–characteristic of human nature, without which human nature is not full human nature. It is part of the real self, of one's identity, of one's inner core… of full humanness" (*Humanist* Vol 27 No.4). Today's radical and postmodern religious humanists might query notions of a "real self" and "one's inner core", but most would be comfortable with the concept of a spirituality that is secular in its this–worldliness, if religious in its expression: an affirmation of faith in the wholly human spirit.

For many, however, there remains a more troubling question than those resolved by a "make believe" or "as if" approach to religious practice and a secular approach to spirituality. The problem that gnaws at their vitals is the age–old one: What secure and objective basis can we deduce for our morality and ethics if we take leave of an objective God as the source of what is good, and as the ultimate guarantor of justice? If that kind of God is dead, and the records of his instructions, commandments and guidance as delivered in the Scriptures are merely the words of men who have claimed to speak in his name, how can we *know* what is right and just? How can we avoid a moral anarchy, an anything–goes relativism? On what *authority* can we say it is wrong to lie and steal and betray our lovers, and right to help those who need help, feed those who need feeding, and generally be nice to each other?

It is worth noting here that the deep need for certainty and security in matters that go to the heart of how we live our lives is not confined to religious believers. Secular humanists, no less frequently than bishops, priests and Bible–belt pastors, voice their horror of moral "relativism", and some no–god men and women have pursued the phantom of an objective morality with no less missionary zeal than the traditionally godly, seeking it in biology, psychology, evolutionary science and Platonist philosophies. It seems to me that these secular–realist approaches to the problem are as misconceived as traditional religious–realist answers.

Realism assumes the existence of a real answer somewhere: in God, in human nature, in the structure of the universe, wherever. If we look long and hard enough, in the right places (scriptures, gurus, genes, nature), we'll find it. Non–realism assumes that there are no permanently fixed, ready–made, one–size–fits–all moral or ethical axioms waiting out there for us to find and appropriate. Instead, we must draw on our human reason and imagination, our individual and community experience, to work out together what is good, right, just, honest. Far from this displaying the overweening arrogance of men playing God, it demands that we be humble enough to acknowledge that we don't have access to absolute truth, and that our efforts to find or forge practical answers will always be fallible, partial, incomplete and provisional – and therefore messy.

There is an obvious analogy in politics. It was once thought in virtually all cultures, and is still thought in some, that there is a single right, true and correct way of organizing political life. Almost invariably, it was a way revealed by God: rule by priests, mullahs, kings or a godly elect. Rebellion against the system was rebellion against God himself. Until the 1640s, it was maintained among the political elite in England that toleration of unorthodox opinion, beyond a very narrowly defined range of permitted discussion, was tantamount to toleration of blasphemy and treason. Freedom of religion was opposed not only because it was considered offensive to God, who had revealed the true way through his kings and bishops, but because it was feared (rightly) that freedom in church affairs would lead inexorably to freedom of opinion in matters of state. Politics had to be founded on the solid rock of some supra–human agency if it was not to sink in the shifting sands of every–man–for–himself.

Today we find such a view outlandish and tyrannical. We acknowledge the need for laws, but we long ago gave up the notion that our laws are made by God or his representatives on earth. It is *our* representatives who make and unmake laws. Politics are a wholly human matter. Of course, that makes them a messy, crude, fallible business, without certainties or absolutes. Just because our laws are human–made rather than God–given and our politics are based on principles derived from human reasoning rather than divine commands, we do not say that we are thereby free to pick and choose which laws we are going to obey, or write our own statute book. We acknowledge that laws are made, changed and unmade by human consensus, and their authority is dependent on that consensus. As times and conditions change, so we change our laws. We have rejected a static absolutism for a dynamic democracy, a political relativism in which we recognize that where there is no bedrock foundation we must work as a community to build as solid a foundation as we can put together over the underlying sands.

And so it is with the moral law as well. This action is "right", that action "wrong", not because some transcendent authority so decrees it but because we human beings, together, in community, have so decided. Some actions – murder, rape, theft, betrayal of love – have such an overwhelming weight of consensus against them that we have chosen to treat them as *absolutely* wrong. But there are many other issues, such as the use of force in self–defence or for just ends, genetic engineering, or the complexities of sexual relationships, on which there is no overwhelming consensus among or even within cultures – or on which consensus is constantly shifting.

We now see that this was always so. If our forebears believed that it was God who laid down the law, moral or political, they were mistaken. We do not escape the human responsibility of distinguishing right from wrong by looking to an absolute and ultimate authority to decide for us, because even when we do that we still have to interpret the word of the authority – God, the Bible, the Church, the Leader – and interpretation is necessarily human, culturally conditioned, provisional and fallible. Morality, then, is a human creation. While we all have a responsibility to our own conscience (conditioned, as we must recognize it to be, by our own experience and by the culture which has shaped our experience), the business of making moral judgments devolves not only on individuals but on communities. It is in community, in dialogue and in association with others, through common experience and culture, that we generate our ideas of right and wrong. It may be a form of "relativism", but this surely is the opposite of moral anarchy and rampant individualism.

If humankind is a moral and ethical species, it is because humankind is the species that reasons and imagines. Our imagination enables us to put ourselves in the place of others, to share their griefs and joys, and thus to recognize that each of us is a part of one human whole. So we suffer with each other and delight in the delight of others. We have the capacity to imagine, and therefore to feel, their fortunes and misfortunes as our own, so we may develop a natural impulse to feed the hungry and care for the destitute: for theirs may be our case some day. It is the reasonable and the imaginative course to treat others as we ourselves would be treated. And we need no supernatural ground for acting reasonably and imaginatively in our dealings with others.

So far, so humanist. But the religious humanist will add a postscript. In so far as the ancient myths and scriptures of the historic religions present us with a prescriptive morality derived from a supernatural, superhuman source, they no longer speak to our condition. But of course that is not the only way to read them. The religious humanist will read them as an unmatched record of the wholly human struggle, over countless generations, to create the moral consensus to which we aspire. If the stories, read literally, appear to make El or Yahweh or a divine Christ the authors of our moral codes, the religious humanist understands that El and Yahweh and the divine Christ are our fictions, our creations, characters in our own imaginative dramatizations of the ways our species has aspired to the good, the true and the beautiful. To privilege the scriptural myths as uniquely sacred or infallible is both naive and dangerous; but to write them off as relevant only to past cultures is to deny our own roots, impoverish our understanding of the wisdom of the ages, and deprive ourselves of the incalculable benefit and pleasure which these products of the imaginative genius are still capable of delivering.

Which brings us within sight of the republic of heaven.

CHAPTER 18

Building the Republic of Heaven

*The republic of Heaven... enables us to see this real
world, our world, as a place of infinite delight, so
intensely beautiful and intoxicating that if we saw it
clearly then we would want nothing more, ever. We
would know that this earth is our true home, and
nowhere else is.*
– Philip Pullman, *Horn Book Magazine*

*Know you what it is to be a child?... It is to believe in
love, to believe in loveliness, to believe in belief; it is to be
so little that the elves can reach to whisper in your ear; it
is to turn pumpkins into coaches, and mice into horses,
lowness into loftiness, and nothing into everything.*
– Francis Thompson (1859–1907), *Shelley*

IN THE PREVIOUS chapters of Part Three, I have delineated a
humanism that is radical in its rejection of half measures, postmodern
in its rejection of absolutes, and religious in its insistence on the ancient
means of making meaning and finding purpose through a fundamental
reinterpretation of storytelling, art and worship. More importantly, I
have sought to make the case that such a humanism can still afford
wisdom and inspiration long after we have abandoned all traces of
supernaturalism and mystification. I have argued that the radical

religious humanist is a secular being, content to live one life in one world. She can tell mythology from history, fiction from fact, poetry from prose, and values them all. She finds that religious language can speak to levels of being that everyday language doesn't have the power to reach. She lives by heart and mind, imagination and reason. She is spiritual in the simple sense of understanding that material satisfaction is not enough: the quest for inner satisfaction, for meaning and values by which to live, is her inspiration. She may or may not belong to a church or its equivalent and participate in the dramas, rituals and make–believe by which a community of faith regularly acknowledges and celebrates things of worth; but she knows there *are* things of worth, and that you can't buy them in the shops.

In these two final chapters I want to make a further argument: that the goal of the radical religious humanist is to contribute to the making of the "republic of heaven".

In Philip Pullman's children's novel *The Amber Spyglass* – the last of the trilogy, *His Dark Materials*, loosely based on *Paradise Lost* – the ex–nun Mary Malone tells young Will how she lost her faith in God and found the experience both liberating and unsettling:

> There's no one to fret, no one to condemn, no one to bless me for being a good girl, no one to punish me for being wicked. Heaven was empty. I didn't know whether God had died, or whether there never had been a God at all. Either way, I felt free and lonely, and I didn't know whether I was happy or unhappy, but something very strange had happened... And I took the crucifix from around my neck and I threw it in the sea. That was it. All over. Gone.

Free *and* lonely. Happy *and* unhappy. And there is the same ambivalence when she answers Will's question about whether she had found it hard to leave the church:

In one way it was, because everyone was so
disappointed. Everyone, from the Mother Superior to
the priests to my parents – they were so upset and
reproachful... I felt as if something they all
passionately believed in depended on me carrying on
with something I didn't. But in another way it was
easy, because it made sense... So it was lonely for a
while, but then I got used to it.

Will asks if she missed God:

Yes, terribly. And I still do. And what I miss most is
the sense of being connected to the whole of the
universe. I used to feel I was connected to God like
that, and because he was there, I was connected to the
whole of creation. But if he's not there, then...

For Mary Malone, God had to go, but his absence was almost
as problematical as his presence. Pullman's trilogy, which mixes fantasy,
philosophy, religion, sexual awakening and quantum physics, tells of a
struggle, both cosmic and human, to replace the authoritarian Kingdom
of God with a people's Republic of Heaven. With the king overthrown,
the realm is no longer a kingdom; but the vision of heaven survives, to
be fulfilled by free citizens of the new republic. And, he suggests, it is in
the collective task of building the republic of heaven that we might
recover the sense of being "connected to the whole of creation."

In an essay entitled "The Republic of Heaven" in the children's
literature journal *Horn Book Magazine* (November/December 2001),
Pullman suggests that some of the best glimpses of the republic may be
seen in the books children read. "If the republic doesn't include fantasy,
it won't be worth living in. It won't be Heaven of any sort". But, he says,
the fantasy has to connect to real life, as in "the great republican fairy
tales such as Jack and the Beanstalk", which is a republican real–life

story "because the magic grows out of the most common and everyday thing, a handful of beans, and the beanstalk grows right outside the kitchen window, and at the end of the story Jack comes home".

Pullman's republic is a place of *joy*, which he says is an alternative word for heaven. It is also the place where the connectedness that Mary Malone missed when she stopped believing in God is restored.

> What I'm referring to is a sense that things are right and good, and we are part of everything that is right and good. It's a sense that we're connected to the universe. This connectedness is where meaning lies; the meaning of our lives is their connection with something other than ourselves. The religion that's now dead did give us that, in full measure: we were part of a huge cosmic drama, involving a Creation and a Fall and a redemption, and Heaven and Hell. What we did mattered, because God saw everything, even the fall of a sparrow. And one of the most deadly and oppressive consequences of the death of God is this sense of meaninglessness or alienation that so many of us have felt in the past century or so.

Children's stories at their best, says Pullman, create worlds of simple everyday connectedness and meaning.

> Part of this meaning that I've suggested we need, the sense that we belong and we matter, comes from the moral and social relations that the republic of Heaven must embody. In the republic, we're connected in a moral way to one another, to other human beings. We have responsibilities to them, and they to us. We're not isolated units of self–interest in a world where there is

no such thing as society; we cannot live so. But part of the sense of wider meaningfulness that we need comes from seeing that we have a connection with nature and the universe around us, with everything that is not human as well. So the republic of Heaven is also characterized by another quality: it enables us to see this real world, our world, as a place of infinite delight, so intensely beautiful and intoxicating that if we saw it clearly then we would want nothing more, ever. We would know that this earth is our true home, and nowhere else is. In the words of William Blake, one of the founding fathers of the republic of Heaven,

"How do you know but ev'ry Bird that cuts the airy way
Is an immense world of delight, clos'd by your senses five?"

...At the furthest extent, this sense of delight in the physical world can blend into a sort of ecstatic identification with it. "You never enjoy the world aright, said Thomas Traherne, till the sea itself floweth in your veins, till you are clothed with the heavens and crowned with the stars: and perceive yourself to be the sole heir of the whole world.

But these glimpses of what it might mean to live in the republic of heaven "need, if we're going to take it seriously... something more coherent and solid. We need a story, a myth that does what the traditional religious stories did: it must explain. It must satisfy our hunger for a why. Why does the world exist? Why are we here?" Evolution by natural selection provides an overwhelmingly powerful republican myth explaining the why of what brought us here: and the fact that we have evolved as conscious beings, conscious of our own consciousness, offers a myth explaining the why of what we are here for:

We might have arrived at this point by a series of accidents, but from now on we have to take charge of our fate. Now we are here, now we are conscious, we make a difference. Our presence changes everything. So a myth of the republic of Heaven would explain what our true purpose is. Our purpose is to understand and to help others to understand, to explore, to speculate, to imagine. And that purpose has a moral force...

We need a myth, we need a story, because it's no good persuading people to commit themselves to an idea on the grounds that it's reasonable. How much effect would the Bible have had for generations if it had been a collection of laws and genealogies? What seized the mind and captured the heart were the stories it contains.

And Pullman ends his article as Jesus might have begun one of his discourses with his disciples, with the elusive enigma of a children's nursery rhyme:

Boys and girls come out to play
The moon doth shine as bright as day;

This is a republic where we live by the imagination. Night can be like day; things can be upside down and back to front and inside out, and still all right.

Leave your supper and leave your sleep,
And join your playfellows in the street –

Not in a private playground with security guards where some of us are let in and others kept out, not in the park that closes its gates before the moon comes out, but in the street, the common place that belongs to everyone.

Come with a whoop, and come with a call,
Come with a good will or not at all.

... We must be cheerful and not go round with a face like a mourner at a funeral. It's difficult sometimes, but good will is not a luxury: it's an absolute necessity. It's a moral imperative.

Up the ladder and down the wall,
A tuppeny loaf will serve us all.
You bring milk, and I'll bring flour,
And we'll have a pudding in half an hour.

We can do it. That's the way it happens in the republic of Heaven; we provide for ourselves. We'll have a pudding, and a good nourishing one it'll be; milk and flour are full of goodness. And then we can play together in the bright moonlight till we all fall asleep.

Of such is the republic of heaven. Jesus called it a kingdom. Having taken leave of the king two thousand years on, we may now call it a republic. It is ours to imagine, ours to make, ours in which to provide for ourselves.

Unaware of Pullman's work (*The Amber Spyglass* came out in 2000), I had published the previous year a very different (and much less significant) book, which I called *Gerrard Winstanley and the Republic of Heaven*. This was a study of the life and writings of the 1640s "True Leveller" leader, who saw the execution of Charles I in January 1649 as the opportunity for the new English republic to rid itself of all remaining traces of "kingly power" and embrace a "new law of righteousness" that

> shall be so plainly writ in everyone's heart that none shall desire to have more than another, or to be lord over other, or to lay claim to any thing as his; this phrase of mine and thine shall be swallowed up in the law of righteous actions one to another, for they shall all live as brethren, every one doing as they would be done by... There shall be no need of lawyers, prisons, or engines of punishment one over another, for all shall walk and act righteously in the Creation, and there shall be no beggar, nor cause of complaining in all this holy mountain.

Winstanley's vision clearly owed much to those of Isaiah, Ezekiel and Hosea, and he elaborated it with references to the Epistle to the Hebrews, the letters of James and I John, and the Acts of the Apostles with its description of the early Jerusalem church as a society whose members had "all things in common". He called his visionary heaven on earth a "Common Wealth" or "Common Treasury". Describing it as the "republic of heaven" was my gloss. My application of the term to Winstanley's project, followed by Pullman's fantasy–fictional use of it, demonstrates how it is open to a variety of creative interpretations – as, indeed, has always been the case with "the Kingdom of God". If theologians cannot agree on what Jesus meant by the kingdom – whether it is "within" us, "among" us, or is, in Tennyson's words, "the one far–off divine event to which the whole creation moves" – we need not suppose that we must pin down the republic of heaven to a single meaning or usage. In fact, I shall argue for a republic of heaven *within* us, a republic of heaven *among* us, and a *future* republic of heaven to be built by its own free, voluntary citizens.

The republic of heaven is a republic because once we have lost our faith in kings, it can no longer be a kingdom. God was traditionally conceived of as King and Lord because kingship and lordship represented supreme power in the everyday world. They no longer do so. We have either pensioned off our monarchs or reinvented them as figureheads. That some of us (in Britain and Canada, for instance, but not in the United States or Ireland) remain the "subjects" of such figureheads is no more than a polite fiction. In truth, they are now *our* subjects. As "constitutional monarchs" they are subject to the constitutional rules, conventions, customs and practices that we impose upon them. They are good for tradition and tourism. As for our lords, we have unseated most of them, leaving them with their titles (and, by mischance, their title deeds), but almost entirely shorn of the fearsome powers they once enjoyed. We no longer tug forelocks or doff hats to them. With W S Gilbert we see that they do nothing in particular, and do it very well. Julius Caesar's arrogation of power turned a government that had been a public affair (*res publica*) into a system run by a *rex (monarch)*. Modern democracies have righted that situation, for our *rex* is now the *public*. The pull of tradition may lead some of us to pretend otherwise, but we know in our hearts that we are a sovereign people, ruling ourselves for better or worse.

But if "kingdom" has lost its force, "heaven" has retained much of its symbolic potency. We long ago ceased to look for heaven above the bright blue sky (though we are happy to revisit that idea as a poetic archaism when we call the skies the heavens), and we no longer suppose that heaven is a place we'll go to, God willing and touch wood, when we die. The heaven depicted in a thousand brilliant frescoes and oils, a place of cherubim, seraphim, virginal choirs and trumpets rampant, is now as quaint, amusing and incredible as its opposite, the hell of fire, flame and fearsome monsters. But the "new heaven and a new earth" of John's vision in Revelation 21, the "new Jerusalem" where there are no more tears, no more death, sorrow, crying or pain, has somehow survived the deposition of the God who was supposed to make these things happen – to make the lion lie down with the lamb and to teach men to beat their swords into ploughshares. This is still the heaven of which we dream, but we know that if "all things shall be made new" we alone can be the makers; and that is why we find ourselves vowing with Blake that we shall not cease from mental fight, nor let our swords sleep in our hands, till we have built this new Jerusalem in what remains of our own patch of green and pleasant land.

God as king and sovereign was a common idea in pre–Christian Judaism and other ancient Near East religions. Psalm 97 celebrates a Yahweh who reigns "high above all the earth" and is "exalted far above all gods". For the Psalmist, the kingdom was always here and now: our god is bigger and better than all others, so there! Gradually, however, and particularly after the fall of the earthly kingdom of David's line, the coming of the heavenly kingdom began to be conceived as an apocalyptic future event. When Daniel interprets Nebuchadnezzar's dream, in Daniel 2:37, he tells him that although the royal dreamer is himself a "king of kings", the day will come when the God of heaven will "set up a kingdom which shall never be destroyed" but will "break in pieces and consume" all other kingdoms, "and it shall stand for ever" (verse 44).

By New Testament times the notion of some kind of spiritual kingdom could be found in the literature of the whole Hellenistic world. The American scholar Burton Mack writes (in "The Kingdom Sayings in Mark", *Forum* 3/1, 1987) that:

> Discourse about *basileia* [the Greek word translated as "kingdom" or "rule"] during the Greco–Roman period was not limited to circles of Jewish apocalypticists, nor, for that matter, to those with specifically Jewish interests. Basileia was a common topic of far–reaching significance throughout Hellenistic culture... in the post–Alexander age... The critical issues now centred on power and privilege, and

on the rights and duties of those that had it... Basileia is what kings and rulers had: sovereignty, majesty, dominion, power, domain... [and] the abstract models constructed in order to imagine the practical issues inherent in the political structures of society could be used as well to think through basic questions about social ethos in general... "King" no longer needed to refer to the actual king of a city or kingdom. "King" became an abstract representation of *anthropos* ("human being") at the "highest" level imaginable, whether of endowment, achievement, ethical excellence, or mythical ideal.

Quoting Mack's essay in his own book, *The Historical Jesus* (Harper San Francisco, 1991), John Dominic Crossan adds that "what is actually at stake is not kingdom as place, be it here or there, but rule as state, be it active or passive. The problem, in plain language, is power: who rules, and how one should".

So when the sage and teacher Jesus tells his stories about "the kingdom of heaven" he is not introducing some strange new concept, but adding a new dimension to discussion of a topic on which there is already lively debate. What is radically different about Jesus' contribution is that it is made not in scholarly exegesis, political debate or literary criticism, but in an astonishingly original and striking set of parables, aphorisms and riddles. Since our republic of heaven must acknowledge its parenthood in Jesus' kingdom sayings, which after two thousand years still have a potent appeal to the imagination, it is worth reminding ourselves of what Jesus is reported to have said and how he said it.

Several kingdom sayings are collected together in the so–called Sermon on the Mount. Here, the power relations of the real world are turned upside down. In the kingdom of heaven, the poor are sovereign.

(Matthew's rendering of "poor in spirit" would seem to be a politically nervous gloss: Luke, more bluntly, has "Blessed be ye poor" [6:20], Thomas has "Blessed are the poor" [Gospel of Thomas 54] and James says it is "the poor of this world" who are chosen to be "heirs of the kingdom" [2:5]). Here the hungry, the distressed, the ridiculed and the ridiculous come into their own (Matthew 5:3f and Luke 6:20f). The rich man and the pious Pharisee have no place here: the rich will find it harder to enter the kingdom than to thread a camel through the eye of a needle (Matthew 19:23f and Mark 10:23–25), and the religious are warned that their ceremonies will win them no entry ticket, as loving care for each other rather than burnt offerings is the new order of the day (Mark 12:33, Matthew 7:21). In the parable of the leaven (Matthew 13:33 and Luke 13: 20–21) Jesus goes so far as to abrogate the distinction between the sacred and the profane – that is, between heaven and earth.

Ernest Renan, one of the earliest critical analysts of the kingdom teaching, in *The Life of Jesus* (1863), gets the measure of it:

> A vast substitution of classes would take place. The kingdom of God was made, first, for children, and those who resemble them; second, for the outcasts of the world, victims of that social arrogance which repulses the good but humble man; third, for heretics and schismatics, publicans, Samaritans, and Pagans of Tyre and Sidon... The doctrine that the poor... alone shall be saved, that the reign of the poor is approaching, was, therefore, the doctrine of Jesus...

– as it had been the doctrine of the Hebrew prophets who had thundered incessantly against the great, and established a close relation, on the one hand, between the words "rich, impious, violent, wicked", and, on the other, between the words "poor, gentle, humble, pious".

For Crossan, Jesus' kingdom of heaven is essentially a "kingdom of nobodies". Crossan tells us that the Greek word *ptochoi* means not simply "poor" in the sense of "those who are not among the wealthy elite" (and that elite includes most of us in the developed countries), but "destitute". "Jesus spoke of a Kingdom not of Peasant or Artisan classes but of the Unclean, Degraded, and Expendable classes... the abused and rejected". Teachers, doctors, Biblical scholars, politicians, journalists and middle management are not obvious kingdom material (though journalists could perhaps squeeze in under "abused and rejected").

I do not take this to mean that one is required to become economically destitute in order to qualify for an entry ticket, but it seems clear that active identification with the poor, the dispossessed and the underprivileged – the active pursuit of social justice – is at least one necessary qualification for inclusion in Jesus' kingdom. James (his brother, according to tradition, though tradition and history are not the same thing) makes the point when he defines "pure religion and undefiled" as "to visit the fatherless and widows in their affliction" (James 1:27); and again, when he reminds the better–off in his community that it is "the poor of this world, rich in faith", who are "heirs to the kingdom" (2:5). "The bad news", writes Robert Funk in *Honest to Jesus* (Harper San Francisco, 1996),

> is that those who think they are leading upright lives
> will be surprised to learn that they have missed the
> messianic banquet, the great supper, because they were
> too preoccupied with misleading and deceptive
> aspects of life. According to Jesus' parables and
> aphorisms, the social roles – marginal versus
> respectable – will be reversed: the first will be last and
> the last first.

The aphoristic references to the kingdom are relatively straightforward, often brutally stark. The parables, however, are more ambiguous. Often, the disciples have to ask what on earth Jesus is talking about, and sometimes he explains, sometimes not. He uses humour, riddles, and shock tactics. He teases both his disciples and his critics, and he loves to make a laughing stock of the know–alls who tried to trap him into making his subversive message so explicit as to risk his being taken out of circulation before his mission was accomplished. As Funk puts it:

> When Jesus talked about this wonderful place, he always talked about it in terms drawn from the everyday, the mundane world around him. The language of Jesus, consequently, was concrete and specific. The scenery of his parables and aphorisms consisted entirely of everyday events and topics, of ordinary times, places, and persons. He spoke of dinner parties, of travellers being mugged, of truant sons, of corrupt officials, of a cache of coins found in a field, of poor peasants, of precious pearls, of the hungry and tearful, of lawsuits and conscription, of beggars and lending, of birds and flowers, of purity and defilement, of the Sabbath, of wealth, and occasionally of scholars. He also referred to common concerns for food, clothing and shelter, of parents' gifts to children, of a speck in the eye, of true relatives, of sowing and planting, of jars with broken handles, of evil demons, of doctors and the sick, of crushing debt, of vineyard workers, of weeds and gardening, and of wedding celebrations. He talked about camels and needles, about friends and enemies, about priests and Levites, about shrewd managers and persistent widows. His images were drawn from the scene he and his neighbours experienced directly on ordinary days. But there was something anomalous about this plain speech: plain as it was, it's meaning was often elusive.

> While he spoke unceasingly in mundane terms, his
> listeners must have perceived that he always had some
> other subject in mind, to judge by their reported
> reactions. His basic metaphor... was God's reign or
> God's estate, but he never [in the parables] spoke
> about it directly. He regularly compared it to
> something else, without telling his followers how the
> two things were alike or related... His language is
> highly figurative. It is non–literal or metaphorical.

Jesus, then, often left his hearers to figure out for themselves
what on earth he was saying about this kingdom of heaven. He threw
out clues and left them to argue among themselves as to how to solve
the riddle. The very nature of the kingdom was such that his allusions
to it were necessarily elusive and enigmatic: "he that hath ears to hear,
let him hear". Like all the best storytellers, Jesus challenged and required
his listeners to share with him in carving out from the stories their full
meaning. He was not a provider of blueprints, or fixed constitutions, or
paper utopias. But the inevitable consequence of leaving it to his
listeners to work out what it all meant was that rival interpretations
soon abounded.

It seems that most of his earliest followers interpreted his
kingdom teaching as prophesying an imminent apocalyptic event, a
supernatural act of God that would take place in their own lifetime.
When this didn't happen, some looked for alternative readings. Firmly
embedded in the tradition were sayings of Jesus that seemed to
contradict the notion of the kingdom as apocalypse soon, and stressed
instead a sense of the kingdom as present rather than future, within and
among us rather than ahead of us. Luke 17:20f has Jesus responding to
a straight question by the Pharisees as to when exactly this kingdom of
his is going to happen, by answering: "The kingdom of God cometh
not by observations [of signs and wonders]: Neither shall they say, Lo
here! or lo there! For behold, the kingdom of God is within [or among]

you". The Gospel of Thomas is more emphatic. Here it is the disciples who ask when the kingdom will come, and Jesus answers: "It will not come by waiting for it. It will not be a matter of saying 'here it is,' or 'there it is.' Rather the kingdom of the father is spread out upon the earth, and men do not see it" (113:2–4).

Another response of Thomas' Jesus to the same question is: "If those who lead you say to you, 'See, the kingdom is in the sky', then the birds of the sky will precede you. If they say to you, 'It is in the sea', then the fish will precede you. Rather, the kingdom is inside of you, and it is outside of you". And again, answering the disciples' question "When will the new world come?" Jesus tells them: "What you look forward to has already come, but you do not recognize it" (3:1f).

So was Jesus' kingdom of heaven in the future or the present – or both? Jesus himself, as portrayed in the literature, appears to give contradictory answers. We are to pray, for instance, that the kingdom that has "already come" (Thomas) *will* come on earth, as it is in heaven. The apparent contradictions, however, are considered – especially by Christian scholars – to be more likely deliberate riddles than unresolved confusions. The riddles came to be solved in different ways. Augustine, for instance, understood the kingdom as the "City of God", and the Church chose to interpret the City of God as a description of itself. The Quakers and radical–reformation sects of the English revolution adopted a similar concept of a "realized eschatology", envisioning their own attempts to build a new heaven and a new earth as both a spiritualized second coming of Christ and tangible evidence of the presence among and within us of the kingdom of heaven.

Readers who have persevered with me so far may be asking why I am spending so much time and space in considering a two–thousand–year–old idea of the *kingdom* of heaven when our subject is suppose to be the *republic*. I do not wish to suggest that our republic is nothing more than the kingdom with a new, up–dated brand name, but it seems clear that although discourse about the republic ought not end with the old kingdom traditions it must at least start with them. The kingdom is the inescapable foundation for the republic. The republic is post–kingdom, as our entire western culture is now post–Christian, moving on from what went before rather than seeking to deny the part the past has played in shaping the present, thereby absorbing the past into the present.

Funk, Crossan and the Westar Institute's Jesus Seminar tackled the continuity problem by looking for a modern alternative to "kingdom" for their *Scholars Version* of the gospels, eventually adopting a variety of renderings, including "God's domain", "God's estate" and even "God's imperial rule". Funk tells us in *Honest to Jesus* that it proved "extremely difficult to find terms that accommodate both the absolute character of the divine reign and the pacific disposition of Jesus. This problem still awaits solution". Late in 2004 he seemed to be settling on "divine domain". Crossan chose to stick with "kingdom" in *The Historical Jesus*, though he tells us he was "not particularly happy with it", doing so simply because most of the texts he was quoting used the term. Don Cupitt sticks with kingdom for much the same reason. Crossan makes it clear, however, that "the focus of discussion is not on kings but on rulers, not on kingdom but on power, not on place but on state... or mode of being".

I do not suggest that "republic" would have been a suitable alternative for Funk, Crossan and those scholars whose task it has been to retranslate the ancient texts. "Republic" would clearly be a mischievous mistranslation of the Greek *basileia*. But we are not here concerned with translation, rather with finding an alternative to the rule of an obsolete king of kings, and we are posing the republic of heaven as precisely such an alternative. What we would be wise to learn from Jesus is that the republic of heaven should be no more clearly defined and prescriptive than was his kingdom. Its full meaning is for us to play around with, knowing that while there must be some things we can say about it, there will be more that is better suggested than asserted.

In his parables in particular, as the American scholar Bernard Brandon Scott has shown (*Re–Imagine the World*, Polebridge, Santa

Rosa, 2001), Jesus offered glimpses of an alternative reality, intimations of how things could be different. Scott quotes the Irish poet Seamus Heaney to apply a striking insight on the function of poetry in general to the parables of Jesus in particular:

> In the activity of poetry... there is a tendency to place a counter–reality in the scales – a reality which may be only imagined but which nevertheless has weight because it is imagined within the gravitational pull of the actual and can therefore hold its own and balance out against the historical situation. This redressing effect of poetry comes from its being a glimpsed alternative, a revelation of potential that is denied or constantly threatened by circumstances.

This is exactly how the poetry of Jesus' parables and aphorisms operates. Jesus's vision does not replace the default world in which we live our everyday lives, but it is a counterweight, counter reality, "a glimpsed alternative, a revelation of potential that is denied or constantly threatened by circumstance". As Brandon Scott comments, "a glimpsed alternative is not a worked out programme. It is always temporary, glimpsed". But if the glimpse doesn't galvanize us into action it will be a daydream, a pipedream, rather than the enabling dream that remakes religion and re–imagines the world.

Readers will have realized by now that my republic of heaven is not as new as it sounds. It has been around for a long time, in various shapes and forms, and under various names. In the final chapter I shall look at the long tradition of paradises lost and found, utopias imagined and mocked, to locate the religious humanist's dream in its historical perspective.

CHAPTER 19

Enabling Dreams

True religion don't take us out of the world but excites
our endeavours to mend it
– William Penn

Fellowship is heaven, and lack of fellowship is hell;
fellowship is life, and lack of fellowship is death. And
the deeds that ye do upon earth, it is for fellowship's sake
that ye do them.
– William Morris, *A Dream of John Ball*

IT SEEMS THAT every culture has its own way of looking back to a Golden Age and forward to its return.

For lo, the days are hastening on,
By prophet bards foretold,
When, with the ever-circling years,
Comes round the age of gold;
When peace shall over all the earth
Its ancient splendours fling,
And the whole world give back the song
Which now the angels sing.

Given the chronic sickness of the world we inhabit, a sickness that hits us between the eyes and jolts the heartbeat every time we open a newspaper or switch on the television, the expectation of an "age of gold", let alone one that is "hastening on", must seem hopelessly naive, if not clinically insane. How does the "war on terror" fit into such an optimistic scenario, or the fact that one in six children is severely malnourished, one in seven has no health care at all, one in five has no safe water, and one in three has no toilet or sanitation facilities at home? What price a better world if we refuse to take measures to halt man–made climate change or reform world trade agreements because such action, however beneficial to the under–privileged, would threaten our precious living standards? What realistic hope is there so long as we allow global politics to be dominated by rival religious fundamentalisms? How do we suppose peace will fling its ancient splendours over all the earth when, from the security of the White House prayer meeting or the Downing Street branch of the Christian Socialist Movement, we arm ourselves to the teeth and legitimize pre–emptive wars? How can we expect to hear the angels sing over the discordant clamour of "ye men of strife" – who are, of course, ourselves?

If, in our quest for paradise regained, for utopia rediscovered, for the republic of heaven on earth, we seek hard evidence that our goal is at least achievable, if not inevitable, we surely seek in vain. The evidence is against us. It is by faith that we are saved. Faith, Paul tells us – and it is worth repeating – is "the substance of things *hoped for*, the evidence of things *not seen*". We must live without guarantees. It is hard – but we must do it. We live by faith that there *is* an alternative to our default–world and that we are at our best, our most human, when we envision the alternative and risk the experiment of living it, knowing that faith without works is dead. Of course we may fall flat on our faces. We usually do, and our faces carry the marks. But better the attempt at realizing the dream than joining the ranks of those who have forgotten how to dream.

I found myself reflecting on this on the fortieth anniversary of Martin Luther King's historic "I have a dream!" speech. With its ecstatic Biblical vision of a "sweet land of liberty" where "every valley shall be exalted, every hill and mountain laid low... and the glory of the Lord shall be revealed, and all flesh shall see it together", the speech commemorated the day one hundred years earlier when the Emancipation Proclamation was signed and black Americans were given a glimpse of a Promised Land in which they too might enjoy the inalienable rights of "life, liberty and the pursuit of happiness".

The vision, and the very rhetoric in which it was expressed, were part of a tradition stretching back to Jesus and the legendary Moses. The Bible begins with a tale of Paradise – a word apparently coined by Xenophon in the 5th century BCE to describe the perfection of a Persian garden – and ends with Revelation's "holy city, new Jerusalem", where sorrow and pain shall be no more. Between them are the promises of a land flowing with milk and honey, the prophets' vision of a world where swords are beaten into ploughshares, and – the jewel in the crown of utopian literature – the visionary kingdom parables and aphorisms of Jesus that we recalled in the previous chapter.

The literary genre at the heart of the tradition has inspired millions: that was always its function. But humans are only human, and the visionary gleam has too often become a fanatical glint in the eye: that is our bitter experience.

Anton Chekhov in *Three Sisters* has his Colonel Vershinin musing that "in a century or two, people will live in a new way, a happier way. We won't be there to see it, but it's why we live, why we work, it's why we suffer. We're creating it! That's the purpose of our existence. The only happiness we know is to work towards that goal". Vershinin's bright–eyed enthusiasm for a better world and his optimistic faith in human nature neatly illustrate the utopian temperament. But by any "realistic" standard he was sadly mistaken. The "new way" that was the lot of Chekhov's fellow Russians, only three or four decades after his fictional character's profession of faith in the future, was not the "happier" highway to heaven he had prophesied, but the hell–bent way of the commissar, the thought police, the gulag.

And, some will ask wearily, isn't that the way of all utopias? The elysian fields of egalitarian socialism, from More and Winstanley to Marx and Morris, metamorphose into the killing fields of Comrades Stalin, Mao and Pol Pot; the American dream sours into Bush's God–blessed brutalism; Israel's land of milk and honey flows with a darker liquid – the blood of the not–chosen who happened to be there first; Muhammad's virtues of tolerance and compassion mutate into the Taliban and suicide bombers; and Jesus' kingdom of heaven degrades to a fiercely authoritarian church redeemed, ironically, only by the civilizing effects of secular liberalism and humanitarianism.

The distressing tendency of human utopias to turn into nightmares is most evident when utopias come to be misunderstood as political paradigms rather than literary creations. The earliest utopians made no such mistake. Plato, the classicists tell us, never intended his model republic to be imitated in Greece – or anywhere else. *The Republic* was a literary conceit, and no one among the philosopher's sophisticated Athenian readership thought to translate it into a revolutionary political programme. This was true of all classical utopias: Euhemerus' *Sacred History*, Plutarch's idealized Sparta and the many Atlantis fables.

Two millennia later, Thomas More's *Utopia* of 1516 conjured up an island paradise where private property was unknown and egalitarian communism prevailed. But More was a deeply conservative Catholic and a fabulously wealthy Lord Chancellor of England to boot; and the last thing on his mind was any intention to put down the mighty from their seats, turn the rich empty away, or spark off a peasants' revolt. That, no doubt, is why he published his book in Latin and thus safely restricted its radical preachment to the very elite he had done away with in his fabulous island. More was a politician whose politics were far from utopian, as well as being the imaginative creator of a Utopia which was far from his politics.*

It was More, of course, who coined the word "utopia", and scholars believe he derived it from the Greek *ou+topos*, meaning "no place". That was the critical thing about *ou*topias: they were nowhere, places that did not and could not exist. That kept them safe from politics, which was about real places that were subject to real change. But *ou+topos* could easily be confused with *eu+topos*, meaning "good place", and was it not every Christian's bounden duty to seek the kingdom of God, which was the best of good places? So *Eu*topia became a good place that was nowhere but might be built somewhere: and that gave a purely literary genre a distinctly political dimension – and one with revolutionary potential. The old Biblical fables of Paradise, the Promised Land, and a kingdom of God "on earth, as it is in heaven" had always threatened change in the real world, as when the hedge–priest John Ball led the fourteenth century Peasants' Revolt by asking, "When Adam delved and Eve span, who was then the gentleman?"

The upheavals of mid–seventeenth century England forced literary and political utopianism, secular and religious, into a common mould. Gerrard Winstanley's *Law of Freedom* (1652) is the world's first manifesto and constitution for a communist state, albeit one with a radically Christianized communism (like that of the early church as depicted in Acts), and also the first political programme to propose the extension of the franchise to all heads of households, without property or class qualification (though unrepentant royalists, speculators and "uncivil livers", including those "wholly given to pleasure and sports", were excluded, and "hireling" priests and lawyers were not only

---

*Strangely, an attempt to create More's Utopia was made in the 1530s in, of all places, Spain's newly conquered territories in South America. Vasco de Quiroga, a devout member of the Spanish ruling council, founded a commune on the outskirts of what is now Mexico City, using More's book as his blueprint. The story of Quiroga and the commune is told in *Thomas More's Magician* by Toby Green (Weidenfeld, London, 2004).

disenfranchised but subject to capital punishment!). Winstanley draws on Biblical liberation mythology to legitimate his utopian politics, but where in his previous works he had relied on a cosmic intervention – "the rising of Christ in sons and daughters" – to usher in the republic of heaven, in his *Law of Freedom* he demands that Cromwell make the revolution that Christ had started but seemed reluctant to finish. There is no indication that Cromwell ever read Winstanley, let alone sympathized with his programme. But, unlike More's communist "no–place" Utopia in a mythical ocean, Winstanley's was a "good–place" Utopia intended for the real world.

French utopias were also overtly political. The ideal states invented by de Foigny, Fenelon and Mercier in the seventeenth and eighteenth centuries all anticipated doctrines and slogans of the Revolution. America too was idealized as a potential utopia, first as pure poetry but soon as pure politics. The poetry was John Donne's *To His Mistress Going to Bed* (c.1600), where "my America, my new found land" is "a heaven like Mahomet's paradise", to be explored and enjoyed "behind, before, above, between, below", as a metaphor for the "far fairer world" of his lover's bedtime body. The political began with G A Ellis proposing in 1820 a "New Britain" that drew on experimental communities in the new American republic. But it was the later nineteenth century that produced political utopian literature that is still read today for pleasure and inspiration, notably William Morris's two socialist classics *A Dream of John Ball* (1888) and *News From Nowhere* (1890), the one evoking an idealized past where sturdy yeomen of England anticipate a future in which all land and wealth is held in common, the other picturing a future anarcho–socialist republic of Hammersmith on the banks of a pure, sweet–running Thames. Both were literary fictions, but Morris in his visionary old age was no "idle singer of an empty day": he had abandoned wallpaper design and laboured to turn his socialist fictions into political reality.

Utopias were always good for a little light mockery. In Shakespeare's *The Tempest* (1611), Gonzalo expatiates on the ideal commonwealth he would create on Prospero's island if he were its king:

> *No occupation, all men idle, all;*
> *No sovereignty...*
> *All things in common nature should produce,*
> *Without sweat or endeavour...*

Meanwhile Shakespeare's contemporary John Fletcher came up with a fine tongue–in–cheek utopia for women in *The Tamer Tamed,* produced around 1600 as a direct riposte to Shakespeare's *The Taming of the Shrew.* In Fletcher's play it is the women who tame the men, demanding a new world in which, "For the good of the common–weal, the women shall wear the breeches". The slogan of these seventeenth–century feminist revolutionaries has a wonderfully twenty–first century ring to it: *"Liberty and Clothes!"*

Utopian idealism remained an easy target for the more serious social satirist, from Swift's *Gulliver's Travels* (1726) onwards. Samuel Butler's *Erewhon* (1872) – "nowhere" misspelt backwards – foreshadowed the more savage satires of a 20th century that witnessed and actively hastened the disintegration of utopias into dystopias: Aldous Huxley's *Brave New World,* George Orwell's *Nineteen Eighty–Four* and A S Byatt's *Babel Towers.* A little earlier, even Gilbert and Sullivan had got in on the act with *Utopia Ltd* (1893), where the ideal republic is described as "Despotism tempered by Dynamite". The king is accountable to a group of Wise Men and the Public Exploder, who keep him in check:

> *If ever a trick he tries*
> *That savours of rascality,*
> *At our decree he dies*
> *Without the least formality...*
> *A pound of dynamite*
> *Explodes in his auriculars;*
> *It's not a pleasant sight –*
> *We'll spare you the particulars.*

And Gilbert, like all good satirists, had a serious point. Checks and balances were what utopias tended to lack. In a perfect society they were hardly necessary. More's, Winstanley's and Morris's ideal states were all static: Winstanley actually made it an offence to change the laws, because any change to perfection would necessarily be regressive. But while that may work in a storybook, we know it is nonsense in the real world, where no society stands still and, Fukuyama or no Fukuyama, there is no end of history. A perfect society may need no mechanism for change, but a society with no mechanism for change ceases to be perfect. Appointing public exploders may take checks and balances a little too far, but without mechanisms for change utopia is not utopia.

Today, utopias are out and dystopias are in. The debasement of the American dream, the unspeakable inhumanities committed in the name of communism and the well–meant failures of "third way" social democracy have convinced many that a "good place" utopia is to be found nowhere, whether spelt forwards or backwards. We no longer believe in an inevitable progress of humanity, onwards and upwards towards that "loftier race than e'er the world has known... with flame of freedom in their souls and light of science in their eyes"; and we no longer look to divine intervention, cosmic benevolence or a miraculous Rapture to give us our New Jerusalem on a gilded plate. Our loss of faith in grand narratives inclines us towards the cynical view that utopias are at best idle dreams and at worst siren fingers beckoning us towards a fool's paradise of discredited absolutes.

So why continue dreaming dreams of a republic of heaven?

First, because we cannot help ourselves. The dream returns, whether bidden or unbidden. It challenges us whether we like it or not. The long tradition of paradises, utopias, new dawns, ages of gold, has not lost its capacity to inspire, despite the long dark nights of repeated disappointments. Republics of heaven inspire not as political blueprints, five–year plans or overarching ideologies, but as visionary gleams, as guides to *what*, if not to *how*. I do not imagine that Winstanley's commonwealth or Tennyson's land of lotus–eaters or Morris's clean, white Hammersmith, peopled by soulful socialists with Pre–Raphaelite faces and fancy dress are achievable, either by ballot or bullet, and I know that if I stumbled into any one of them I would soon be a rebel in the counter–revolutionary underground. I know that the fully perfected City of God is not going to happen in this world, which means it is not going to happen. But I'm with Blake. I'm damned if I'm going to cease from mental fight or let my sword sleep in my hand, content to leave New Jerusalem a mere province of cloud–cuckoo–land. Utopias are the stuff of the dreams of the young and the visions of the old, without which the people perish.

Utopias are texts, stories, the stuff of imagination. They are poetry before they are politics; art before they are science. Like Jesus' kingdom stories, they are *inspirational* before they are *instrumental*. They suggest *what*, leaving us to work out *how*. They are the stuff of dreams: not the idle dreams and fantasies of our sleep but *enabling* dreams which pick us up when we fall, refresh our faltering faith, energize the wholly human spirit. If we can *imagine* a better if not a perfect world, we might convince ourselves that we can take a tiny step or two towards *making* one.

And we do not need to convince ourselves that we shall succeed. I repeat that there is no objective guarantee in heaven or on earth that we can build our republic, our new Jerusalem – or, if we do, that it will turn out any better than the old. William Morris recognized this in *The Earthly Paradise*, where paradise lies in the attempt rather than the achievement. Fiona MacCarthy, Morris's latest biographer, calls the poem "an epic of resilience... suggesting that contentment can consist in creative interaction, our human exchanges of experience and perception. Love usually fails. Heartfelt hopes are often shattered. *The consolation rests in the intelligent attempt*" (my emphasis). The British composer Michael Tippett makes a similar point in his Third

Symphony, where he invokes past dreams from Beethoven's setting of the *Ode to Joy* to King's Lincoln Memorial speech, asking, "What if the dream crack?" and answering "Re-make it! Dream a new dream!"

Martin Luther King was no daydreamer. He did not dream to escape the real world but to remake it. His was an *enabling* dream. And while he certainly aimed high, he did not set his Promised Land, his republic of heaven, above the bright blue sky or in the fabulous mountains of the sweet by-and-by but in "the prodigious hilltops of New Hampshire, the heightening Alleghenies of Pennsylvania, the snow-capped Rockies of Colorado... and every hill and every molehill of Mississippi". Blake set his Jerusalem on England's mountains green, Winstanley tried building his on St George's Hill in Walton-on-Thames, Surrey, and Morris set his a stone's throw from the Hammersmith flyover in London. Utopia is "the consolation of the intelligent attempt" to fulfil the dream, and Utopia really is no place if not in our own back yard.

There is much that I would be happy to import into the republic of heaven straight from the kingdom of God (much as the newly independent American republic imported many customs, rules, statutes and modes of living from the rejected mother-kingdom of Britain). The republic of heaven, like the kingdom it seeks to replace, proposes an overturning of the old order that will put down the mighty from their seats, privilege the hitherto unprivileged, see the hungry fed, give the unhappy cause to laugh. Membership is offered to those who sign up for the transformation, the overturning – and that may include many who don't lead respectable lives and are no better than they should be. The religious who say "Lord, Lord" will have their membership suspended till they stop talking and start doing. Children, at Philip Pullman's insistence, are honorary members already – not because they are "innocent" (which every parent knows to be a fantasy) but because they haven't lost the power to imagine. Nice middle-class people who go to church or temple or synagogue, pop the odd coin in the collection plate, take out standing orders for Oxfam or Greenpeace or Save the

Whales and express their disillusionment with Britain's New Labour and America's Rapture–riders will be excluded if they suppose these attitudes give them an automatic right to citizenship, for those who believe they deserve it thereby demonstrate that they don't.

What the republic will not import from the kingdom is the notion of blind obedience and abject subjection to a divine lord, master and king; for lordship, mastership and kingship belong to the past. The republic is to be built, stone by stone, by the free citizens of the republic of heaven, fully aware that they alone are responsible for what they are building and how they build it. The republic is to be the masterwork of the wholly human spirit, and the fruits of the human spirit are the religious virtues of mercy, pity, peace and love; but there are also religious values and impulses which can have no place in the republic. As Rabbi Sara Blumenthal puts it in E L Doctorow's novel *City of God* (Little Brown, 2000), "the impulse to excommunicate, to satanize, to eradicate, to ethnically cleanse, is a religious impulse. In the practice and politics of religion, God has always been a licence to kill" (as he is for both the terrorist suicide bomber and the western politicians and their supporters who bomb and blast their way to victory over the very enemies their Bible tells them to love). So the republic must embrace values which we may not think of as religious: independent–mindedness; freedom of thought, speech and action; liberty, equality, brotherhood and sisterhood; romance, laughter, generosity and tolerance; common decency and common welfare; creative imagination and reason – each valued for itself, and not because a sovereign lord so decrees.

The republic, then, is:

- *within* us when we cherish these virtues;
- *among* us wherever women and men struggle for social justice and the rights of the poor and dispossessed; and always
- *before* us as a future state of which we may dream, an aspiration towards an ideal world that we know will never be achieved but that somehow feels like home.

It is Isaiah's peaceable kingdom, Jesus's world where the first shall be last and the last shall be first, John's new heaven and a new earth. It is echoed in Thomas More's utopia, Gerrard Winstanley's common–wealth, William Morris's idyll of the past in *The Dream of John Ball* and his model for the future in *News from Nowhere.* If it is a dream, it is not an idle daydream. Rather is it an *enabling* dream, inspiring action. It is the vision without which the people perish.

And who can doubt we need the vision? Two thousand years after the Jesus stories, millions live in a world that might reasonably be considered closer to a kingdom of hell than of heaven. The long sigh and shriek of misery, grief, pain, anguish, sickness and despair threatens to tear the world apart. By the middle of this century, if the demographers are right, ten billion people will inhabit the earth, most of them in vast mega–cities where life is consumed by the struggle to control the planet's diminishing resources.

If the earth's present population were envisaged as a village of one hundred people:
- 80 villagers would live in houses unfit for human habitation;
- 70 would be illiterate;
- 50 would be seriously malnourished;
- 6 would own 60% of the village's land and wealth;
- 30 would be white but would consider the other 70 ethnic minorities!
- 10 of these thirty would be actively polluting the village on which the remaining 90 depend for their living.

Where among them are the rebels, agitators and outsiders, the partisan recruits to the underground army of subversion whose loyalty is pledged to the republic of heaven, the City of God?

Yes, the City of God! For here's a paradox: even for the religious humanist God does, after all, have a place in the republic of heaven! God understood as the protagonist of the fictional god–stories, as our incarnation of mercy, pity, peace and love, as the sum of our values embodied as a being with whom we can have a relationship – that God tosses away his crown and joins us in the messiness and absurdities of our human lives. Nor is this some domesticated caricature of a God in Heaven who would be of no earthly use to anyone. This is the God who plants his footstep in the sea and rides upon the storm, the ancient of days, no less: the most powerful of all the potent symbols ever created by the symbol–making species called humans.

That's the trouble with God: she can't be written out of the script. So since she won't go quietly, let us retain her in the capacity of honorary consultant–adviser, to help us create the hallowed secularism that is the hallmark of the republic of heaven.

INDEX

OF NAMES AND ORGANISATIONS